In the Trickster Tradition

In the Trickster Tradition: The Novels of

Andrew Salkey, Francis Ebejar and Ishmael Reed

Peter Nazareth

BOGLE L'OUVERTURE PRESS

For

My wife Mary

Who has flown to curious places with me

First published in 1994 by
Bogle-L'Ouverture Press Ltd
P.O. Box 2186, London W13 9ZQ

Typeset by Contour Typesetters, Southall, Middx
Printed and bound in Great Britain by The Cromwell Press,
Melksham, Wiltshire.

ISBN 0 9045 2197 4

'Who
was that stranger by the sea?'

Man, he is your memory,
that each sunset moves among
the jetsam of the tribe

Wayne Brown, 'The Witness', *On the Coast*

There are parts of me I myself don't know and
the thought of them fills me with dread. Certain
parts of me give me a cold shudder I often cannot
control. And these parts of me I myself don't
know what they are.

The narrator in Francis Ebejer, *Come Again
in Spring*

The West African spider-god, *Ananse* . . . the
Yoruba god, *Esu, Ikto-mi* ('Spider') of the Dakota
and Sioux Indians . . . are all expressions of the
unpredictable nature of the Unconscious, which is
capable of both creative and destructive activity.
The relationship of this 'trickster-god' to the
paradoxical figure of *Mercurius* or *Hermes*
in alchemy . . . has been pointed out by C.G.
Jung . . .

Michael Gilkes, *Wilson Harris and the
Caribbean Novel*

With your glimpse of my penchant for
ambiguity and ambivalence, I would have thought
you might have twigged to my method of
characterization and narrative. Yes? No?

Letter from Andrew Salkey

No one says a novel has to be one thing. It can be anything it wants to be, a vaudeville show, the six o'clock news, the mumbling of wild men saddled by demons.

> The Loop Garoo Kid to Bo Shmo and his
> neo-social realist gang, in Ishmael Reed,
> *Yellow Back Radio Broke-Down*

Raven of the haunted woods, our ancient guide along the paths to nowhere.

> Daniel Sloate, *Words in miniature and other words*

Is only those who take chance with land and water, who go way far from home and roam world views, who stretch distance with foot, who for ever making home out of homelessness and drift, no matter what, that can see what Anancy seeing, here, right now.

> Andrew Salkey, 'Middle Passage Anancy', from
> *Anancy, Traveller*

Readerji, by bending, yes-Masta, yes-Masta, you follow me colonizer-critic to his bed!

> Yasmin Ladha,
> *Lion's Granddaughter and Other Stories*

Contents

Acknowledgements

I should like to thank the University of Iowa for making it possible for me to write this book by the granting of an Old Gold Summer Fellowship during the summer of 1987. I should also like to thank the American Council for Learned Societies and the University of Iowa Foundation for grants to travel to Singapore to present a paper on Andrew Salkey's *A Question of Violence* at the Seventh Triennial Conference of the Association for Commonwealth Literature and Language Studies (ACLALS), National University of Singapore, June 16–23, 1986. I should further like to thank the Foundation, directed by Darrell Wyrick, for a grant to make publication of this book possible.

I must thank Fred Woodard, at the University of Iowa, and Edwin Thumboo Chair of the African-American World Studies Program, former Dean of the Faculty of Arts and Social Sciences at the National University of Singapore. Both are old friends whose ideas and help, literary and otherwise, cannot be appreciated enough.

The paper presented at Singapore has been published in *Jamaica Journal*, ed. Olive Senior, Kingston: The Institute of Jamaica, Vol. 19, No. 4, November 1986–January 1987. The section on Salkey's third novel was presented at the Twelfth Annual Meeting of the African Literature Association, East Lansing, April 16–19, 1986 under the title 'Sexual Fantasies and Neocolonial Repression in Andrew Salkey's *The Adventures of Catullus Kelly*'. The paper is published in *World Literature Written in English*, ed. G.D. Killam, Toronto: University of Toronto Press, Vol. 28.2, Autumn 1988.

The first section of the chapter on Ishmael Reed was presented as a paper under the same title as is used for the chapter at a conference entitled 'Of Our Spiritual Strivings: Recent Developments in Black Literature and Criticism', University of California at Los Angeles, April 23, 1983. The paper was published in *The Review of Contemporary Fiction*, ed. John O'Brien, Elmwood Park, Illinois, Vol. 4, No. 2, Summer 1984. A shorter version, the one used for the oral presentation at the conference, was published under the same title in *The Toronto South Asian Review*, ed. Moyez Vassanji, Vol. 4, No. 3, Spring 1986.

The section on Frances Ebejer's *Requiem for a Malta Fascist* was presented as a paper at a Plenary Session entitled 'Text and Context: Literature and History', *26th Modern Literature Conference: Third World, Diaspora, and Revolution*, Michigan State University, East Lansing, November 11, 1988.

The epigraphs are taken from the following sources: Wayne Brown, *On The Coast*, London: André Deutsch, 1972, p. 48; Francis Ebejar, *Come Again in Spring*, New York/Washington/Atlanta/Los Angeles/Chicago: Vantage, 1979, p. 174; Michael Gilkes, *Wilson Harris and the Caribbean Novel*, London/Trinidad/Jamaica: Longman Caribbean, 1975, p. 41; Andrew Salkey, letter to Peter Nazareth dated November 25, 1981; Ishmael Reed, *Yellow Back Radio Broke-Down*, New York: Doubleday, 1969, p. 36; Daniel Sloate, *Words in miniature and other words*, Québec: Les Editions Maisonneuve, 1972, p. 20; Andrew Salkey, *Anancy Traveller*, London: Bogle-L'Ouverture Press, 1992, p. 11; and Yasmin Ladha, *Lion's Granddaughter and Other Stories*, Edmonton: NeWest Press, 1992, p. 1.

The quotation from 'Hard Headed Woman', a hit by Elvis Presley in 1958 used in the chapter on Ishmael Reed, is used by permission. As instructed by the copyright holders, I have provided the acknowledgement on the copyright page.

There are more people to thank: Narendra and Usha Sood, for introducing me to many things, including Larry Abraham, *Call it Conspiracy*; my Godmother, Uncle Frank, Aunt Diana, Brother Joe, Cousins Margaret and Tom and Joan Francis for their support; Andrew Salkey, who made a suggestion about the title of the work, which I received.

Good people have gone on who unfolded uimbrellas during storms: Darwin Turner, Jawa Apronti, and Ali Shalash, and someone who was a literary role model when I was a freshman,

Jonathan Kariara. They are sorely missed but their good works are remembered.

I had hoped that the three writers of the text would discover that in juxtaposition, their books knew more about them than they did. This is the discovery of Raven. Tragically, Francis Ebejer passed away in Malta on June 6, 1993. May his work resonate in our minds.

Introduction

When I wrote one-act plays at Makerere University College in Kampala, Uganda in the late fifties and early sixties, I was trying to change society. I took it for granted that this was the function of literature. My father had been a leader of the Goan community, Goans having come to East Africa chiefly as civil servants under British colonial rule; unlike most Goans, my father always had books around the house, including joke books. He was a very good public speaker and always had an appropriate joke for the occasion which made the people feel good as well as giving them food for thought. So I was used to the idea that writing and speech and humour were inter-connected and all had a serious social purpose.

Social reality was not simple. I was aware that there were many different ways of seeing reality. This must have come from my unique background. I was an African and yet not an African; an Indian and yet, because Goans in East Africa were Roman Catholic and came from a Portuguese colony, not an Indian; and a Goan and yet not a Goan in that my mother was born in Kuala Lumpur, Malaya, where my maternal grandfather, a professional musician, had settled so that while other Goan children heard stories from their parents about mythic Goa, I heard stories about two different places. If, then, there were many ways of seeing reality, it meant that many people missed seeing essential elements of reality because of their background and moment in time. They were blind. The audience was not outside the problem. How could I make it see? The problem was to break past the defences, to trick the audience into seeing.

As an English Honours student, I wrote an essay on Jean Anouilh's *Antigone*, which was a reworking of the classic

Sophocles play written while France was under Nazi occupation: Anouilh deliberately broke the illusion that the audience was watching real life because he wanted it to think about occupation by an unjust ruler while he was maintaining the illusion that this was a classic so that he could get it past the censors.[1] The first time I wrote about a *novelist* playing tricks was when I wrote about the fiction of Kole Omotoso of Nigeria under the title 'The Tortoise is an Animal But He is Also a Wise Creature[2].' By a close reading of each of Omotoso's published fictions, I showed how we the readers drew the wrong conclusions until we suddenly were made to realize we were wrong and then had to retrace our steps. After discussing Omotoso's *The Edifice*, I said,

> The author has led us into a trap by letting us identify too closely with Dele. Then he breaks the continuity of our expectations, just like the dramatist Jean Anouilh in his reworking of Sophocles's play *Antigone*, to jolt us out of our complacency into a new awareness. We are forced to reassess Dele, and we realize that he has always been obsessed with whiteness.[3]

I continued,

> 'The comment the Hungarian poet, Agnes Gergely, made about my novel *In a Brown Mantle* applies equally to *The Edifice*: It is a tricky book. It cheats you. You start reading it and find it easy to read. Just the way you put a knife in butter and feel it going through. But then you suddenly stop and come to the core. It's hard. In the end you come to the conclusion you are trying to break a piece of stone.'[4]

After analyzing Omotoso's third novel, *Sacrifice*, I said,

> But is this really a solution to the problem? Once again, Omotoso will not let us have things so easily . . . *Sacrifice* is a riddle we must solve for ourselves.[5]

At the time the essay on Omotoso was written, I had not thought of using the term 'trickster', although it was clear I was working in that direction since I quoted Agnes Gergely using the word 'tricky.' Even more important, I compared Omotoso to the tortoise of African tales. Although I was unaware of it at the time, the tortoise is also a trickster. In an African version of the story of the Tortoise and the Hare, the tortoise defeats the hare not by being patient and plodding along but by placing relatives at strategic points along the route, relatives the hare did not know about. Like Anouilh, Omotoso is concerned with fighting oppression by opening up the minds of the audience/reader; but unlike Anouilh, Omotoso is a Third World person who is concerned with the consequences of colonialism.

What is the thing called the Third World? Some people have identified it through an economic definition: the First World is the developed West plus Japan, the Second World was the Communist bloc and the Third World is the rest. Perhaps that is more of a political definition than the economics one, which is made in terms of the Gross National Product, so that a few people go on to posit a Fourth World, a Fifth, and so on. Yet others such as the Caribbean novelists Sam Selvon and Wilson Harris reject the notion of the Third World: in the space and nuclear age, it is clear that we are all living in one world, and besides, some people confuse 'Third World' with 'third-rate'. But I find the term useful, although I agree with the cautionary advice of Robert Stiller, the Polish critic and translator, who told me that whenever you start a movement, you should be on the other side trying to stop it because it will get out of hand.

Some thinkers have therefore rejected the term in favor of 'South' (versus 'North'). A monthly news-journal published in London is called *South*, sub-titled, 'The Third World Magazine[6].' The first use of the North-South relationship to my knowledge is in a novel, *Season of Migration to the North* by Tayeb Salih of Sudan, published in the late sixties.[7] For my purpose, 'the Third World' represents those areas of the world, and those people, that have had the experience of colonialism, whether of the direct or indirect kind. Writers from these areas of the world and these experiences in dealing with *their* world have also to deal with the relationship to the 'mother country', that is, the colonizing power, since the two are intimately linked. First World writers can neglect this colonial relationship since it is to the advantage of those benefitting from colonialism to be blind. Jonah Raskin says of Conrad's *Heart of Darkness* in *The Mythology of Imperialism*,

> After Kurtz dies Marlow must return to Europe and visit his white
> fiancée. He lies to her. We know the truth, but she never will.

> Kurtz's fiancée is the blind citizen of the mother country. She knows
> nothing of the truth about colonialism. Her existence rests on the
> Third World, but to her that world is invisible.[8]

Marlow was unable to tell her about the brutal exploiter Kurtz
had become in Africa in order to build up his mother country, her
country, but we note that *the story* brings the truth back home.[9]
So *Conrad* is not blind. But Jane Austen is in *Mansfield Park*. The
patriarch goes away and it is never explained exactly how he
makes his money. Omolara Ogundipe-Leslie asks this question in
'To a "Jane Austen" Class at Ibadan University':

> Do you ask why India grieves?
> From whence the much-loved stones
> in your much-loved crowns in London?
> Do you tie our rote-learned tales of
> the Navigator's men, Clive's antics,
> routes traced and gained to time spent
> and time stolen in Mansfield Park?[10]

Jean Rhys felt that the story of Charlotte Brontë's *Jane Eyre*
needed the presentation of the colonial connection to be
complete: Rhys provided the other side of the story in *Wide
Sargasso Sea*.[11]

Some of the best Third World writing, then, deals inescapably
with the so-called First World and should therefore be of concern
not only to people in the Third World but also to those in the First
World who want to know the truth. And many people in the First
World do want to know the truth, as the Iran-Contra hearings
indicated while I was writing.

Some Western readers tend to assume that Third World writing
is, by definition, protest literature. I do not want to rule out the
idea of protest: one of the best examples of protest fiction is Alex
La Guma's *A Walk in the Night*.[12] In the way it structures
language, uses metaphors, and shows the impossibility of achieving manhood in the colonially oppressive system of *apartheid* in
South Africa, the novella is a truth that is still valid three decades
after La Guma wrote it.[13] The problem with the idea of protest
literature is that it is just against something and not for something
(although 'protest' can also mean 'to affirm'). To insist that all the
Third World writers can do is to write protest literature rather

than incorporate the element of protest into a larger framework is to suggest a one-sidedness, an absence of an internal value system on the part of the colonized; it is to suggest the impossibility of Third World literature incorporating a *dialogue* with the West; it is to suggest that the West and the non-West are fixed and separate and unchanging.

But the West has always had a relationship to the non-West, it has always incorporated elements from the non-West. We have seen in *Heart of Darkness* how the ivory of the Congo builds up Brussels. Umberto Eco's best-seller, *The Name of the Rose*, shows us a medieval European monastery translating texts from the non-West, chiefly the Arab world, from which come translations of the Greek texts, getting ready for the rise of Europe.[14] The novel is a mystery novel, a thriller, a who-dun-it (and a 'how-dun-it'). At the heart of the novel is a search for a missing text: which is at the heart of Ishmael Reed's *Mumbo Jumbo*, published a decade earlier. In fact, Eco's novel gives literary proof that Reed's Berbelang may be right when he sees that the Faust myth haunts the West because Faust was a mountebank, a charlatan who suddenly found the magic working. After that, Faust kept drawing from the non-Europeans but always lived in fear that he would be found out.

In using the term 'Third World', I am not assuming an identity of cultures among the different countries. Just because I am from the Third World and acknowledge it instead of wanting to climb into the First World, a temptation Ayi Kwei Armah deals with in his novels *Fragments* and *Why Are We So Blest?*, it does not mean that I automatically know or understand, every Third World country.[15] I have had to learn about these countries. I have not been to Jamaica or Malta. I had not been to the United States until 1973 and although I grew up on American culture – country and western, rock 'n' roll, comics, movies – there was still more to learn when I was here, particularly about African-Americans. When I came across the work of Ishmael Reed, Andrew Salkey and Francis Ebejer, I had to read and re-read the texts.

Well, then, what connects these three writers? Is it that, as a reader said of my second book of criticism, that I am saying, 'Hey, look, I have found these interesting writers and I am going to write about them?' Yes. I am not claiming that Salkey learned

from Ebejer or that Reed learned from Salkey. It is probable that
Reed has not read Salkey and Ebejer (although his reading is
enormous: he has taken his name seriously). I know that Salkey
has read Reed, but I doubt he has read Ebejer. Ebejer first heard
of Reed when I started working on this book – I sent him a copy of
Mumbo Jumbo since the Knights Templar play a key role in the
novel as they did in the formation of modern Malta. Ebejer wrote
to me on February 9, 1984,

> What a book! Certainly a great talent there, though I must confess I
> found it a bit disconcerting where allusions were too 'in' . . . It's a
> big finger in America's yawning wound.

So there is no direct literary connection between the three
novelists. The connection is one I, the critic, am making. *I* am
saying that they have something in common and that studying
them is of value.

How is this different from what F.R. Leavis is saying in *The
Great Tradition*?[16] Leavis was the backbone of my studies when I
received an Honours degree in English from the University of
London, granted through Makerere University College in
Uganda in 1962. Jonah Raskin pins Leavis ideologically down for
us, effectively if a little brashly:

> Tradition, the dominant idea in the minds of modern critics, is a
> fraud. What have you got when you possess a Great Tradition?
> Nothing. F.R. Leavis, the major British critic of the forties and the
> fifties, heard Eliot's sermon, responded to the plea and wrote his
> own version of the tradition in his study of the English novel. He
> insists that Jane Austen, George Eliot, Henry James, Joseph Conrad
> and D.H. Lawrence are the major English novelists. Leavis issues
> them cards in the Great Tradition Club. He turns down Dickens's
> application. From the start there is a gaping hole which cannot be
> filled. The machinery which generates Jane Austen, he says, also
> generates Joseph Conrad. Leavis does not account for social or
> cultural changes. He does not illuminate either Jane Austen or D.H.
> Lawrence by putting them together in the same bag. He is left with
> an empty bag. It appears that Leavis did not notice sex. It is a cruel
> joke to have lusty Lawrence embrace frigid Austen. She would run
> away shrieking. The word 'fuck' is not in *Pride in Prejudice*, but is in
> *Lady Chatterly's Lover*. Leavis's tradition cannot explain why it –
> and the act of making love – appears in one and not the other. It
> puts a clean sheet over the naked man and the naked woman. It

covers up the sexual revolution in society and the orgy in the English
novel. Lawrence watched Victorian men and women getting into bed
with each other. He saw them making love and he knew something
was wrong. There was a dead thing between them as they lay
together in each other's arms. Englishmen conquered the world,
constructed an empire, but between English men and women there
was an emptiness. Lawrence began filling the gap with a new,
quivering force. We draw silent too when we ask why Conrad's
world is unlike George Eliot's. Leavis has not gotten his fingers into
the mud of imperialism and so he cannot feel the extraordinary
forces of Conrad: his extremes, his terrors, his darkness, his
revolutions, his explosions. George Eliot's planet Earth was
transformed by Conrad's contemporaries. He mapped the changes:
he followed the bulldozer into the jungle. He pried open the future
while Eliot excavated the past. He voyaged to the Congo while she
sat in London.

Leavis tells us that Austen, Eliot and Conrad share a 'reverent
openness before life.' But *The Great Tradition* blocks the exits to life.
It is containment criticism. The three writers Leavis toys with are
yanked away from society and hung up to dry on a literary
clothesline. Soon enough he has hung them to death. They exist for
him only insofar as they converse with each other and plug into his
worn moral circuit. They are sealed off from their cultures and their
nations.[17]

Leavis was working within the English Puritan tradition and was
conveniently overlooking the colonial underpinning of that
tradition. Armah suggests in his *Why Are We So Blest?* that sexual
disfunction at the centre is a direct consequence of the brutality of
colonialism, a factor that Lawrence and Leavis do not consider.
Furthermore, Leavis's selection of writers is one *he* is making:
look, he is saying, I have found these writers who are interesting
because I say so and I am going to prove it by analysis. While
Leavis's great tradition is bolstered by British colonialism, I am a
product of that colonialism. I therefore have to roam the whole
world looking for the pieces to make sense of my world, which
was fragmented by colonialism and made to fit into the needs of
the metropolitan center's rising capitalism, industrial and
financial.[18]

I have found Salkey, Ebejer and Reed. And yes, I am saying
that they are valuable and I am going to show the reader why. I
am focusing on novels. To date, Salkey has published five novels
(plus nine children's novels), Ebejer six novels (with a new one, *I
Lucian* – and the Baron, in the wings) and Reed nine. The three

novelists inhabit different parts of the world but have in common the experience of being colonized, of belonging to people who have been made to serve the needs of Euro-American capitalism. All three deal with the experiences of having to struggle against the idea of powerlessness and of decisions always being made elsewhere. They deal with history and hold a dialogue with it. To echo Joyce, colonizing man's history is colonized man's nightmare: all three novelists are trying to wake their people up into creating their own history. At the beginning of Ayi Kwei Armah's first novel, *The Beautyful Ones Are Not Yet Born*, the protagonist is asleep; at the end, he is wide awake, alert and energized.[19]

If novelists such as Armah, Ngũgĩ wa Thiong'o, Wilson Harris and Gabriel García Márquez also attempt to wake colonized people into history, why have I chosen Salkey, Ebejer and Reed? It is because these three novelists use the *form* of their novels to get the reader to participate in the process of creating meaning. Each of them creates novels which give the readers a nudge, a start or a shock to shake them out of dangerous fixed perceptions so that they will see and think. Critics who refuse to recognize that they (the critics) too are part of the problem instead of being outside it will end up misreading these writers.

I myself am particularly aware of the problem of a text being read 'straight' and thus being misread because I have experienced it with my fictions. As I said earlier, from the beginning, I considered the audience/reader perception to be part of the problem: so I constantly played tricks with that perception. In my one-act play, 'Brave New Cosmos', produced at Makerere University College in 1961, I was under the influence of Chekhov. I believed then that everything on the stage had to appear to be just as inconclusive as things in real life but that behind the words of the characters, things were happening that were having earth-shaking effects on their lives and, by extension, on the lives of the audience. It was up to the audience to work it out. The clue I provided was in the *dramatis personae* in the program: I used the 'k' sound to have Kaggwa, Karanja, Kiwanuka and 'Chorus – the Audience'. Some members of the audience got the play, others did not: I heard comments like, 'So what happened? Three characters appeared on the stage and talked.' The play was produced by the B.B.C. African Service.[20]

At the request of the B.B.C., I wrote a play just for its African

Service. The play was 'The Hospital', it was a radio-play, and it was written under the spell of Kafka's *Metamorphosis*. The play presented an enclosed, nightmarish world in which people were turned into ciphers: it was up to the listener to decide what was to be done once the play had ended. Next in line was my radio-play *X*, written under the impact of Brecht and his 'alienation effect'.[21] I wanted to show the brainwashing effect of colonial rule, which turned the élite into ciphers and split personalities. I wanted to demonstrate the brainwashing techniques used through the medium of radio, I wanted to show that choices could be made once one recognized the methods of mind-control. It was as though a hand came out of the radio every few seconds to deliberately show the listener that he had been brainwashed and to show him how this had happened. But O.R. Dathorne, a prolific novelist and critic, analyzed the play straight by only considering the character within the play created by the narrator and not paying any attention to the narrator who had deliberately created that character or the narrator's thought-processes and the techniques he used to make the play. Dathorne analyzed the cipher, not the person and not the techniques of the art-form, thus ending up misunderstanding the play.[22]

My first novel, *In a Brown Mantle*, was in the form of a confession.[23] The readers' response was similar to that of Philip Roth's *Portnoy's Complaint*; Roth said, 'a novel in the guise of a confession was received by any number of readers as a confession in the guise of a novel.'[24] I was obliged to point out the difference between my own life and that of my protagonist.[25] The narrator is confessing, feeling guilty in exile in London after reading about the attempted assassination of the political leader of his country. The point about the Catholic confession is that one is trying to confront the truth about one's sins and also trying to slide by it.[26] The function of the Father Confessor is to draw the sinner's attention to what he/she is trying to dodge; but there is no Father Confessor in the novel, although there is an idealistic priest. So the novel is really a dialogue the protagonist is holding with his conscience, with various characters rising up to be part of that dialogue. Too many readers identified with the narrator because he seemed to be such a nice guy, he spoke their language: and they assumed the narrator was me. One person wrote me a letter saying he was going to take legal action against me because he just took it for granted that one of the characters was his (assassinated) brother, although the names were different!

With *The General is Up*, based fictionally on the expulsion of Asians from Uganda by Idi Amin in 1972, the trick is in the conclusion and the epilogue. One of the first critics to understand the trick in the novel was J.R. McGuire, who says,

> Even before reading the disorienting epilogue, one is sceptical of the fantastic, improbable and rapid-fire flourish of events that end the novel. It is in fact the preposterous final chapter followed by the equivocal epilogue that urge the reader to retrace his steps through the novel and reevaluate [sic] the text he has just read. These final two sections superimpose a new optic on the preceding pages, forcing the reader to interrogate drastically, and perhaps modify, his initial perception of the book.[27]

Prior to McGuire, most critics tended to assume that the novel was taken directly from the real world. For example, Lambert Mascarenhas, a Goan novelist, said of the novel,

> Even if the author, who was born in Uganda, calls this book a 'work of the imagination' the ordeal suffered by the Indians when they were suddenly uprooted from that country is real, a fact.[28]

In a long essay Ebejer published on his novels in the Maltese journal *Civilization*, he discusses his novels in chronological order. About his fifth novel, *Requiem for a Malta Fascist*, he says,

> The Countess Elena pulls Lorenz one way; his deformed cousin, and very Maltese, Kos, the other. Kos is the matrix: does he represent the old Malta with its hardships and perhaps unattractiveness, clamouring for attention and suitable cultivation even in the face of the threat from the beautiful foreigners?[29]

Notice that even in the explanation, Ebejer is asking a question and leaving it to the reader to interpret and decide. Later in the same essay, talking of his sixth novel, *Leap of Malta Dolphins*, Ebejer comments,

> Alas, the now fully emancipated Maltese woman presents another type of problem: not as specifically herself; more in the near-mythical manner in which Marcell and a few others regard her.[30]

Here is another problem Ebejer is pinpointing: the danger of people mythifying things and people that should not be mythified or mythifying incorrectly and thus repeating old patterns that come from habits of powerlessness under oppressive rules.

Albert Wendt, the Samoan novelist, says in his introduction to *Lali: A Pacific Anthology*:

> Like a plant, the artist through an unconscious process of osmosis draws his mana (his artistic and imaginative energy) from everything surrounding him as from a birth sac – the aesthetic and cultural traditions into which he is born, his personal relationships, even the food and drink he consumes. This mana he transmits back into his community in a reconstituted form. How well he does this depends on his talents and on the willingness of his society to receive his paintings, or poems, or songs. Factors such as censorship, the reaction of critics and those who control the community, and the need to earn a living can influence, hamper, and even stop that transmission.[31]

The artist must inspire, must make the people who have been suppressed have confidence in themselves; he must not undermine before doing this or else he will be contributing to the low self and group esteem brought in by colonialism. Yet if he goes to the other extreme, he would end up falsely glorifying his people and underplaying the impact of the colonial relationship. Wendt himself has had some problems with his Samoan readers because while they are happy he brings them honor, they are unhappy he does so by telling the truth, by undermining the myth which has been imposed by the West and which they have tended to accept that they are a simple and innocent people living in paradise. Some artists see that it is not enough to identify the problem or to show the way out. The way the people see must be broken through.

Near the end of *Season of Migration to the North*, the narrator opens the room in the southern village belonging to his nemesis, Mustafa Sa'eed. He finds artefacts and photos recreating his life in England, including a fireplace, and he finds a whole collection of books whose titles are listed. Yet none of these books, not even the most radical, helps him understand the mystery of Mustafa (and of himself). My interpretation is that the author is telling the reader that in order to understand the story of Mustafa Sa'eed, not only must the story be put together by the narrator but also the reader has to find relevant books so that by juxtaposition, we can understand the story of Mustafa, the colonial seeking revenge against the colonizers yet unable to wipe out the North in himself, just as the women he seduced in England were inescapably attracted to what they saw as the South in him.

Once I accepted my Third World identity, I had to re-educate myself, to read, and sometimes create, those books which, when placed in juxtaposition with one another, throw light on one another and on the complex world of the colonial. Since the South must be explored in its relation to the North, the exploration has meaning and significance to both the South and the North. In an unpublished novella, *The Murmur in the Depths of the River* by Violet Dias Lannoy, the English teacher in a secondary school in Kenya turns out to be an intellectual agent for the West who is learning all he can from the non-West, in this case Kenya, including other ways of understanding the secrets and myths of the West. He knows that any society that can only see things in one way is in danger: there has to be more than one way of seeing reality and of seeing one's own culture.[32]

Some readers may make the hoary statement when they find many details and quotations in my text that I am incapable of conceptual thought. The problem for a Third World critic is well put by Henry Louis Gates, Jr. in his introduction to *Black Literature and Literary Theory*. He says,

> *we must often resurrect the texts in our tradition before we can begin to explicate them.* To render major contributions to contemporary theory's quest to 'save the text', in Barthès's phrase, is our splendid opportunity. Unlike critics in almost every other literary tradition, much of what we have to say about our literature is new. What critics of the Western tradition can make an even remotely similar claim? Jeremiah could speak only to the Jews; we, however, must address two audiences, the Jews and the Babylonians, whose interests are distant yet over-lapping in the manner of interlocking sets.[33]

If one mentioned 'thirty pieces of silver', the whole story of Christ's betrayal would immediately come to mind: the story does not have to be retold but can be taken for granted. But would a Christian readership catch the meaning of a brief reference such as 'Karna's kavach' from *The Mahabharata* without the story being told first? Would Kurtz's fiancée understand that 'the civilizing mission' would not have the same meaning for the Africans as it does to her? Would her compatriots be willing to understand the truth about that mission without Marlow having to sneak in the story in a framed, hedged and qualified way?

Yet I am going to provide details without relying heavily on plot summaries: many early reviewers of Andrew Salkey's fiction did provide plot summaries such as David Haworth's of *The Adventures of Catullus Kelly* in the *New Statesman* which, by their very nature, distorted the meaning of the text, even when the reviews were complimentary such as Graham Hough's of *A Quality of Violence* ('a remarkable first novel . . . the ever-present vitality of the writing . . . a vigorous, imaginative and quite unusual novel') and *The Times Literary Supplement*'s of *The Late Emancipation of Jerry Stover* ('an energetic narrative of ceaseless and swarming dialogue . . . His sense of place and intense recreation of a specific social mood make this a strong book').[34] Instead of relying on plot summary, I shall provide extensive quotations, which I shall then examine. Or I may do something else. I shall behave like Professor in Wole Soyinka's brilliant play, *The Road*.[35] He picks up pieces of newspaper, road signs and other kinds of writings without any distinction between 'high' and 'low' literature. His intention is to put all the clues together in order to find the missing center, the center that has vanished since European colonialism created its imperative. The center can be found through The Word.

Chapter I

Those Who Won't See Can't See: The Fiction of Andrew Salkey

Andrew Salkey's first novel, *A Quality of Violence*, deals with the drought in Jamaica in 1900.[1] While the importance of the novel was recognized right away, the same cannot be said for the nature of the novel. For example, Ivan Van Sertima praised the novel in his series of broadcasts on Caribbean writing over the B.B.C. in 1962, three years after it was published, but said,

> Of Salkey himself, little may safely be said at the moment. Narrative is not his strong point and he cannot command the power and style to carry the burden of such an ambitious intention and attempt. But his dialogue is as vital and vigorous as in a good play and his characters stand out as vividly as the violence. The book as a whole can almost take the form of a play. Scene after well-constructed scene move [sic] swiftly to a powerful dramatic crescendo and the last scene, in the words of one of his critics, is 'the most tremendous theatre.[2]

What Van Sertima is referring to by 'such an ambitious intention and attempt' is the response of the people in the village to the drought. 'In their predicament the people turn to the one source that seems to offer them some kind of hope and salvation,' he says.

> That source – Religion. But here it is that a dangerous mix-up and perversion occurs. A confusion and perversion that has to do with a people who have been forced out of one continent and culture into another, who have lost in that uprooting the crucial nerve-centre of

their world and soul and are seeking in an emptiness and drought-time for new spiritual values and foundations.

Having outlined the problem, Van Sertima expects Salkey to deal with it straightforwardly. He expects 'narrative' and does not pay sufficient attention to the author's use of drama. He says, 'The literature of the West Indies has so far been largely a literature of sensation and surfaces.' He seems to be thinking about the achievement of Wilson Harris when he goes on to call West Indian literature largely,

> a literature that has made full use of the peculiar and exotic natural furniture of the region but has seldom ever touched on or exploded the deeper collective psychic experience of its people. Yet this experience, this unique psychic property and feature, this strange spirit and genius aprowl in the place cannot forever be ignored.

Kenneth Ramchand takes Salkey's novel more seriously. In his pioneering work, *The West Indian Novel and its Background*, he says:

> The socio-economic depression of the masses and the 'great emptiness, somewhere in their life, that gnawing at them and beginning for plenty plenty satisfaction' (p. 59), underlie Andrew Salkey's handling of pocomania cultists in *A Quality of Violence* (1959). The spectacular elements of drums, rhythm, sacrifice, flagellation and spirit possession occur. But Salkey sets the novel in a period of drought and aridity in the land: this is the clearest of indications that the author has larger artistic uses for the frenzied manifestations of the cultists.
>
> The pocomanians find the substance of their lives breaking up beyond control in the endless drought. Dada Johnson their leader sees their faith in him collapsing, and the deputy is looking around for the right moment to make a bid for primacy. These motives operate in the spectacular dance ('the Giant X') in which the dancers equate their bodies with the land, each whipping himself in an attempt to banish the barrenness of the land and that of the earthly body: 'We must lash the devil out of the land. We must lash good water into the land.' The rivalry between Dada and his deputy spurs each man to the more and more incisive self-laceration until both collapse exhausted and expiring. The Giant X claims both as sacrificial victims. But the rains do not come.
>
> This fierce vision of human aberration under burning stress, and the deafness of the gods is placed within *a more conventional ordering of experience* in the novel. But although the solid virtues and values

of the Marshalls and the Parkins help to disperse the pessimism in
the work, it is Salkey's exploration, through the sacrificed and
suicidal cultists, of the irrational elements in human existence that
makes the work such a powerful one.[3]

Through the phrase I have italicized, we can again see Wilson
Harris haunting the critic. Ramchand takes Dada Johnson to be
the leader of the group while we know he – Johnson – is a conman.
Ramchand also takes the Marshalls and the Parkins at face value,
overlooking the fact that the wives quarrel with their husbands so
that we know that the even-temperedness of the husbands is to be
questioned. The phrase 'the irrational elements in human existence' makes the novel much too broad and overlooks the quite
specific crisis within which the characters are trying to find
solutions.

Gerald Moore also misses the point when he says,

> Ma Johnson, the leader of the cult, finally dominates the action of
> the novel by her willingness to die, stoned by her own followers, in
> order that the kind of power she represents may live.[4]

Bill Carr gets closer to understanding Salkey when he says that
when he first read this particular novel, he had one response but
when re-read it, he responded differently. Carr is right when he
says of *A Quality of Violence* that Salkey 'wants his readers to
sense for themselves the presence of a defining history'.[5] But he
begins to go off the track when he says,

> The book offers little in the way of character. The protagonists are,
> rather, disparate points of view, conflicting figures in a pattern
> whose design is the form of the book.

No: there definitely are characters, as we have seen from the
critics quoted earlier. But Carr is onto something when he thinks
of the design of the book: he has almost got it when he says the
novel is 'choreographed' and that it has a 'complex irony.'

Salkey himself provides us with clues as to how to read. In his
Author's Note to *Anancy's Score*, he says:

> Where would Afro-Caribbean folk tales be without the seminal
> support of the African Anancy? Indeed, how could this book ever
> have been written without it, or without Anancy's historical

authority, or without my having tapped Anancy's score in his first home country?

The traditional Anancy is a crisp, cool calculating spider, a persuasive, inventive, anarchic spider-man.

I have wilfully used his name, and even more wilfully tried to understand his nature, and remoulded it for my own ends.

I have plucked my Anancy from the great folk tales of West Africa and the Caribbean, and I have made him inhabit both worlds, the old and the new, locked deep in my own imagination; he also inhabits the ready minds of children, *and crashes the defences of most adults.* He holds no reservations; makes only certain crucial allowances; he knows no boundaries; respects no one, not even himself, at times; and he makes a mockery of everybody's assumptions and value judgements.

In this personal collection, the language and plots are mine; and the twists, turns and flights of invention are also mine. *The journey and the critical eye are yours.*[6]

In this note, Salkey is telling us two things of great importance. First, he is drawing our attention to the Anancy story, the Anancy way of reading. Anancy is a trickster: one function of the Anancy story is to bring buried contradictions to the surface.[7] In 'Anancy and Andrew Salkey', Mervyn Morris tells us that in the traditional Anancy stories,

Anancy is a cunning spider-man, often greedy, lazy, envious, as well as shrewd. He often outwits some formidable adversary. Though sometimes bested, he is the great survivor . . . *Is Anancy meck it*: a reminder that the West African ancestor of Caribbean Anancy was an Akan Creator God.[8]

Morris continues,

Salkey explicitly acknowledges a debt to the traditional Anancy story. But, as the 'Author's Note' to *Anancy's Score* makes clear, his creative mission is to reconsider, revise and extend the tradition, to use Anancy in new ways.

In *A Quality of Violence*, Salkey deliberately draws our attention to the Anancy story:

Before Linda would go peacefully to her cot, her mother had to tell her an Anancy story . . . "You know, Linda, I despairing plenty-plenty of your treatment of the word of the Lord. Everything you

think of have to have some connexion with that fool-fool spider,
Anancy. I want you to understand that Anancy and the Lord who is
God son is two different people, entirely. The Lord is no Anancy
story. I want you to understand the serious thing that the Lord is.
(pp.25/6)
[Brother Parkin] remained with the girls for about ten minutes.
They laughed and chatted freely with one another. They liked him
and they adored his stories about Anancy and Brother Tacuma and
the jokes and Duppy stories he told . . . (p. 88)
Brother Parkin was a spider called Anancy, thought Linda.
(p.91)

Through such thoughts, statements and references, Salkey is
letting us know that his novel is an Anancy story.

The second thing of importance in Salkey's Author's Note to
Anancy's Score is his address to the reader. 'The journey and the
critical eye are yours.' The problem is not only out there: it is also
inside, inside the mind. Colonial rule took away the centre of
control and placed it somewhere else, far out of reach, or so it
would seem. Salkey makes reference, appropriate to the story of a
Caribbean island, buccaneers, pirates and buried treasure, to
having to dive deep to find that centre: in his introduction to
Breaklight, he says,

> A truly sensitive and compassionate awareness of people, place and
> history in our spiritually-fragmented Caribbean, is a very difficult
> level of consciousness for most of us to achieve; it almost seems a
> treasure, set securely in our midst yet utterly out of our reach.[9]

He continues,

> Surely, our poets may be the first to discover how to identify, anew,
> that awareness, and give it back to us.

In *A Quality of Violence*, the text says,

> Marshall knew hidden meanings in the Bible stories he read from
> time to time and he was anxious to see what new twist the meeting-
> yard might give to them.
> (p.59)

A Quality of Violence was published in 1959, when the Third
World seemed to be rising up to throw off the shackles of

colonialism. Yet over three decades later, with starving people and military coups and assassinations of idealistic leaders and corrupt leaders, it is clear that the throwing off of the chains was largely an illusion. The chains were also in the mind. Salkey knew the battle would be long. As an epigraph to his *Georgetown Journal*, he quotes Elsa V. Goveia:

> Whether in education or in history, good intentions are not enough, and the road to hell is paved with authoritative half-truths. No one is ever educated or liberated from the past by being taught how easy it is to substitute new shibboleths for old.[10]

Salkey wants to wake his readers up by refusing to let them have any clichéd perceptions of the world for these perceptions come fundamentally from colonialism. Let me rephrase that: he *does* let them have the clichéed perceptions of the world, their world, and then he undermines those perceptions so that the readers are forced to think. As Martin Luther King says of Socrates in his classic 'Letter from a Birmingham Jail', Salkey finds it necessary to create a tension in the mind so that individuals may rise from the bondage of myths and half-truths.[11]

The people Salkey is dealing with in *A Quality of Violence* are chiefly the peasants of St. Thomas in Jamaica. The drought causes serious problems for everyone. When Miss T. comes to complain to the Marshalls about how their little girl mistreated her little girl, she says:

> We is all in the same boat. We is all living on the land, and we is all tie-up with the land. When things like drought and earthquake happen, it make we know that we is all on the same level. The land is the thing that make we one class-a-people. Another thing that you Marshall people had better remember is that we is all next-door relative to slavery that just leave the land yesterday. If we have one class, that one class is to be call the slave class or something like that.
> (pp. 98/99)

The suffering of the people and their relationship to the land are well presented and we are made to sympathize with the people. Yet we know from the earlier section that the Marshall couple, who are thinking of dealing with the problem of the unending drought by going away to a better life, perhaps to Haiti, do not in fact think of themselves as better than the other peasants. What we see in the speech by Miss T. is transference – the transference of frustration onto an object that is nearby. This is a serious problem. Salkey warns us to pay careful attention to such transference in the short, dramatic Prologue which sets the scene sharply before us:

> When the drought comes to the land, it comes like a carrion-crow, circling at first, circling slowly and far above the water on the land; then it descends frantically at an angle, diving for bounty which it never earned.
> Naturally, the carrion-crow can smell the dying land from a distance and hasten its death; and when the land is dying, those whose lives are nearest to it smell of death also, and, being contaminated, resent it.

Salkey starts out naming a drought that actually took place, then uses a simile, 'like a carrion-crow', and then it turns into a 'concrete' metaphor: drought *is* a carrion-crow. In the third paragraph, we see that the desperate people

> pray in their own way, make bargains with the carrion-crow, and, after a while, begin to look and act as if they, too, were at an angle, diving towards the land with their claws bared.

The last two paragraphs are crisp:

> The drought brings a touch of madness to the land, a kind of rebellion, and a quality of compelling suicide which Calvary once witnessed.
> Drought first began on Calvary.

By now, we know the drought has become something else. In fact, the middle paragraph had warned us: 'Then, the land becomes a mirror!' Imagine the Prologue being read over the radio. It would work very well: the paragraphs are short and dramatic and evoke pictures before our imagination. And yet, thanks to their brevity, they are mysterious, if we stop to think. After the reference to the mirror comes the longest paragraph, entirely metaphorical:

> No man ought to feel the desire to look at it. No man ought to search for his reflexion in it, because if he did he would only end by

> resenting what he saw; and by discovering his awkward image, and
> so discovering his loneliness, he would hold the mirror high above
> his head, fling it from himself in disgust, and smash it on some
> unsuspecting rock.

The word 'reflexion' is spelled with an 'x': it means both the
mirror image and the reflex action to smash the mirror because
the man does not like what he sees. The scene has its echoes of
Moses smashing the Ten Commandments because he did not like
what he saw, and the Biblical reference becomes important, as
does the 'x'. More important now is to ask where the Caribbean—
or, in broader terms, colonial – man's reflex action comes from
since colonialism was also an attack on the mind. And so we are
told that those whose lives are nearest to the carrion-crow – the
drought – sometimes resent it 'with a blind, hurricane hatred.'

In his prologue, Salkey is doing an Anancy on us: giving us a
tricky story which we misread if we take it 'straight'. We are being
forewarned. And once the story starts, it has twists and turns that
leave us going one way while it goes another.

Mr Marshall, a small planter, has decided to leave the area but
he is not sure whether it is wise to go to Haiti. His wife is not keen
on leaving. He decided to ask Brother Parkin for advice. Brother
Parkin is a small planter and usurer. He is thought of as a man of
ideas. His cousin Biddy, who does his accounts, thinks of him as a
usurer with a soft heart and a very hard head. Brother Parkin
thinks there is nothing wrong with going to Haiti because at least
there is no drought there. His wife disagrees vociferiously
because, she says, Haiti is the land of duppy and Voodoo. Parkin
rather fancied his even-temperedness and fine reading. But his
wife does not always agree with him and now they have a loud
quarrel over whether the Marshalls should go to Haiti or not.

So Brother Parkin takes Marshall along to see Missa Johnson,
a healer. Parkin knows that Johnson is a con man who is thriving
on the problems and psychic needs of the community. (He even
'cures' the problems of the women through sex.) But Johnson
presents a case for himself as a person who is actually doing good
to the community. He shows Brother Parkin some letters:

> Well, this one is from a man who used to go to the hospital for a
> sore on his back which he had for over three years. It just wouldn't
> heal and the doctors try all sorts of things on it. In the long run, he
> start to get poorly and he lose a lot of weight and look like death

self. He come to me, one day when I was holding meeting in the yard, and ask for treatment. So I say yes. And we arrange some 'dues'. The wife and me give the man some bush baths over two weeks' period and the man begin to get well like magic take him. The sore dry up more and more. The herbs and bush in the baths start to take effec' and the man start to get flesh all over. In a month from time to time he come to see me, he fix up nice as ninepence, ole man. He was so happy in him mind that he write me this letter thanking me for what I do for him. He enclose a whole heap of money as an extra 'dues' which I didn't even ask for. In the letter he tell me how I am a doctor that should get Government help to establish a Poor Hospital in St Thomas and that I should have plenty places name after me. He say that he give the name of Johnson to his son who have a name already and if he have a girl pickney he going to name her after my wife. (pp. 50/51)

By this point, we believe him and we almost forget that he is a con man. His assistant is a con man too. The two of them go through a complex game of flagellation to exorcise the spirits of the suffering people. The ritual is supposed to bring rain. Marshall protests to Brother Parkin,

> Them look like them going to murder each other, out there! *You can't see that, man? Is blind you blind or what?*
> (p. 58, my italics)

Brother Parkin refuses to stop it because he does not think they are in trouble. He warns Marshall to say out of it:

> You see all these people here! Every man and woman expect to see this thing. They live on it like bread and what is more if they don't get it Dada Johnson in real trouble.

We believe Brother Parkin. After all, he reads, he knows the community, so he must know what he is talking about. Furthermore, three pages earlier, we had seen the thoughts of Dada Johnson through the omniscient author. He knew his assistant was rising up to challenge his power:

> Yet, Dada Johnson was not worried. He would always be the master of the meeting-yard. His worshippers knew him well, and he was aware of the authority he held over them and their lives. His strength, *he knew*, lay in the personal relationship he had fostered in the days when he was starting the meeting-yard – the private

commissions he had undertaken without payment, the family secrets
he held, the intimate knowledge of family histories he shared, and of
course *his own indomitable self-assurance.* He merely smiled as he
watched his deputy fighting for a place he would *never* be able to
have. He smiled and he became more certain that usurpation of his
position would *never* be one of his worries; if his deputy, he thought,
were an older man, he might be worried, might even be willing to lay
traps for him, or on the other hand, just simply dismiss him from
service in the meeting-yard. *His smile became a wide grin* as he
followed the words of the deputy who was still standing on the table
and proclaiming his position as the second-in-command.
(p. 64, my italics)

From the words I have italicized, which we read quickly and
respond to without evaluating carefully, we believe that Dada
Johnson is very sure of himself. Our feeling is confirmed by the
experienced Brother Parkin and we doubt the inexperienced
Marshall when he tells Parkin after the 'fight' that they should go
because he is sure the two men are dead. Parkin says, 'Don't tell
me that you want to go before the resurrection. I wouldn't believe
you, at all.' (p. 70) A few short paragraphs later, it turns out that
both men are dead. We are stunned. How did it happen that
Brother Parkin was wrong? That Dada's assurance was wrong-
headed? How did *we* believe that nothing would go wrong? The
answer is partially contained in the lines I italicized. We also got
fooled by the self-assurance of Dada Johnson; we did not realize
that he had conned himself. There was no Resurrection. The
Biblical reference is deliberate and so is the frustration of
expectations, Calvary is mentioned in the Prologue, but his is a
Calvary without resolution for nothing comes out of the suffering
and sacrifice: the sacrifice is only play-acting, but worse because
the players themselves get carried away. We should have been
warned: the two fought on what is called the Giant X, the giant
cross, the crossroads, the 'x' we noted in the Prologue.[12]

The theme is repeated on other planes. The children hear about
the double sacrifice and they play a game in which Dada Johnson
has now become a Christ-figure. Doris, Marion and Linda have
formed a secret society. Brother Parkin comes across the three
when they have gone through secret rituals. Marion tells him that
Linda believes that 'Missa Dada Johnson look like him is Massa
Gawd Son.' When he says that that is all wrong, Doris replies,

> But, plenty-plenty people in St. Thomas don't think so, though . . .
> They think like how Linda and me think. And so much people can't
> be wrong, you know, Brother Parkin.
> (p. 89)

Linda explains,

> I don't think that a man like Missa Dada could ever dishonest at all.
> Too much people follow him and did love him. He dead. I know
> that. But he dead like the good death that Massa Gawd Son did dead
> on the cross. I know that and a whole-heap-a people know that, too.
> And I have a rosary that I find, that tell me so. Him too good. Him
> two hands stretch out and drip-drip a-blood running down his head
> side. (p. 81)

Parkin, who knew Johnson was a con man, now sees the
mythifying process at work. Doris says,

> Brother Parkin! We find out a way to fix the drought, you know. We
> going to fix it good-good. You wait and see if we don't fix it.
> (p. 90)

Linda gets mad that Doris is giving away their secrets and calls
her a Judas. They begin a bloody fight and are separated by
Parkin. All this happens under the Banyan tree, which seems to
have mythic significance.

That evening, Miss T, Doris's mother, comes to the house of
the Marshalls to fight with them over the way their daughter
Linda mistreated her daughter. She has a transference of her
anger, as we saw earlier. Someone comes to say that Doris is ill.
Now Miss T blames the Marshalls and their daughter. Parkin tries
to calm her down but she fights with Mrs Marshall.

Mrs Johnson now takes over her dead husband's role and
begins to treat Doris. She says the mother should not seek the help
of the doctor; she causes blame to be placed first on the Marshalls
and then on Brother Parkin. Parkin's good Samaritan attempt at
separating the fighting girls is now described as sinister. Three
men high on ganja go to fetch him; he is brought back in the style
of Christ, beaten up, bare-chested. Like Christ, he is unable to
answer his accusers and torturers. Just when we think he is going
to be killed, and we are angry with the cruel Mrs Johnson, things
turn around. Doris dies, the blame is put on Mother Johnson, and

the group turns on her. Soon, our relief that Brother Parkin is not
going to be sacrificed after all turns to shock when we realize that
the crowd is going to get Mother Johnson. We were sympathetic
with Parkin when he tried to open the eyes of the crowd:

> Listen, everybody! All this woman is doing is quite clear to me. She's
> trying to take her husband's place. She's using Doris's illness as a
> platform. That's all, believe me! She's seeking power which she'll use
> to imprison you the way Dada used to do. I know her only too well!
> She's nothing but a trickster who's on to a good thing, which she
> knows will keep her in money and good living as long as she can
> hold up the pretence of being a true and inspired healer. She's a
> common obeah woman! Black magic and a lot of nastiness are the
> things that she thinks important. And she'll do more than that!
> She'll blackmail you without thinking twice about it.
> (pp. 136/7)

We wanted the crowd to listen to Brother Parkin. We believed
that Mother Johnson was evil and we wanted to be curbed. Yet
when the crowd turns against her, we are alarmed. Miss Gatha
now converts Parkin's suffering into a sacrifice which will bear
fruit. Mother Johnson is now led in a march with the people who
are going 'to some destination not really understood by anybody'.
Parkin sends Miss Gatha to fetch Marshall to stop the crowd.
  Then follows a parody of Calvary:

> The three addicts knelt before Mother Johnson and begged: 'Do
> something, now, Mother. Do something now, nuh.'
>   The leader was silent. The others continued: "You naked you
> know that, Mother? Yu' clothes gone, same so! Put them on again
> and make we see. Beg you, love. Put them on and make we see, nuh!'
> (pp. 182/3)

Of course, the crowd does not see. Parkin tells the people that they
are heading for murder and appeals to them to think of what lies
ahead. The response is,

> So you think you above we, Brother Parkin? You think you cut on a
> different bias, eh, King Solomon Parkin?
> (p. 193)

The leader of the pack turns to colour difference. Marshall arrives
and gives it his best shot. Parkin gets into the act:

You think that you, Parkin, really can save anybody? You think that
you are like Dada Johnson? Is who playing God, now? Who?
(p. 202)

She refuses to keep quiet. 'You think that you and your wholesale
mercy can get things on the right side, eh?' she says. She refers to
her husband and mythifies him: 'Dada dead but him live in me.
Him is here right now with me and him laughing after you.'
Echoing what Linda had said about Doris, she calls the people
'Judas people'. She calls on them to kill her, to 'Stone me like the
bible say.' So they do. The last sentence of the chapter is one of
hope: 'Then, for the first time that night, she relaxed, and waited.'

But the hope held out in that sentence is false. The brief,
dramatic Epilogue denies us any solution or resolution. The first
paragraph reads, 'The drought continued for a long time.' The
second one, 'Rain threatened, but that was all. The third tells us,

> The procession and the others drifted apart. She moved to other
> parts of St Thomas-in-the-East, some to the other parishes, some
> nearer the coast, and some to the other islands. The Marshalls went
> to Haiti.

Structurally, the novel is down-playing the departure of the
Marshalls: it is a failure. And the novel ends cynically:

> Yet, for those who remained in St Thomas-in-the-East, there was
> something else to which they could look forward. They had the
> Great Earthquake of 1907 which somehow would make them forget
> the carrion-crow.

Compare the conclusion of *A Quality of Violence* to that of
Ngũgĩ wa Thiong'o's *The River Between*.[13] In both cases the
people sacrifice a person they had followed only just before: but in
Ngũgĩ's case, the person is a martyr whereas in Salkey's, the
sacrifice is meaningless and worse times follow. Wilson Harris
comments on this meaninglessness in 'The Writer and Society':

> Sacrifice for whom and for what? That is the question. It is the
> rigidity that appeals, one that masks every concept of sacrifice, and
> may spring from the death-dealing sanction of tradition, yes, but
> which defeats the very object and mystery of all capacity in the end,
> in that it makes of the spontaneity of living sacrifice something

already 'given' (rather than something belonging to unpredictable experience), something which loses its 'negative' film or state of possibility.

It is as if the negative film or suspension of the ground of reality was never a series of creative distinctions at all, but a cunning fiction, a hardened process in itself, incapable of genuine or free expression and development.

Andrew Salkey in his novel *A Quality of Violence* touches on this theme of the ultimate meaningless of sacrifice in a remarkable way. The religious one who is stoned to death – and it is upon this the novel closes – suffers the lack of all meaning, the triumph of all meaninglessness. A far cry from Saul's Stephen for whom the heavens shower grace. For here – in *A Quality of Violence* – is the enforced multiplication of sacrifice for its own sake which one finds in the derisive breath of the contemporary theatre, Ionesco, Beckett, Pinter and others.[14]

Although Harris comes close, he too, like the other critics we saw earlier, misses the point. It is not just sacrifice that is at stake. It is the way people fall into ritual patterns and find a sacrificial logic where there is actually no meaning, either in the preconceived act or in its consequences. Brother Parkin is beaten up for nothing. His suffering leads nowhere: he is not even able to stop the crowd from killing Mother Johnson. Mother Johnson gets caught up in the ritual pattern and follows through to the end, having totally forgotten the original problem, which is how to end the drought. Things were triggered off by a con man and his assistant who got involved in a fake ritual to fool the crowd but who got carried away by the ritual and killed each other. *At the same time, and of greater importance, the reader has expectations because the language invisibly contains and imposes a pattern, expectations that are frustrated.*

In Ishmael Reed's *Flight to Canada*, three slaves have escaped while the fourth one, Uncle Robin, stays on with Massa Swille, the slaveowner who is also a multinational. One of the slaves, Stray Leechfield, is earning money through various schemes such as taking part in pornographic photos, planning to buy his freedom with the money. He refuses to believe Raven Quickskill, another of the escaped slaves, that Swille does not want his money, he wants him. Swille considers Leechfield to be his property and sends his slave-catchers after him. Leechfield is caught and brought back: to find Swille dead and Robin owning the estate.

Robin pays the slave-catchers and frees Leechfield, saying,

> Did you think you could just hand history a simple check, that you could short-change history, and history would let you off as simple as that? You've insulted history, Leechfield.[15]

Margaret Atwood says,

> The problem facing all of us writers, insofar as we are concerned with this area of our experience is: how to describe the Monster – in all its forms, *including those in our heads* – accurately and without being defeatist?[16]

The people in Salkey's novel are always referring to history. They are chiefly black people who come out of slavery and remember those times. They particularly remember the neglected Africa. Yet this is not enough for colonial history is in their heads. The scheme by the colonial rulers to destroy local culture and supplant it with an imposed, colonial version of the culture of the mother country was largely successful. It was most successful in the implantation of ritualistic patterns from outside, chiefly the Christian ones. Mother Johnson follows through with the Christian pattern: she demands that she be stoned to complete the pattern. The problem is the inability to think and break out of the imposed pattern. Hence the drought becomes a metaphor for something much larger: Mother Johnson

> was the target, the link between Dada Johnson and the people in the drought, the drought of their faith on the land, and the drought of rational action.
> (p. 164)

This, I keep stressing, is also a problem for the reader: Salkey sees the reader as part of the problem. There are chains on the reader's mind: Salkey knows these chains have to be broken or the reader will refuse to see. Salkey wrote to me that there is a saying in Jamaica, 'Those who won't see can't see.' So he lets the reader deceive himself and then forces him to look back to find out where he went wrong. This is a technique Salkey uses more extensively in his other novels, as we shall see. Margaret Atwood's statement might be extended to read, how do we remove the monster from our heads?

One of the problems is that no matter what the writer does, critics who are trained in the European tradition think they are approaching literature objectively whereas their minds are conditioned to ritual patterns too. This is not to say that the critic cannot understand Salkey: it means that Salkey has to keep playing tricks to break through the barrier. Of course Anancy will not reveal his tricks. When I asked Salkey a question about *Come Home, Malcolm Heartland*, he wrote,

> Can't help you, I'm afraid! Those books of mine, the ones you are considering, indeed all my books, are *done* fictions, really forgotten stories, which I can no longer see clearly or remember point for point, or argue cases for; it's up to the critic to bring them alive, again . . . Let the critic go!

* * *

> The name's Sobert. Johnnie Sobert. Jamaica. R.C. Middle class. Or so I've been made to think.
>   There's hell below my room. A small Hampstead bed-sitter. Private tenement kind of hell. Six rooms below mine: an Indian, not a Trinidadian Indian, just an Indian, the kind that caused Columbus to make his *fortunate mistake*; and four Londoners.

The first novel ended with escape from the island: the second one, *Escape to an Autumn Pavement*, begins with escape having taken place to the Mother Country.[17] There are differences between the two novels. The main characters in the first were attacked for considering themselves privileged above the other peasants though they were from the same class: this time we have someone who is from the middle class, although, as he explains with anger, this is a peculiar type of middle class, an invisible or absent one. 'Can you imagine a middle class that doesn't exist, but is actually a part of the thinking of a people in a society?' he asks Fiona, an Englishwoman who wants sex with him (p. 46). This was said before Frantz Fanon had published his classic analysis of the Third World bourgeoisie in his *The Wretched of the Earth*.[18]

The second novel is even more dramatic and spare in language than the first. This is because the story is being told almost in the form of notes by Sobert, a name that echoes 'sober'. He is working as a waiter in a bar frequented by colored people, chiefly black American G.I.s. The owner of the bar is a white woman,

Sandra, and both she and the waitress, Biddy, like and help him. Although from the middle class in Jamaica, Sobert did not get a higher education before escaping to England and he is now a worker plus, although he downplays this to the point of invisibility, a hustler and producer (p. 28). Thinking about the Indian girl, whom he calls Miss Goolam Chops, he says/writes,

> Coloured territories (shameful epithet that) in the near future will be thick with wigs and gowns and silks, dear God, and not a damn' soul qualified to look after a simple thing like the land – nobody worries about Agriculture in mainly agricultural countries or islands. Dirty thing, the land! Not for middle-class aspirants!
> (p. 13)

He is carrying a great deal of suppressed anger within, as we see from the way he names people ('Fish Face', etc.) and from the fact that almost everyone he meets says he is carrying a chip on his shoulder: 'You are angry, aren't you?' asks his landlady (p. 11). When Gerald Trado asks him for his overdue rent on behalf of the landlady, he thinks,

> Hit him! Hit him murderously hard and be done with it. Bash whatever little brains he has left and feel like a man afterwards. There's only one way to get out of this with any satisfaction, and it's done with a touch of violence.
> (p. 21)

Gerald Moore is right when he says,

> Johnnie Sobert is in flight from Jamaican middle-class values, which he feels to be not only shoddy in themselves but not in any way validated by the social realities of the island's life.[19]

Bill Carr points out that none of the British reviewers seemed to realize that while Johnnie Sobert was just a black immigrant in England, at home in Jamaica he was middle class and therefore 'clearly defined as apart from the Negro mass of the population.'[20] So even more than the West Indian workers who come to London (for example, those we see in Sam Selvon's *The Lonely Londoners*,[21] Johnnie came to England mythifying the English middle class and became even more of a loner because he was not really accepted by that class. He comes across two racist pamphlets, the second read to him by Fiona:

> Mentally the Negro is inferior to the white man. The sutures of the
> Negro's skull close quite early in life, preventing the further
> expansion of the brain . . . What is true is that many of the
> immigrants come here partly to find a white wife – often for reasons
> of prestige; and that most of them find means to have trial runs.
> Obtaining white women is not only a matter of desire but of
> necessity as well . . .
> (p. 135)

Thanks to his class origin and education, Johnnie has been
created in the image of the English middle class yet here he is
being rejected in crudely racist terms. Where is he to turn? He says
to Fiona,

> Africa does not belong to me! There's no feeling there. No bond.
> We've been fed on the Mother Country myth. Its language. Its
> history. Its literature. Its Civics. We feel chunks of it rubbing off on
> us. We believe in it. We trust it. Openly, we admit we're part of it.
> But are we? Where's the real link?
> (p. 48)

Although he depends on immigrant West Indian workers for
friendship, Johnnie does not really identify with them.

His only means of dealing with the world, then, is, as Carr
points out, a slick, at times sarcastic, language, occasionally but
not too frequently ironic. This is not the humor that we find in
Selvon, the humor of survival and involvement with life: it is the
defensiveness of the sacred loner demonstrating that he is
mentally superior when he is actually afraid of the English middle
class. The example Carr quotes is as follows:

> Sexy-boy Trado is sprawling in an armchair. Quite obviously reading
> *The Observer*. Quotes Ken Tynan the way a Jamaican peasant quotes
> the Bible. Sexy-girl Trado is toying with the handle of the old lady's
> vacuum cleaner. Also sprawling in armchair number two. Carpet by
> mantelpiece a trifle threadbare; just the spot where jolly Trado takes
> his stand after a hard night at the pub and lays down the law on
> anything *The Observer* had made clear to him the Sunday before.
> (p. 19)

In this kind of superior language, Johnnie is showing that he is both of the class of the Trados and superior to them because he can identify them and make comparisons from above. He knows *The Observer* and Ken Tynan, yet he can see the English people from a perspective they cannot have. He is also distancing himself from the Jamaican peasant. And he is doing so by his mastery over the language imposed on the colonies as a weapon of enslavement. But, as Carr notes, Johnnie's is a rootless idiom. He is the unhappy outsider. His rudeness towards the Indian girl in the building appears to be sexist but is really an indication of the fact that although he knows he has some Indian ancestry, he feels rootless in a nationalistic sense: she has the confidence of coming from a country that has been independent for over a decade and has had an identifiable culture for centuries, even though she is a colonial like him. She does not realize that this is why he is so angry at her: he resents the fact that she comes from a real middle class.

Gerald Moore is more correct than he realizes when he says, intending it as a form of criticism, that Johnnie Sobert

> is adequate as a character but not as a window on the world, *unless the limitations of his vision were exploited more deliberately by the author.*
> (p. 107, my italics)

Precisely: the author does exploit the limitations of Sobert's vision. How do we know that his vision has limitations? By paying attention to his way of telling his story. William Riggan says:

> First-person narration is . . . always at least potentially unreliable, in that the narrator, *with . . . human limitations of perception and memory and assessment, may easily have missed, forgotten, or misconstrued certain incidents, words, or motives.* Furthermore, precisely because the narrator sits before us as a human being – albeit a fictionalized one – we naturally react to him in varying degrees in human terms *and not just as a disembodied voice* providing us with information. Much of what he tells us *also gives us an idea of what he himself is like . . . Emotional ties also enter into such assessments and reactions on our part as auditors and readers of his account.*[22]
> (my italics)

We have to add to Riggan's list of possibilities the idea that the narrator may be blocking things out of his story because he is blocking them out of his consciousness. He could be only giving us things from his consciousness. Are things going to burst through from his unconscious? Or is he, with his education and ability to control the language, going to be able to keep such things out of his story? Sobert says,

> Words are such bastard dissemblers. Ancient convenient hypocrites.
> Still, we got to live by them, toe to toe, consequence for
> consequence, hurt for hurt, and so on right down the flaming hill.
> (p. 99)

He is actually fighting with language. 'Fifteen rounds with Muhammed Ali,' as Edwin Thumboo said of Adrian Roscoe's analysis of Okello Oculi.[23]

Johnnie's mother senses something is wrong. She writes to him,

> Your letters tell me that there's something troubling you. You must
> remember that I'm *good at reading between the lines*. I've had enough
> experiences: first your father, and now you. I sense a certain unrest.
> A certain, shall I say, nervousness and anxiety? Yes?
> (p. 127, my italics)

This is a clear message to us to read what is not being said.

The suppressed problem is brought to the surface by an inescapable choice Johnnie is forced to make. Fiona seduces him; and she falls in love with him. But he is ambivalent about the sexual relationship and tries to escape it. He moves out of the building to share a flat with Dick, an Englishman who 'has all the nervous energy of his class, or rather his class come-down-to-ground-floor level.' (p. 8) Dick is English lower middle class. We begin to realize that Johnnie must have a latent homosexuality that he is not bringing to the conscious level but which is sending out signals. For example, early on, he is angered by Trado's demand for the rent and says/writes: 'Ignore him. He's lonely. He's anxious. He's insecure. He's bisexual.' (p. 20) He uses the word 'gay' several times, though we must note that this was before the word became a popular synonym for homosexual. Fiona and Dick arrange a confrontation where he must choose between them. He dodges choice for as long as he can. He even tries to get Larry, the West Indian barber who acts as West Indian adviser and communicator, to solve his problem, but Larry won't exactly do this. At the end, when he goes to his flat, he finds that Dick has left – and left him with the problem of having to choose, only after which he can join him.

So is *Escape to an Autumn Pavement* a novel about latent homosexuality or bi-sexuality before it became acceptable in modern literature? I would not rule this out. But since the novel is about escaping island imprisonment, an imprisonment brought about by colonialism, and since the novel is full of references to colonial rule – the novel was written just before many British colonies became independent – we have to decide whether the tension of having to choose between Fiona and Dick is not more than just having to choose between a white woman and a white man. Anthony Boxill says:

> In the novel . . . the central character, Johnnie Sobert, a Jamaican who lives in London, wrestles with the problem of deciding whether he is a homosexual or not. Certain commentators suggest that it is a relief to find a West Indian novel dealing with a problem other than colour and the exile of West Indians in London. Such commentators have refused to look below the surface for, in explaining Johnnie Sobert's predicament, Salkey talks as much about the colonial situation, which includes colour, and about the West Indian's reason for being in London, as any other West Indian writer. Admittedly, such themes are not obvious and obtrusive, but they are there for the reader who wishes to trace them.[24]

For Johnnie to acknowledge either that he hates white women – or hates women – or that he is a homosexual is not pleasant to him. Boxill notes that this is the problem for the emasculated colonial, the colonial who cannot be a man because of colonialism. Loving a white man also carries the implication for the colonial of loving the white master, who displaces the father as a role model for manhood. Note the scene when Johnnie has sex with Fiona for the first time:

> 'You seem so withdrawn, Johnnie. Why?'
>   'Nothing.'
>   'Aren't you enjoying me?'
>   What the hell does she expect me to say to that? I suppose she wants to purr affectionately, curl up beside her and say:
>   'Yes, Mummy darling. You make Cream of Wheat the *bestest* in the whole wide world.'

> Enjoying?
> It's such a quiet, intimate word, isn't it? Entertaining, too.
> Enjoying what?
> Enjoying hot soup? Steak? Soufflé? A saucer of milk? Sleep?
> 'Aren't you with me, Johnnie?'
> 'Sure.'
> You bet I'm with you, Jezebel, Ramona, Dolores of the lonely
> hills. I'm with you like a thorn in the backside. I'm with you in the
> same way Dick's with me. It's all in the mind, as the man in the
> Goonery department would say. (p. 105)

This is the first time he has had sex with Fiona yet he thinks of her in terms of his mother and he thinks of Dick. As Raven Quickskill thinks about Harriet Beecher Stowe in Reed's *Flight to Canada*, 'Watch what you put down on the page.'[25] So Johnnie does not really like sex with Fiona and is therefore *not* the classic colonial black man coming to England for white women, as Fiona notes (p. 134). Johnnie's explanation to Larry the barber for why he is not thrilled about being involved with Fiona is, 'She's the grabbing, gobbling type . . . She makes me feel caged up. Frightened. Nervous. Inadequate . . .' (p. 174). There could be some truth in what Johnnie is saying since Fiona told him that she once loved a Nigerian, Joseph, whose child she had had (just after he had left her) and who used to say that West Indians were 'halfies' (p. 42). It would seem as though, like the white women in Tayeb Salih's *Season of Migration to the North*, Fiona is sexually attracted to black men. Yet we discover later that Fiona loves Johnnie, so he was being unfair to her. And she cannot be easily dismissed because, in some respects, she turns out to be as wise and profound as his mother, as we see when we compare what his mother writes with what she (Fiona) says. For example, it is Fiona who draws out of him his hatred of his non-existent middle class and the fact that he is always escaping (p. 133). Later, Johnnie thinks of Dick,

> he had been trying his best to be my friend; to be an anchor; to be a
> bulwark against my attacks, my frequent attacks of escapism.
> (p. 158)

But it is Fiona who, while she wants Johnnie to probe her sexually as deep as possible, probes his wound. She says, 'you don't know what you want out of life.' She tells him that he is carrying a monster, as she is (p. 121). She also tells him that unlike her class, he has mythified the Mother Country. He says,

> Surely it takes much more than a hundred and twenty-eight years after the Abolition of Slavery for a middle class to evolve? . . . When I look at your middle-class structure and I think of mine back there, I want to laugh and cry, all at once.
> (p. 47)

She replies,

> But that's not sensible, Johnnie! Britain's a nation of people, old and well formed. Too well formed, as a matter of fact. I can't see how you could possibly think of Jamaica in terms of this country!
> (p.47)

Johnnie always escapes from decisions and from himself: to escape Fiona, he rents a flat with Dick, but she tracks him down, and he does not break from her but pays her a (sexual) visit, which angers Dick when he later finds out. Johnnie wants someone else to solve his problem, so he asks Larry,

> Do you think that the mere fact that I went with him to the flat is a kind of admission that I'm that way without knowing it?
> (p. 175)

Larry does not provide a definite answer. Later, Larry tells Johnnie:

> You're a self-seeking man. A real old-time selfish, ever-grasping individual . . . You're looking for a sort of mirror which will make you out to be somebody worth while. You want an identity like. You want to feel that you have a nation behind you, a nation that you can call your own, a national feeling is what you looking for. You would like to walk proud like how the German or the Frenchman or the Englishman can walk proud knowing that they have tradition and a long history behind them to give them a real identity. You feel lacking in all that because you're a colonial boy with only slavery behind you. So you bound to be confused. You bound to want to escape.
> (p. 199)

Later, Larry backtracks and tells Johnnie he was thinking of himself, not of Johnnie when he said what he said. Are we to believe him? The mirror image is to be found elsewhere (e.g. p. 30) so it seems that Larry spoke the truth. It is significant that when he finds Dick reading yet another historical novel, Johnnie says he has read only one (p. 179). Johnnie says at the beginning of Chapter Eleven:

> *If only I had known* is such a bastard of a thing to say, anyway. I knew all along that I was looking for more than just a choice between Fiona and Dick; between greed and contentment; between unambitious sentimentality and unambitious tranquility; between sexuality and intelligent, ordinary living. I knew too a little about myself, not much; I knew that I could be stupidly hesitant, fiercely if not self-consciously honest, overbearingly brash, fairly considerate, resentful of being bored, riddled with pretensions, preoccupied with making a go of my escape to England, I knew that I was searching, like a hundred million other people, for something to pin my tiny flag to, in order to be recognized as a right and proper claimant to happiness, however overworked that myth might be.
>
> I knew all that, and yet I didn't try hard enough to do anything about my condition. Everything seemed too pointless. Wasted. Finally, I realized that I was headed nowhere like a hundred million others: I had escaped a malformed Jamaican middle class: I had attained my autumn pavement; I had become a waiter in a Dantesque night club; I had done more than my fair share of hunting, rejecting, and condemning; and I had created another kind of failure, and this time, in another country.
> (p. 145)

From the above, we notice that Johnnie is using balanced and complex rhythms. He is coming closer to acknowledging his inner problems. 'Another country' refers not only to England but also to the title of James Baldwin's novel about the people who inhabit 'another country', including homosexuals.

We have seen that Sobert's problems arise to a large extent from belonging to a colonial middle-class, Jamaican variety. Fanon was to characterize the middle class in the most scathing terms in *The Wretched of the Earth*, published in French in 1961, a year after Salkey's novel, and in English translation in 1963:

> The national bourgeoisie will be quite content with the role of the Western bourgeoisie's business agent, and it will play its part without any complexes in a most dignified manner. But this same lucrative role, this cheap-Jack's function, this meanness of outlook and this absence of all ambition symbolize the incapability of the national middle class to fulfill its historic role of bourgeoisie. Here, the

dynamic, pioneer aspect, the characteristics of the inventor and of the discoverer of new worlds which are found in all national bourgeoisies are lamentably absent. In the colonial countries, the spirit of indulgence is dominant at the core of the bourgeoisie; and this is because the national bourgeoisie identifies itself with the Western bourgeoisie, from whom it has learnt its lessons. It follows the Western bourgeoisie along its path of negation and decadence without ever having emulated it in its first stages of exploration and invention, stages which are an acquisition of that Western bourgeoisie whatever the circumstances. In its beginning, the national bourgeoisie of the colonial countries identifies itself with the decadence of the bourgeoisie of the West. We need not think that it is jumping ahead; it is in fact beginning at the end. It is already senile before it has come to know the petulance, the fearlessness, or the will to succeed of youth.[26]

While noting the emptiness of the imitative Jamaican middle class, Salkey does not dismiss the class, not only because he belongs to it but also because this is the class that has the opportunity to see the Western middle-class it is imitating, on whose behalf it is acting. The Jamaican middle class is essentially blind but a thinking, *sober* member of that class is in a position to look through the sham and to recognize his links to the peasants and working class. The problem for Johnnie Sobert is that he has no self-knowledge and is able to trip blithely if unhappily along, torn by the contrary desires for acceptance and rejection. This is why he does not see the sense in the letter his mother writes to him. True, she does not understand his circumstances and his difficulties, but she knows something is wrong. She is right when she says,

> And above all, son, see to it that you do not get involved in any political rows or, for that matter, any racial nonsense. You never had the intelligence or cunning to deal with either topic.
> (p.51)

But instead of sifting through his mother's advice, he dismisses it with as much 'tough' cynicism as he dismisses everything else: 'Pride of family name, first. And my bloody happiness last, eh?' Salkey was the first writer, to my knowledge, to articulate the crisis for the middle-class colonial who is in the Mother Country for the first time.

Earlier in the novel, Larry had told a story about a West Indian friend deserted by his English wife and pointed out the moral, which Johnnie finally saw as applying to himself: 'Our deeds shall follow us from afar, and what we have done shall make us what we are.' (p. 63)

Salkey provides us with a valuable note to the novel:

> Although all the characters and situations depicted in this novel are fictitious, I'm obliged to point out that the character called SHAKUNTALA GOOLAM might, indeed, cause some offence in that, quite unwittingly, she has been given an improbable Indian name. Apparently, SHAKUNTALA and GOOLAM belong to different worlds.
>
> After naming her, I learned that SHAKUNTALA (Sanskrit) is Hindu, and GOOLAM which is properly GHULAM (Persian) is Muslim. Because of this I should like to say that there has been no attempt on my part to embarrass anyone, or to utter propaganda on behalf of Hindu-Muslim Unity, or anything of the sort.
>
> In the first instance I plead ignorance, and in the second innocence. If I'm allowed a third I plead invention. As it is, SHAKUNTALA GOOLAM barely exists in name, therefore, she has no other life and exerts no influence whatever beyond her appearance as a minor character in this novel.
>
> A.S.

Unless one concludes that the author does not know that he could correct the name before going to press, one must suspect that he is doing an Anancy on us (note the first initial). It is a clue that we might miss: until we look back to the fact that the protagonist, Johnnie Sobert, is ignorant and innocent in the sense of not knowing and is inventing in that he is controlling the words. *Sobert* could be making up the name of Miss Goolam to maintain his pose of superiority. But it is a pose that is challenged by the end.

* * *

The Late Emanicipation of Jerry Stover, Salkey's third novel, follows the pattern of home/exile.[27] This time, the action is in Jamaica. The protagonist is Jerry Stover, a young man in his early twenties. He has a great deal in common with Johnnie Sobert: he too is middle class, he too has been brought up by his mother (his father being away in Cuba, where Jerry and his elder brother Les was born). The mother later writes him letters containing a lot of solid sense when he needs it: and one of her letters makes the connection with Sobert for it reads at the end, 'Think soberly, seriously.' (p. 142) In fact, the connection with the second novel is emphasized right through the novel for an early comment by the mother on Jerry's tone applies equally to Sobert's: 'Flippancy is a child's way out.' (p. 33)

At the time, it was fashionable to deal essentially with the peasant and working classes in the Third World and to dismiss the middle class, as Fanon did in *The Wretched of the Earth*, as imitators, hucksters. Bill Carr says,

> Perhaps it isn't surprising that his [Salkey's] public comment on his first book should be in the nature of a cynical aside, that it was written to catch the market for "peasant" novels.

But the second and the third novels focus on middle-class protagonists for Salkey sees, like Wole Soyinka in *The Interpreters*, that the educated middle class is not to be dismissed since it has power and it not only runs things but also has hegemony.[28] And after all, in Jamaican society, for most people, the gap between middle class and worker/peasant is not a great one, and certainly not an old one. This is why Miriam the housemaid says to Jerry (who sleeps with her),

> We the same black people together, Missa Jerry. We really the said same, only you're different when we get up an' go outside. You' different only 'cause of you' mother.
> (p. 114)

And Glissada Maycroft, the secretary to Rybik, the leader of the Government, says of the Rastafarians' demand for better treatment and recognition,

> A very thin line divides me from the lunatic who came to see you the other day. We've got the ol' skin in common. I should be terrified of the closeness.
> (p. 199)

The middle class in this case means chiefly the Civil Service. When the British were preparing to 'hand over' power, the chief weapon and sign of achievement was the Civil Service. And it is with the

Civil Service that Salkey begins his third novel, in his usual crisp and dramatic way. As before, Salkey places the novel clearly within the framework of history:

> It was a long time after the New Constitution of 1944.
> It was the time of public anguish for parents whose sons and daughters were not selected by the Civil Service Appointments' Board for employment in one of the approved offices of the Island Treasury and the Colonial Secretariat (the status of the other departments was always a matter of doubt).
> It was also the time of the coming élite of the Ministries.
> Indeed, it was the time when to be a civil servant, however *unestablished* the post, however *temporary* the clerkship, was clearly to be on the winning side (not to be a civil servant was to be considered an acknowledged failure: a limp, damp thing inevitably headed for the sinister depths of commerce and industry in some back room along Barry Street, or even deeper still, along Port Royal Street).
> It was the time when nobody bothered to discuss the challenge of private enterprise, when nobody cared to work in it, except of course the immigrant Chinese, the Syrians and the Jews; it was the time when almost everybody was busy sneering at farming and large-scale agriculture, except the East Indians and the British expatriates.
> It was, in fact, altogether a splendid time for the desk, and a rotten time for the land.

A time was to come in Third World writing when private enterprise was condemned as part of neocolonialism, as part of working with outside interests against the workers and peasants. But at this time, Salkey sees the essential uncreativeness of the Civil Service as worse, as a place for dead wood: or so it would seem from the prologue. At any rate, Jerry Stover and his friends, most of whom are in the Civil Service, although some are of the same generation and outside, feel frustrated by their lack of creativeness. They try to rebel against this stifling system. But how do they rebel? By drinking, wenching, etc. They deceive themselves into believing that they are eating away at the system:

> Six months before that afternoon in the Niagara, while Jerry, Silba, Albert and Paula were discussing the doubtful merits of the Kirby-Rybik Kingdom, NEXUS, Prudence Kirby's literary review, and class and caste in the Island, it occurred to Jerry that all they were really doing was trying to bore away at the *status quo* over cheap rum and water, and he said so quite strongly.

'If that's the case,' Paula suggested, 'why not let's think of
ourselves as termites, threatening the system in the afternoon?'
'Right!' Albert said. 'Right!' Albert said. 'We're Termites from
now on, *to rass*!
They accepted his obscene comment.
(p. 26)

This is the point at which we see that Jerry has possibilities above
the others. He is not happy about being called a Termite. 'After
we've helped destroy the Kingdom, what do we put in its place?'
he asks. There is no good answer forthcoming. The novel thus has
to do with the awakening and growth of Jerry. First, he must drop
out of the safety net of the Civil Service, then he must move to the
bottom of the society, as he does when he goes to stay with the
Rastafarians, and then he must surface. There has to be a process
of real education as opposed to what passes for education.
Mason, who is white and who has a degree from Oxford like his
father, disposes of some illusions. Paul says,

> Look, Mason, you're an intelligent man . . . you're educated. You
> can think like an adult. The Termites are all small boys, *rassed* up by
> the Island and floundering like bitch, man.
> (p. 51)

Mason replies,

> Oxford meant a list of books to read, lectures to go to, essays to
> write, tutorials, and imitation . . . What you really want are loads of
> reformers, teachers, philosophers and moralists, opening shop all
> over the Island. I'm only one of the returned grey blobs, and one
> without a vocation.
> (pp. 51/2)

Jerry feels close to Mason: but he is different from Mason. He is
not white, he has not been to university, and he is not been off the
island. *Getting off the island is the sub-text of the novel.* Jerry's
father is off the island, on another one, Cuba, and seems to be on
the verge of return when he suddenly wins the national lottery, for
the second time it seems, and does not return. Jerry's brother,
Les, *has* been off the island: he studied at Julliard in the U.S. but
returned to find his plans of being a composer with an orchestra
frustrated:

> Jerry knew that many of Les's plans had been frustrated but he was
> unable to make the first move to sympathise or even talk things over
> with him. Les, in turn, was also aware of Jerry's attempts to escape
> the Island's extreme colonial strangehold, but he, too, was unable to
> make the first move to show his understanding of the situation . . .
> Jerry respected Les's love of music and Les's ability to live with his
> unrealised dream and carry on in spite of his blighted future.
> (p. 14)

While Jerry wants to do something, he is wasting his life because
he does not know what he wants to do. Something is missing, as is
emphasized by the description of the mother of his part-Syrian
girlfriend, Carmen:

> For a moment, she reminded Jerry of a middle-aged household fairy,
> forever on the move, forever in search of a wand she had lost in her
> early youth.
> (p. 72)

The novel is about Jerry's search for the missing something – and
about whether he finds, or is on the verge of finding it.

The company Jerry keeps has an in-built problem of social
identity, Jamaica's problem, reinforcing the deeper question of
whether the people have a centre. Van Farson is half East Indian
and half Negro (the term 'Negro' being used in the novel instead
of 'African' or 'black', except when the Rastafarians talk about
themselves), but chooses to identify with his East Indian half.
Wyn Stone is Ex-RAF and East Indian; Sally Dawes is part Carib,
part Jewish, part African. Albert Ley, Silba Lane and Berto
Sabyo are black; Mason Donne-Jones is white. Mason's wife
Jenny is an English blonde, as is Paula Watt. In a society that
judges class and caste with a finely-tuned color consciousness,
black people are at the bottom of the heap. Hence living on the
Dung'll are the Rastafarians. They identify with Ethiopia and
want repatriation to that country. (In the past, 'Ethiopia' meant
'Africa' to many people.)

So people have to work out a national identity. Jerry sees the
Rastafarians' desire to go to Africa in terms of an escape, both in
the sense of being an unrealizable dream and, if realized, of being
a way of letting the national government off the hook. To stress
the problem of race, color and class, Jerry's two lovers are
Miriam, his maid, who is black and from the country, and

Carmen, who is part-Syrian and urban and who leaves to study at Julliard. He discovers on the same day that he has impregnated both of them: he finds out about Carmen as she is leaving for the United States and when he gets back from the airport, he finds out about Miriam, who says she will leave and return home since she knows he will do nothing to help her situation.

Jerry cannot make any progress in self-knowledge while he remains in the Civil Service, which is a treadmill:

> Hundreds of civil servants had been celebrating as they usually did on the night before pay day, taking everything on credit, signing fantastic wine cards, borrowing extravagantly. They did this simply because they knew that during the next day between mid-day and four o'clock in the afternoon they would be disappearing from their offices before their eagle-eyed creditors, the past month's money-lenders, bill-collectors, food-vendors, merchant tailors, traveling salesmen, car dealers, night club waiters, barmen, barmaids, estranged wives, divorcées, cast-off sweethearts, the usual assortment of dependents and near-relatives, touts and trusting prostitutes had time to catch up with them and humiliate them by asking for what was owed, promised or otherwise coming to them.[29]
> (p. 4)

We know Jerry is tired of the meaningless round with the Termites because he is the one who suggests giving up drink for Lent, accepting his mother's criticism about the drink without realizing it. The person who gives him the push is his senior in the office whom he had always despised as a failure, whom he had always poked fun at, Randy. Randy tells Jerry that he cannot fit into the civil service. He explains that Jerry has not seen his (Randy's) situation for what it was. He says he worked with his father behind a fish-counter and served people, learning to completely forget self:

> After a few years of that I started to study on my own, in secret, without my parents knowing a thing about it. Had I been caught at it, it would've seemed to them like a form of betrayal, treachery, in fact. After all, I was there to carry on whenever my father saw fit to hand over to me.
> (p. 102)

He says he could have moved higher up the civil service a long time ago if he had wanted to, but he decided that he had had enough of hauling himself up the ladder. He knows 'The world's packed with people in the wrong jobs.' (p. 103) He says to Jerry,

> *You* have had it far too easy, all your generation, your so-called privileged friends, all of you. You've had all the obstacles removed. No guts, Stover. That's the result. No sense of responsibility. No grit. No stick-to-it-tiveness. You'll begin to rot inside. *You'll lose your moral centre.* You'll lose the fight and you and your pals will be trampled in the mad rush for the dung hill. That's what your kind of education has done for you, Stover.
> (p. 101, my italics except for the first 'you')

He hands Jerry a pen, and Jerry resigns. And then he respects Randy. Jerry is next to be told to resign from another group, the uncreative literary board of the significantly named *NEXUS*, run by Prudence Kirby, the wife of the Leader of the Opposition. The journal is only a tourist attraction when it does come out, what one might call airport literature rather than literature probing the soul of the country. It is no wonder Prudence feels threatened when an American woman, Caroline Selkirk, turns up with plans to edit her own journal. Jerry welcomes Caroline, an act Prudence considers as betrayal, so Jerry is forced to resign.

Jerry moves to the Dung'll, a way of escaping the island inwards. He had first gone there when Paula wanted to write a story about the Rastafarians and that is how he had met Bashra and the others. Now he collapses drunk on the street and is saved by Marcus, a Rasta, waking up a week later in Bashra's hut. Bashra says the people on the Dung'll have been trying some home remedies and hoping for the best. Just before quitting the civil service, Jerry had gone to see Bashra while he was not drinking. Bashra knew something was on his mind. So Bashra had offered him marijuana cigarettes and told him when they reached a certain point, he would give a signal and both Jerry and he would have to speak from the heart and state what was worrying them:

> He was gradually sensing his own presence, the bulk of his thighs, the space he was occupying in the hut, the whole weight of his body. An energy, which he had never known before, made him aware of all this; it seemed concealed in the pit of his stomach. It stirred and leapt out in spurts. It dictated to his will. It guided his limbs. He found it easy to regard himself from the inside. He stood and

discovered that his surroundings were different; he also discovered
that he was someone else. *He felt that he had no weight, no ballast to
keep him fixed to the floor, no centre, no hold over himself.*
(p. 98, my italics)

When Bashra whispered, 'Go!', Jerry said, as though he had been
waiting for the signal all his life, 'No culture. No tradition in doing
things.' When Bashra spoke, he said, 'Africa is home for me and
all my people.'

Jerry now decides to stay with the Rastafarians and teach them
to read and write and do mathematics. He changes his identity.
Later, he sends for Mason to join him. It is then that his
correspondence begins with his mother: in the past, he was always
on the run and did not pay attention to her. Jung says,

> Because the mother is the first bearer of the soul image, separation
> from her is a delicate and important matter of the greatest
> educational significance.[30]

In addition to sending him money and food for the body, she
provides food for the soul, and mind, through written words:

> The surest way to fight for your cause is to acquire a good sound
> sense of politics together with a flair for welfare publicity and an
> acumen for impressing the conscience of the Government and the
> middle classes. All the sentimentality and wishful thinking will get
> your cause nowhere.
> (p. 174)

She writes further,

> I think you really ought to be laying the foundation for a specific
> apprenticeship; the basis, I am certain, ought to be partly academic
> and partly humanistic: an intense course of study in some chosen
> subject, and then, living to the full, intelligently, and with an
> awareness of the problems of humanity and with an appreciation of
> the elegance of the highest achievements of others. After that, and
> only after that, will you be able to attempt the sort of political and
> social reformative action *which you're now merely playing at.*
> (p. 175, my italics)

It is the italicized statement that is of key importance. Jerry and
his friends are always playacting, even when Jerry gets serious.

This is what he thought earlier when he saw Van come out of Randy's office:

> His manner was remarkably easy. He held his head high. Jerry noticed his entrance and realised that he, too, was playing to his waiting audience.
> (p. 82)

Later, when Carmen is introduced to the Termites, she says, 'Are they real?' (p. 89)

So far, it would seem that *The Late Emancipation of Jerry Stover* is the 'straighest' of Salkey's novels. Indeed, one of the best critiques of the novel takes the novel entirely straight. This is by Gareth Griffiths in *A Double Exile*, although Griffiths makes a mistake in the title and right through the novel, calling Stover 'Stoker' (Griffiths told me that this was an error on the part of his publisher). He says that Salkey shows a 'compassion for the confused, well-meaning young men and women' who have to live in his generation. He adds,

> we get a detailed and valuable inside picture of the deadness of the new society for those who are trapped in it, a deadness brought about not by lack of intelligence or will-power, but by the overwhelming sense that the issues which face them are painted dummies see-sawing inanely above a sea of apathy, indifference, and cynical outside manipulation.[32]

Griffiths continues,

> as a study of the floating world of Kingston and the imperceptible way its delights shade off and cross the barriers of class and race, providing a welcome, if superficial, escape from the problems the new West Indian élite faces, it has its purpose and its point. Gradually Jerry begins the slow rejection of this temporary solution weaning himself off the continual Black Seal rum 'pitches' and seeking alternative consolations, first in a love affair, and finally, in a relationship with a Rastafarian brother whom he meets, a resident of the Dung'll, a shanty town refuge for derelicts and outcasts. At first his intention is to live on the Dung'll with Bashra, the Rastafarian, and teach, to provide the illiterates with the education denied them by their society. But he is quickly involved in the realization that the only possible solution to the problems posed are political.[32]

But precisely because Griffiths overlooks the trickster element, he finds fault with the novel. He says,

> Salkey's novel is often rambling and over-emphatic, drawing out its
> effects too generously, and capping over-long descriptions with a
> too-neat narrative comment.[33]

Griffiths does not analyze any passage to prove his point, and
because he takes the novel straight, he misreads the ending. He
says,

> In a rather theatrical ending the Termites are killed in a car crash
> whilst returning home from a 'pitch' up-country and Jerry is left to
> contemplate his failure and to wonder if 'someone with more
> experience [would] take over, and work at it?' It is clear, though
> unstated, that Jerry Stoker's next move will be the journey out from
> the islands to that exile which, though no solution, is at least a
> temporary ease to the pain of life in the troubled Caribbean.

Salkey's 'too-neat narrative comment' is just that. We take it to be
the author's objective judgement of the person or situation when
in fact it is subjective. A good example is Randy, when we first
meet him:

> Jerry Stover was early. With three minutes to spare, he was leisurely
> climbing the winding stairs at the back of the Resident Magistrate's
> Courts at Half Way Tree, when he ran into the Clerk of the Courts,
> R.A.D. Randax-Lee, affectionately called Randy. A Negro Chinese,
> fifty-three, balding and a zealous civil servant, he was Jerry's only
> work problem. Unnoticed, socially unimportant, and entirely
> predictable, Randy had been the Clerk of the Courts at Half Way
> Tree for seventeen years. He had never been thanked, praised, liked,
> and for seventeen years had never been promoted. Randy knew his
> job but he was qualified for nothing more than the position he held.
> Barristers came, went, and became Resident Magistrates, but Randy
> remained the Clerk of the Courts and served them faithfully, and in
> some instances, openly resentfully. He was highly sensitive about his
> Chinese ancestry and deeply regretted his Negro blood; altogether he
> disliked the way he looked.
>   He bullied Jerry because he could do so to no one else in the
> office; everybody had long ago learned to resist Randy's attacks.
> (p. 15)

As readers, we go along with his judgement, not realizing that it is
Jerry's subjective and slick judgement rather than that of the

omniscient author. So we, too, write off Randy. But later Randy is the person who tells Jerry to quit the civil service, letting him know what he (Randy) had to go through to get where he did. Jerry is being given the challenge that he really needs, not to opt for something safe but to build on the achievements and sacrifices of those who have gone before: but Jerry only realizes this later and is forced, then, to re-evaluate Randy. And when he does so, Randy becomes one of his heroes. We allowed ourselves to be tricked by the 'too-neat narrative comment.'

Jerry is right that he is bothered by the lack of tradition, of a way of doing things. Yet the problem is deeper than Jerry thinks. Right through the novels, we find *an absence*: always references to something lost, a missing centre, but nobody knows what it is or is entirely aware that it is missing. Given the importance of the missing centre to the Caribbean, years later, V.S. Naipaul was to use the term as the title of one of his books.[34] There is a mental block: it is impossible to get at what is missing because of this block. This is tied up with memory, not only personal but also national and therefore historical. We see the problem of memory quite early in the novel. This is when Jerry comes home after a drinking session in the morning and sleeps with Miriam before entering the house for breakfast. It is his turn to say the grace:

> He realised quite suddenly that he had forgotten the opening
> sequence of words of the recitation. He stared in front of him,
> through the space between his mother's furled linen napkin and the
> heaped plate of buttered toast, and hoped. It seemed an age. Thelma
> shifted uneasily.
> (p. 9)

Jerry's predicament is to be found in the words of Trinidadian poet Wayne Brown in 'Insomnia': 'staring/Like a just-dead man trying/To haul himself back along a memory/He cannot quite remember . . .'[35] It takes a long time but his mother insists:

> At last, his mind, his murky Wednesday night memories of past
> delights, secrets, violence and indelicacies began to clear. Then,
> gradually and easily the grace came back to him. It came sincerely,
> word after word, every emphasis correctly placed, the entire
> recitation ordered and felt. It slipped piece by piece into a pattern of

near-song. Jerry was surprised. At the end of it, his pause came
naturally and well-punctuated.
(p. 10)

The point of the incident is the difficulty of remembering, and yet
finally the ability to remember. So it is really *memory* that Jerry is
searching for: and to do so, he has to remove a mental block. *This
mental block takes a physical form at the end of the novel.* Griffiths
misses the point when he says,

> In a rather theatrical ending the Termites are killed in a car crash
> whilst returning from a 'pitch' up-country and Jerry is left to
> contemplate his failure and to wonder if 'someone with more
> experience [would] take over and work at it?
> (p. 134)

The ending is meant to be theatrical. Salkey works with dramatic
scenes *which he places before our eyes because he wants us to see*,
although he knows we are not going to see without being given a
shock. It is not a car-accident, though. Everyone is driving back
from P.D.'s place at Dallas the morning after Christmas, drunk.
Nearly everyone is on an open haulage truck. Only Jerry is riding
behind with Caroline Selkirk, the American editor; he, too, is
drunk and she has decided to drive Mason's station wagon and
has asked him to sit beside her to direct her. This is what saves
Jerry. As she says when she keeps waking up in the hospital, the
whole mountain ahead of them seems to move and suddenly
covers the truck. 'Who moved the mountain' asks Wayne
Brown's 'The Approach'. 'Who moved the mountain?'[36] If Jerry
will not quite come to the mountain, the mountain will come to
him, we could say. The mountain is a physical representation of
Jerry's mental block.

Why was Jerry saved? For one thing, he had befriended Carole
when she had arrived to show Prudence he was his own man: he
was not willing to settle for clichés, exploitation, kowtowing to
the big people. He wanted to be involved with the journal because
he was potentially a thinker. The Termites brought their disaster
on themselves with their 'rebellion' that always took the form of
drinking and casual sex. Jerry's toast turned out to be prophetic:
'To an early death!' (p. 29)

It is commendable that Jerry gets involved with the Rastafarians at a point of searching in his life, when he has quit his civil service job and regurgitated all he has drunk. But how can Jerry help the Rastafarians when he does not know himself? True, he teaches them to read and write. He organizes them so that he can make an appeal for help to first the ruling party and then the Opposition. Jerry is not wrong to disagree with the Rastas about repatriation to Africa: he feels this is an easy way out for the government, although the Leader of the Opposition says that emigration has always been the solution to problems of employment in the West Indies. But Jerry overlooks another side to the desire to return to Africa. Bashra says, 'Take a dream from a man an' *you*' got a big responsibility for life, maybe.' (p. 177) He organizes the Rastas into a silent march: the result, Rybik tells Glissada, is that it is harmless, completely harmless. The problem is, as Earl Lovelace's Aldrick Prospect says near the end of *The Dragon Can't Dance*, that the dispossessed are always appealing to the ones above them instead of looking within.[37] Some of the radical Rastas refuse to join the march:

> Marcus raised his right hand. 'Peace an' love, Brother,' he said sympathetically.
> 'That same shit goin' kill you one day,' the spokesman told him.
> (p. 196)

It happened. Jerry's involvement with the Rastas brought first the Termites and then the mountain down on them. The Termites nibbled at a mountain and the mountain squashed them. So Jerry, with his inadequate knowledge, is responsible for bringing death to the Rastafarians who helped him: he helped tame the moderate ones so that the government was then in a position to send the police to attack and kill the more radical group.

The solution to the problem is not simple. We know this because of the fact that Jerry finds out on the same day that he has impregnated a black working-class girl and a lighter-skinned middle-class girl. What solution can there be once Jerry has been so irresponsible? He loses Carmen by his inaction and he keeps searching for Miriam without success. There is an interesting coincidence here with *No Bride Price* by David Rubadiri, published in the same year as Salkey's novel.[38] Rubadiri's protagonist, Lombe, meets a black girl, Miria, in a night-club and makes her his housemaid and mistress. When she gets pregnant, he treats her badly and she leaves; thereafter, he keeps trying to find her but the woman he thinks is her turns out not to be.

The problem of being trapped on a little island is a hard one to solve. For example, note the relationship between Mason and his English wife, Jenny. When they are dancing at P.D.'s place for the first time, we have the following scene:

> Jerry stood behind the table and held a tall drink. He spotted Mason and Jenny and waved his glass. He admired them. In all of the chaos of Termite life, Mason and Jenny had managed to remain faithful to each other. The Termites took their mutual fidelity for granted.
> (p. 58)

Yet *the very next page*, Sally is upset to find Berto in the station wagon having sex with Jenny. If this seems too contrived, it is so in the way in which Reed makes a point T.V. sketch-style in *Flight to Canada*. Jerry has no basis for concluding that Jenny and Mason would continue to be faithful to each other because he had no inbuilt value system or knowledge, he did not know what brought them together and therefore did not know what would drive them apart. We discover much later that Jenny's problem is not unlike Jerry's. After she had started having an affair with Neddy Lazar, she asks him to whip her while she is wearing Mason's gown. When he leaves, she thinks:

> It had always been like that for her: England, during her
> adolescence, had been mainly the London postal areas of warmed-
> over tradition, trumped-up heroes, controlled chauvinism, and
> imported American popular entertainment; then that, in turn, shrank
> to the size of one small postal area of London, tired Hampstead, and
> after a time, that contained only one attractive experience: meeting
> and falling in love with Mason. Shortly after that, he broadened into
> the Island which narrowed within months into the Termites; Neddy
> had been merely a breakaway splinter attraction. And now, after her
> exchange of one island for another, she was alone again.
>   She closed her eyes and chuckled softly.
>   'There's still the safety of the Termites,' she told herself, placing
> her feet on the veranda rail and hugging her breasts through the
> multiple folds of the academic gown.
> (p. 162)

Griffiths believes that Jerry's solution to being trapped on the island will be the classic one, that Jerry will leave the Caribbean. But Griffiths seems to have reached this conclusion because it fits into the thesis of his book. It is unlikely that Jerry will leave. He knows from his brother that going away can lead to frustration too. He knows from his father that going away makes coming back almost impossible. When he thinks about Jenny, as he must since the incident of her unfaithfulness happens only minutes after he had admired her faithfulness, he must realize that exchanging one island for another is no solution.

Some of the key happenings in the novel are not happening in the novel at all. We are given clues to what is happening behind and around in the carefully selected epigraphs to each section. For example, the epigraph to Book Two, which ends with Jerry on the Dung'll:

> . . . what can we recall of a dead slave or two except that when we punctuate our Island tale they swing like sighs across the brutal sentences and anger pauses till they pass away.
> (p. 67; the epigraph is from Dennis Scott, *Epitaph*.)

Everyone is running away from the slave past, from slavery. In their restlessness, their drowning themselves in drink, in small talk, in cynicism, everyone is dodging the mental block of slavery. Yet without coming to terms with this mental block, everyone is doomed to move around without a centre. Ayi Kwei Armah in *The Healers* has the collective voice that narrates the novel say that while there are painful times that make forgetfulness necessary for survival, too long a forgetfulness is dangerous.[39] Jerry constantly gives indications that he wants to stop escaping. For example, when he is with the Rastas and is reading his mother's long letter, he thinks: 'Indeed, it was his first experience of honestly loathing escape and external help.' (p. 175)

The mental block finally moves when many of Jerry's illusions are destroyed. He is left with a series of questions, but he is now in a position to ask them, with no props. Will he be able to ask them? This is where his name is seen to be deliberate, and Griffiths's error with the name distorts the meaning of the novel. Jerry is trying to avoid being more colonial cannon-fodder ('stover'). This is emphasized by his first name, which suggests 'jerry-built'.

He is now in a position to look inside, inside himself, inside his society. Though late, he is mentally emancipated.

* * *

The *New World Dictionary of the American Language* defines 'adventure' as follows: (1) the encountering of danger; (2) an exciting and dangerous undertaking; (3) an unusual, stirring experience, often of a romantic nature; (4) a venture or speculation in business or finance; (5) a liking for danger, excitement, etc.[40]

All these definitions apply to the story of Catullus Kelly.[41] He is an honours graduate in English who, after spending a year in America, goes to England at the age of twenty-five. Yet he is not an emigrant in the classic sense. As we discover, he has not gone for good, that is, permanently, but for a short period. He intends to return home: and at the end of the novel, having spent four seasons in England, he does go back to Jamaica.

Why has he gone to England if not to study, work or make money? This is where he is different from nearly all the other West Indian immigrants in England. He does seek jobs and he does work in London, but he has something to fall back on: his mother sends him money from back home. (Once again, the mother is the stable point in Salkey's fiction). So Catullus Kelly has gone to England for some other reason: and other people he comes into contact with notice. Dulcie, one of his lovers, says, 'You're obviously on some sort of quest.' (p. 109) She is not the only person to notice it.

What is this quest? It is tied up with something that comes to Catullus's mind after he receives his mother's letter telling him to come home:

> If he stuck to his original plan, it would take a quality of skill and fortitude which he lacked to carry it through to the end of his exile. (p. 45)

His quest, then, has something to do with his desire to end his exile: and to the end the exile of Caribbean man. This is not as simple as going home physically. It is linked up with the colonial relationship with the mother country, that is, England. As we see from Ayi Kwei Armah's *Why Are We So Blest?*, published after

Salkey's novel, there is imperfect knowledge within the colony of what is being done to it. One needs to get to the mother country, in this case England – although America is taking over: note Catullus's visit to America – to find out what is going on in order to end exile. He is the latter-day counterpart to Columbus. He is the adventurer. His true quest is to discover the missing pieces of the puzzle. Thus a great deal of what he does is done in a spirit of curiosity and inquiry. While most other people avoid the bookstore of the White Defence League, he deliberately goes there, on the advice of Erasmus, his landlord, fellow-countryman and servant from past days.

Erasmus is like his namesake: he is a humanist, well-balanced, not given to extremes; as an erstwhile member of the working class, he is able to act as mentor to Catullus and give him insights into the colonizing beast. He says that nothing is the way it seems to be in England, where it is a cardinal rule not to call a Spade a Spade. Erasmus knows that Catullus's education has not prepared him to understand the reality of England:

> Well, the new education up there don't even begin to give you what this London or any other European metropolis, for that matter, have to offer . . . you believe that the garden, early days as it is, really help' you to see the colonial thing round you? Or the hate thing? Or even give you a look-see at you'self? The lovely garden surroundings doing well in exam-passing . . . Between the garden and this other Godless London, here, all that's happening is question-paper watching and exam-writing and degree-grabbing. What happening to the personality side? The side that can conquer hate. What happening to you after the exam-room lock up and you leave the garden and start to face the blows?
> (p. 20)

Erasmus is talking about the campus-type élitist education of the British colonies which isolated the clever exam-passers from the other people, turning them into the exceptions that were going to be admitted into the pantheon of the gods, as Armah shows in *Why Are We So Blest?*. There is the problem of not having true knowledge of the nasty side of the mother country, and just as important, of not having any real knowledge of the self and all its possibilities. One could have built up the personality through a false understanding of reality, or, to use a word that recurs in the novel, a *fantasy* understanding of reality. Although Catullus was given his name when he used to translate the poems of Catullus as a student, we note that naming is very important, particularly for those who have come through the experience of slavery, where they were denied the power to name themselves. Catullus is indeed like his namesake: he tends to be lyrical and to bestow his attentions on the unworthy who let him down.

While Catullus is engaged on his adventures in the outer world, there is something going on in his head that he does not realize. For example, his response to Chico's places him on top of events:

> *Praed Street, Chico's*: sea-change implies language-change; the boys are up against it, naming the shit out of London after their own fashion.
> (p. 59)

Yet we know that what is going on in the barber's shop while Catullus is making his mental snap judgement is more complex than he is able to cope with. Like his namesake, he is being less than realistic. This gets clearer when he gets to his flat and actually makes the diary entry:

> *Praed Street, Chico's*: some of the boys, a handful of the ghetto-bound ones, the real despairing 'cats', seem, in part, a pathetic lot; what little impression they've made on their London exile would appear to have been done with the fragmentation of language, the 'naming of parts', foreign parts, and a kind of *cuntish* irony.
> (p. 68)

His slickness places him on top of events, when he actually notices what is happening and even more when he shapes the language to deal with it. Compared to Johnnie Sobert then, there are two levels of misunderstanding of reality. For he is missing what is really happening at Chico's, as we shall see. How he reacts to reality is a reflection not only of the reality, not only of his use of language, but also of his fantasy life, so much so that a number of things that happen to him, we eventually realize, are fantasies. We do not realize this at first: and when we do, we discover that we have been taken for a ride, that we have shared his fantasies because they are ours.

Let us take a simple example. Chapter 3 of the first part is entitled, 'Catullus Teaches'. Winter is nearly over, Spring had 'broken loose'. And

> Catullus had gone out to teach at an unsuspecting and hopelessly under-staffed comprehensive school in Fulham. His first morning was not altogether eventful. It began with an English grammar lesson, partly on clause analysis and partly as Catullus's own introduction of himself to the form; he believed that, by merging both tasks, he would, indeed, be conserving his energy and, at the same time, varying the formal pattern of the lesson, by striking a blow for personal relations; a sound, practicable pupil-teacher relationship and something that Catullus instinctively trusted and genuinely wanted to foster.
> (p. 70)

Right away, we think of E.R. Braithwaite's *To Sir, With Love*, which had been made into a popular movie starring Sidney Poitier.[42] We have a sense of *déja vu* – then the novel deliberately reminds us of the connection:

> 'Sir?' the first boy said.
>   'Your name?' Catullus asked.
>   'John Bowen, sir.'
>   'Yes, John. What is it?'
>   'Sir, did you write that book?'
>   '*That* book, John?'
>   '*To Sir, With Love*, sir.'
>   'No. I did not.'
>   'It was made into a film.'
>   'I hardly go to the cinema, John.'
>   'It was at our local.'
>   'Indeed.'
>   ''E's a darkie like you,' the same girl said. 'The writer, ain' 'e?'
>   'Braithwaite,' John said.
>   'A good un-darkie name, too,' Catullus suggested.
>   'I'd hate an African name,' the girl decided, looking round the form for approval.
>   'By the way,' Catullus said, 'what's your name?
> (p. 71)

We, the readers, know *To Sir, With Love* and expect things to go a certain way. First, the students will be rude to the teacher. Then he will fling off all formal attempts to teach them for exams. He will begin instead to teach them about life: and in the process he will win their respect. And things do go pretty much according to plan. We do not realize at the time of reading the account that there is a vagueness to the whole experience. We do not realize it because while the language is very precise, *we*, the readers, are the ones supplying the connection. That needs clarification. The language is precise, but because it is so brief, it is vague in the sense that the words are what Christopher Booker calls 'nykto-morphic' words: words which are like blanks *we the readers* fill in out of our own experience since these words carry little meaning in themselves.[43]

Of course we filled in the blanks because of *To Sir, With Love*, but what if that novel and the movie are fantasies without the author realizing it because he is not getting to the bottom of the colonial relationship, to what the nasty elements in colonizing England actually are, and to the fact that the problem is so deep in his own psyche that it is impossible for him to really solve the problems of working-class English children? It is no accident that Salkey uses as epigraphs quotations from Kamau Brathwaite's *Rites of Passage*. Brathwaite is frequently confused with Braithwaite. But Brathwaite has been a relentless pursuer of the truth in the colonial relationship. It is also deliberate that Salkey brings in the reference to *To Sir, With Love* because he wants to show us that like Catullus, we have a fantasy perception of reality. Catullus solved the problems too easily. What precisely did he do to win the respect of the students? What did they learn by being taken to movies that were almost X-rated? It is a fantasy solution to a real problem: and therefore it was a fantasy perception on the part of Catullus.

The most sustained fantasy in the novel is sexual. Catullus has sexual adventures with several white women; Olga, a prostitute; Dulcie, an art student; Philippa, the wife of the owner of the coffee-shop where he works; Lope, a librarian who turns out to be the daughter of a rich man; Portia, Lope's friend and co-conspirator and a woman he knows as Lilith. There are others too, but these are the ones named and the ones he returns to. We are prepared for his adventures with the women by a few well-placed comments and scenes. In the Prologue, we are told, 'He was an enthusiastic amateur womaniser and a professional drinker.' When he goes for an interview to the studios of the Temperate Broadcasting Unit, the following takes place:

'A few words for level, please,' the studio manager requested, keeping her voice coolly down and detached. 'First, from you, Mr Kelly, and then from your guest. Thank you.'

Catullus imagined what she looked like. He ran his hands up her thighs. They were long, smooth and firm. Her hips were vast. Fortunately for his progress, she was without her panty, but she was kinkily wearing a suspender belt.

He cleared his throat, thought of something to say, cleared his throat again, leant forward and remained speechless.

'Ready for level when you are, Mr Kelly,' she urged sympathetically.

Catullus twanged her suspender belt in celebration of the pantyless discovery and tried to part her thighs. There was ecstasy there, he thought.

He cleared his throat again, quietly suppressed a sudden surge of panic, relaxed and then said, 'One, two, three, four, five, six . . .'
(p. 48)

This scene is set out as reality leading to fantasy – and while we read it, it is real since we are experiencing it through language. *We are being given a clue that other sexual encounters in this novel are also fantasies.* These fantasies are important. In an article entitled 'Hot Secrets' in *Playboy*, the appropriately named David Black says:

Like dreams, sexual fantasies are played out on an internal stage: unlike dreams, they tend to involve the real world in a direct way – as though the mental burlesque show were being performed by members of The Living Theater. The fantasies may be compelling shadows, but what thrills us is what is casting those shadows, the exotic who bumps and grinds around the corner of the imagination in the light of reality – the phantom Juliet who discovers in us her flesh-and-blood Romeo.

Such a fantasy woman, part succubus and part anima, mysteriously satisfies our deepest longings. In her many guises – blonde with pubic hair shaved off, brunette flaunting a peekaboo bra, redhead in sheer panty hose – she stirs up in us not merely lust but a kind of nostalgia. Thinking of her affects us like Proust's *madeleine* the little cake whose taste unlocked a world of sensuoous memory – as if the sex she offered were a place from which we had been exiled a long time ago . . .

In fact, sexual fantasies are always with us, flickering on and off as we go through our daily routine. They are our secret sharers, an entire *commedia dell'arte* cast waiting in the wings for the change to flash, leap, tumble, fly, hop, juggle, clown, slink, twirl and cartwheel into awareness.

> Why does our unconscious cook up scenarios that our conscious
> mind may reject? Where do such dreams come from? While they are
> often entertaining, sometimes they are also unsettling. What function
> do they serve? What, in fact, is a fantasy? Is it a sexual dream? A
> fleeting sexy thought? An elaborate erotic script? . . .
>   Environment and culture may play a greater part than gender in
> determining what people fantasize. For people in a culture that has a
> taboo against showing a breast, breasts will become objects of
> fantasy. For people in a culture that has a taboo against showing a
> face, faces will become objects of fantasy.[44]

As Frantz Fanon has shown in *Black Skin, White Masks*, in a
colonial society in which black is the negation of the ruling white,
the white woman becomes the object of desire because she is
completely out of reach in the black/white manichean world of
colonialism; the black man feels that he can become the equal of
the white man by possessing and being loved by a white woman.[45]
Notice that all Catullus's sexual encounters or relations in
England are with white women. This can partially be explained by
the fact that there were very few black women in London at that
time, but not entirely. He does meet one black woman, and when
she propositions him, he turns her down, letting her believe that
he is a homosexual, which he is not. True, she is a prostitute: but
then, he had not rejected the first white woman who propositioned him although she was a prostitute.

The white woman, calling herself Olga, propositioned him
soon after his rejection at the fascist bookstore where he has seen
a book entitled *The Shape of Skulls to Come* by Aethelstan
Gordon-Venning. He was not permitted to buy the book, or to
enter the bookstore, and thereafter his surface quest, the one he
thinks he is on in London, is to find out what he can about
Gordon-Venning and to get the book. The following happens
after he leaves the scene:

> Catullus strolled aimlessly along Bayswater Road. It was about three
> o'clock. The afternoon was cold and bracing. He admired the highly
> polished body of a white Jaguar which drove slowly past him and
> stopped a few yards away from his position at the edge of the
> pavement. As he drew nearer, a fur-wrapped head and face shot
> through the window and a hoarse voice said, 'Going my way?'
>   Catullus nodded and got in beside the young woman and smiled at
> her. She did not return the courtesy. The Jaguar slid up the road and
> turned left into Leicester Terrace.

> 'Short time, a fiver,' the driver said casually . . .
> (p. 14)

After the sex:

> She uncrossed her thighs, half rolled on to her side and leapt off the
> divan. 'You're forgetting something,' she said. She opened her
> handbag and held up his folded five-pound note.
>   He took it and left. Outside, he patted the Jaguar and narrowed
> his eyes, arrogantly, heroically, like Othello before the handkerchief.
> (p. 17)

The white woman drives a white Jaguar (whereas the jaguar, the
cat, is not white). Catullus so satisfied her that she returns his
money: so the relationship was no longer one of prostitute and
client but of white woman and superstud black man. There is a
complete absence of details about the actual act of sex. Combined
with his literary idealization of himself in terms of Othello, we
have clues that all this is fantasy. Without thinking about it,
Catullus has accepted the definition of the black man imposed on
him by the whole structure of colonialism. Fanon says,

> A prostitute told me that in her early days the mere thought of going
> to bed with a Negro brought on an orgasm. She went in search of
> Negroes and never asked them for money. But, she added, 'going to
> bed with them was no more remarkable than going to bed with white
> men. It was before I did it that I had the orgasm. I used to think
> about (imagine) all the things they might do to me: and that was
> what was so terrific.'[46]

Just as Catullus is unable to penetrate his own psyche, he is unable
to get below the surface of the world around him despite receiving
'messages':

> He listened to his darting inner voice. It accused him of tasting the
> surface of London life. It raged against his sexual light-footedness. It
> roared self-conscious guilt. He chuckled quietly. Dulcie pinched him.
> He crushed her with his bulk. She sighed rapturously. He thought
> about the surface of things. Dulcie's skin. Philippa's. The froth of
> the thousand *capuccinos* he had made. The sooty patina on Nelson's
> column. The book-jacket layout of *skulls*.
>   He coaxed himself into believing in the delight of being outside
> everything he touched and saw round him. He was not alone. There
> were millions of others who were also outside everything. Most

people were looking on, touching and seeing at a distance. They owned nothing. They were ripe for alienation. It was very nearly a noble condition.

It had been the same in New York. There, the distance between himself and the fantasy objects, in Manhattan particularly, was infinitely more tantalising; the surfaces were glossier; the costing was very nearly everything and the prices were grotesquely prohibitive; failure was more oppressive and there was a kind of concealed violence everywhere. But he did not mind being outside in America. The outsider seemed attractive to him, if only because the others appeared earnest and embattled, conforming and living up to trend, herd-fashion and drama-style, and prospering neurotically inside it.

London's equation was more than marginally different; the margin was a chasm. Conformism could hardly be popular in the face of the unwritten freedom which Catullus fondly imagined most people moved about in, day by day, failing or succeeding.

(p. 110)

So Catullus sometimes knows that he does not know. But since he cannot penetrate the depths, he wears different masks to help him deal with different situations, masks he has drawn from his wide experiences. But through his sexual adventures, he eventually gets into a situation where he cannot find the right masks: and at his most troubled moments, he cannot cut himself off from the peasant background that is not too far under his middle-classness. It is Philippa who is the catalyst to Catullus:

She jerked his head upwards. 'Stop it,' she said, flattening his face against her sweat-filigreed bosom.

He was the Grand Duke of Tuscany.

She squirmed flatteringly.

He was Sidney Poitier.

She cried out.

The centuries rolled back and forth for him. He was living on an extremely plush scale. The tropical light was blocked by green wooden blinds. The plantation sounds were distant. No threat. No tradition of lynching.

'Do you ever once think of the Negro in Birmingham, Alabama, or of your countrymen in Nottingham and Notting Hill?' Philippa asked.

'If it improves the performance, yes.'

'You're vile.'

'On and off.'

She slapped his face, took off his clothes with inspired intimacy and massaged his shoulders. He brought her down to the carpet. He

> disliked the slender ornate leg of the dressing table. It stood and
> watched him. It pierced the carpet arrogantly. He disliked it
> intensely. He had to distract himself from the sugar-cane stem.
> (p. 108)

Catullus is lying: he is thinking of the peasant and slave past and
its world-wide ramifications. In fact, in the scene at school where
the girl prefers the Western name to an African one, Catullus
quickly asks for her name because he knows that the Western
name was given by the slave master. Notice the 'sugar-cane stem'
coming from the days of monoculture in Jamaica. When he is
working at Philippa's coffee-shop as what her husband calls an
'Atmosphere Man', he is most like a slave: he is given a different
name, Beano, coming from the thing he has to work with, the
coffee bean, and he has to wear fantasy clothing. He comes to
realize that his country and others like Kenya grow coffee and are
therefore monocultures over which the colonials have no control.
The first time the coffee-making machine breaks down because he
was not watching it closely, he is sacked. In his sexual escapades
with Philippa, he lets himself fall into the role she wants, a role he
was not even aware had been planted in his mind just as the coffee
and sugar cane had been planted for the benefit of the outsider:

> 'You haven't called me Beano,' he said wistfully, blotting out the
> offending leg.
>   'You're *my* Catullus,' she told him frankly, 'my black
> reincarnation.'
>   'Didn't bring any poems with me.'
>   'You've brought more than enough' . . .
>   Philippa shifted niftily, beautifully. He followed like a hunched
> panther. They slithered towards the vast bedside rug. He thought
> instantly of dog. She hugged him viciously.
> (p. 109)

There is worse to come in his relationship with women. Even
though he has a more-or-less steady relationship with Dulcie – she
has even given up her English boyfriend for him – he decides to
accept the invitation to a party by Lope, short for Penelope, who
was the librarian at the library he had gone to return books to
(which he had borrowed on the cards of Peregrine Danquah, a
Ghanaian also staying in the flats belonging to Erasmus). Talking
to Erasmus about it, Catullus felt a tug on his conscience about

Dulcie.' (p. 141) But Dulcie does not object to his going so he goes: and has a series of unsettling experiences. First, the guests decide to smoke 'mellow yellow', a 'banana joint':

> 'What's that, for God's sake?' Catullus sensed, fearfully, a passage from informed innocence on to devastating experience. How could he, from a banana-growing area, from the old agricultural world, not know about the mellow-yellow banana joint?
> (p. 143)

Lope hooks her hand into his trouser-waist and tugs and drags him towards a room at the back of the flat. He finds all the walls covered with shelves of books from the floor to the ceiling. She pats one volume, *The History of the Decline and Fall of the Roman Empire*. Right through Salkey's novel, books are named and assume the importance they do in Salih's *Season of Migration to the North*. Is Catullus, who belongs to the side of the colonized, reading the right books in order to make sure these empires do come to an end?

> 'Are you wondering about the establishment?' Lope asked, her timing precisely matching Catullus's nagging curiosity.
> 'I am, I'm afraid.'
> 'My father's.'
> 'Where's he?'
> 'New York, Washington, California. Who knows?'
> 'Salesman?'
> 'Of a sort?'
> 'Academic scientist.'
> 'Very academic?'
> 'Profoundly.'
> 'Does he share your collection?'
> 'Now and then. He has his own, in his bedroom, with his priceless *Histortia Ecclesiastica Gentis Anglorum*, all five books, perched over his bedhead.'
> 'Scientist-Latinist?'
> 'Father's "fix".'
> (p. 146)

Who is her father? He is rich, which means she has wealth from her father. Where is he? Taking care of business interests all over the world, as part of the new empire? He is taking care of business, his business, while Catullus is fooling around with his daughter.

And not even for sexual/colonial revenge, as in the case of Salih's Mustafa Sa'eed. Catullus is allowing himself to be used. True, he enjoys himself sexually, but the sexuality gets out of his control. An olive-skinned brunette with green eyes, calling herself Portia, gets into the study, and we have the intriguing comment, 'Catullus was Victorian bemused, out of his native century, useless driftwood. Lope and Portia were wicked C.I.A. actresses in reverse.' (p. 148) Catullus is thrown for a loop. He

> was accustomed to women who ruled by right and dictated the lives of their lovers, husbands, sons, brothers and all the other free-wheeling males in his society. But he was able to bear the tender domination because there were always the available local Kingston masks which were usually very effective.
> (p. 148)

He now looks for a mask but before he can find one, Portia orders the lights be turned out. Catullus is now scared:

> There they were, poised, white furies, yellow with mellow, ageing with welfare-state boredom, in love with cool, imitating Village style and vocabulary, and controlled.'
> (p. 151)

He is told to get Portia. He crawls on his hands and knees, naked in the dark, totally helpless. How is this different from the way slaves were treated? He looks for inner strength from a blues, then tries to find the Jamaican equivalent from a *mento*, but all he can come out with is the popular 'Man smart;/But woman smarter/ Than man.' As he crawls, he touches an ankle:

> The lights blazed. They were blinding. Catullus blinked. Lope was standing by the switch. Portia was sitting in the chair. Lope was dressed. Portia was not. Both girls laughed. Catullus frowned.
> (p. 153)

In a situation in which one person is dressed, the person who is naked is at a power disadvantage. This does not apply to Portia since she is the one controlling the game. Catullus has lost; and he is commanded to make love to Portia. He thinks, 'He identified with her. She was as split as he was.' This is not altogether satisfying: he is trying to reassure himself and put himself linguistically in control, once again. Portia tells him that as a research assistant in industrial psychology, she has been able to identify his type: he is prone to ritual, trusting, optimistic, easy fodder. This game, which ends with their making love, puts Catullus at a further disadvantage, of being known and not knowing in return. No wonder 'Gibbon slept. And Coleridge.' (p. 155)

Catullus is not ready or willing to discuss this experience so he gives Erasmus a 'cautiously edited report.' We see the limitation of Erasmus's down-to-earth solidness when he comments, 'The young people, today, bafflin' bad.' Yet it is more sinister than that. The two women may have been agents: they obtained vital information about Catullus's psyche and behavior and are in a position to pass it on to the industrial laboratories belonging to the people who own the present-day empire, such as Lope's father. So who says the Roman Empire ended rather than getting transformed? 'An establishment which had been in operation for 2,000 years had developed some pretty clever techniques,' says Ishmael Reed's *Mumbo Jumbo*.[47]

We are prepared for the most sinister experience Catullus has, one he goes into blindly because of his unquestioned belief that he is highly desirable to white women:

> She was a tall, brooding, blonde nymphomaniac with an elegant flat in Holland Park. In her own words, she had a predilection for the 'lurking potency of jet-black men'; the blacker the lover the deeper the predilection the more passionate the involvement. At first, Catullus was flattered and eager for the continuing reassurance of his black excellence, which he was given, performance after performance. But as the weeks passed, what began as a blissful sexual extravagance progressively became an ugly brutal threat to his coolth. For one thing, the young woman would not tell him her name . . . There were moments when Catullus wondered if she existed; there were, of course, the overwhelmingly physical interludes when there was absolutely no room for doubt. Then, on a Sunday afternoon, just after they had had a frugal lovers' tea, in the bath, she said soothingly, 'Call me Lilith.' Catullus refused to take the name seriously . . . Lilith seemed absurdly neo-classical, forbidding, an ill omen. He long felt that Olga was teetering on the credible, though actually sounding a little assumed. He accepted that Dulcie was wholly believeable. He knew that Philippa, for her very specific demanding role, was 'classical' and right. And so was Penelope, even abbreviated to Lope. He suspected that Portia was, somehow, far

too apposite, ringing appropriately with her mask and personality,
neat and permanently fixed. But Lilith, after her thrilling diffidence
and awful silence, was much too improbable, and worrying.
(pp. 160/1)

Catullus is preparing to return home and he has a kind of sexual
reprise with all the women. The last chapter, entitled 'Catullus
Leaves', begins as follows:

Christmas Day was cold, windy and bleak. Lilith was stale drunk,
wild and inventive to a fault. She had stretched herself unsparingly,
and Catullus too.
(p. 180)

She leaves the flat at nine o'clock, promising to be back at
midnight. Catullus occupies himself with words and phrases for
Christmas diary entries. Once again, he thinks he is in control
because he is controlling the language by which he will record
events. He falls asleep and is awakened by a terrifying ring. He
walks around, goes to the writing desk, finds an opening in the
wall-panelling, prises it up – and finds thirty-two copies of *The
Shape of Skulls to Come*. The phone rings again: it is Lilith. He
calls her 'Æthelstan'. She says she will be home in a minute but he
hangs up and leaves. Æthelstan is the unifier of the English
people, and one meaning of 'Lilith' is a night witch who menaced
infants. Catullus has found out who the fascist is: and he has to
digest his own role in permitting the fascist to be successful. But
he has no time to do so until he gets back to Jamaica. Making
goodbye talk at the airport, Erasmus raises the question of what
Catullus will do back home: 'To civil service or not to civil
service?' (p.184) Peregrine suggests that he teach. Catullus then
tells Erasmus that the author of *The Shape of Skulls to Come*
turned out to be a woman. Erasmus makes a remark the others
find surprisingly tolerant:

if you ain't got love in your life, then you' got you'self a big
problem, youngster. No love? No proper life. That's 'ow I see the
world', an' that's 'ow I sum up the business o' Skulls, whosoever
write it, man or woman.
(p. 185)

The Epilogue begins, 'Six months after Catullus's departure from

London, Erasmus received a letter from Catullus's mother.' (p. 181) He reads the letter and his early recollections of Kingston come back to him: the smallness of the enclosed areas of everyday living, the conflicts of class, the penalties of poverty, the slights, the closed doors, etc. He reads the letter to Bridget, Dulcie and Peregrine. Within a week of arrival, Catullus began to behave strangely, the letter says. He used to read aloud from his London diary to anyone who would stop and listen to him. Then he left home and used to read in the park from *The Shape of Skulls to Come.*

> Then he took to assaulting passers-by with the book, telling them that he was Winston Churchill's representative in the Island. He also said that he was General Franco's representative, Napoleon's. And Alexander the Great's. We lost sight of him for about a month. Then he reappeared as a Rastafarian preacher, with beard and matted hair and ragged clothes to match. His father was extremely distressed.
> (p. 194)

He began to curse everybody, including his father and the working class. He began to quote Erasmus, whom his mother thought at first was the Dutch humanist. Then he became a public nuisance because he preached about the virtues of touching and finally gate-crashed a garden party and touched the Governor-General's wife on her hips and thighs:

> We went from one extreme to the other and one day, two weeks ago, he walked naked into the House of Representatives during a debate on the mechanisation of agriculture, and demanded to speak on the sociological implications for the mass of the people on, what he called, the unloved land. Needless to say, he was arrested and it grieves me to have to tell you that, last week, he was comitted to the lunatic asylum at Bellevue.
> (p. 195)

The last words of the novel are those of Erasmus who says it is a sin, a 'cryin' educational shame', and asks, 'Where's the profit?' The last sentence is, 'He looked compassionately at Dulcie, went up to the window and held out his hands and warmed them.'

So what has happened to Catullus? The Epilogue does not give us his experience from the inside; we have to infer it from the outside, chiefly from not his language but his mother's. Like most of the mothers in Salkey's fiction, she has solid, down-to-earth sense, but she is lost in the face of an experience she cannot imagine. We the readers have now to interpret. *The Shape of Skulls to Come* finally gets through to Catullus. Although we do not know what is in the book, it is not difficult to infer what it is about: it is a 'scientific' book about the inferior – read 'colonized' – races who have smaller skulls than the 'superior' races and that is given as the reason for their development getting arrested, not colonialism. Catullus's reason for going to England was that he was on a quest, we recall. He has finally recognized, as Armah's Modin does in *Why Are We So Blest?*, that as the educated élite, he is being prepared to serve the role of the 'factor', the middle-man responsible for handing over his people into slavery to the white man. In this sense, he is an agent of Winston Churchill and all the other colonizers. He recognizes that the old empires did not die: they just transformed themselves. He tries to find a way out, as Jerry Stover did, through Rastafarianism, but this is not the answer. His mind goes through a further 'breakdown' and he does what he had played at doing with Olga: they had discussed the idea of walking naked through the land. This was her romantic idea while the reality of the land had intruded into Catullus's consciousness: the robber-baron hotels, the mineral resources taken away, and the unloved land. Now his mind fastens on bringing the naked truth to the politicians. But the people will not listen: they say he is mad. This is the colonial Catch-22: Catullus is mad because he is sane.

We must backtrack to understand further what has happened to Catullus. Quite early in the novel, the barber Chico, who is Jamaican, says,

> Don't ask me 'bout darkies and buildin' nothin'. No patience, man. No guile proper. *No Anancy tactics.* No schemin' European mentality no how. An' wha' is worse, no self' interes'.
> (p. 62, my italics)

A few pages later, one of the persons Catullus questions about *The Shape of Skulls to Come* is Spider, originally from St Lucia, whom he meets in the barber-shop. While the others call Spider a 'fascist', he seems to know something: Anancy is a spider, we recall. In reply to Catullus's question, he is on the verge of a reply when the others annoy him and he leaves. After that, Catullus receives a number of enigmatic phone calls from him, the longest of which includes the following exchange:

> *Spider*: The time is twelve o'clock, Kelly. Midnight, man.
> *Catullus*: That you, Spider? Where're you calling from?
> *Spider*: You really want to know, Kelly boy?
> *Catullus*: Certainly. Where?
> *Spider*: From a little o' asylum in Kent.
> *Catullus*: A mental home?
> *Spider*: You can call it that, brains.
> *Catullus*: How long've you been there?
> *Spider*: In a way o' speakin', for years, since I' born, Kelly man. But, in fact', jus' some months now.
> *Catullus*: But how? What happened to you? When did you go in?
> *Spider*: We're all *in*, Kelly. We're all guilty, pardner. Vietnam is the t'ing. We're Vietnam an' Vietnam is we. They'll catch up wit' Chico an' the res' sooner or later. Tell that to Erasmus, hear me?
> (p. 90)
> *Catullus*: Why phone me then?
> *Spider*: Jus' checkin' up on you.
> *Catullus*: Why?
> *Spider*: 'Cause I want to be certain 'about the date an' time o' night or day they come for you Kelly.
> *Catullus*: Are they coming for me?
> *Spider*: They' goin' get you all, yes. An' you know wha' else? They' goin' get the Conservatives an' the Liberals an' the Socialists . . .
> *Catullus*: The House of Lords?
> *Spider*: The greates' debt-collectin' agency in the worl'. (p. 92)

When Catullus asks him what he can get him, Spider replies,

> A single 'andful o'dirt from St Lucia. Jus' a little piece o' St Lucia, Kelly. Tell them to sen' it in a' airmail envelope. That's all I want.

Two paragraphs later, we are told, 'It was not until the end of the week that the report of Spider's suicide was published in the *Daily Express*'. The exchange with Spider and his death unsettle Catullus and he gets depressed, but he lets it roll off, just as he was able to easily solve the problem of the troublesome students in the school. We the readers cannot dismiss it so easily: and it turns out to be prophetic of Catullus's fate in that every unheeded warning becomes a prophecy. Catullus discovers the truth at home. While he thought he was outside the problem, the problem was in him:

he was contributing to the continued enslavement of his people, and of himself, by his fantasy-based sex-life, by allowing himself to be the stereotypical black man who was a sex machine. He does not change the stereotype: the woman with whom he performs best turns out to be the person who wrote the book justifying the myth of white superiority over black. The woman who was using him to get her sexual kicks was providing the ideological justification against miscegenation on the grounds that it was destroying the Anglo-Saxon race. And she seemed to have connections with the mysterious fascistic organization that had exploited the non-white people throughout history.

There was a problem with Catullus's self-assurance, with his 'two-way *Weltanschauung*' which he thought placed him in control. We are told about it in the Prologue: it is

> his Kingston-dialect mood, and his Standard English mood. He had romped through what he called 'dingy Brooklyn', and had resolved to do the same in what we had heard was 'foetid London', alternating between his two *moods*, using the one, suppressing the other, back and forth, never becoming tedious, never sacrificing originality, and always being impressive while doing so, at any rate to himself.

And the end-result of this two-way *Weltanschauung* was his slowly evolving *négritude*:

> And, his *négritude*: the end product of his *Weltanschauung* which, when properly developed, would give him the dignity of an *Africoid*; that is, all black men raised to the superlative degree of blackness, as all white men have been raised to the superlative degree of whiteness: in essence, like Caucasoid like Africoid, like Africoid like Caucasoid. (pp. 121/2)

This comment is slick and places Catullus in linguistic control: but it is a false perception of the self. This two-way *Weltanschauung* in fact cracks before the reality. This is not what Catullus had expected to find in the mother country.

But now that he has discovered the truth, Catullus tries to bring back to his people: and they do not want it. In a short story, 'The Coming of the Whiteman', Albert Wendt presents a Samoan who returns from New Zealand and is considered by the people to be a whiteman because of his magic suitcase. The suitcase contains shaving equipment and stylishly designed towels: he would go through an elaborate ritual of shaving, showering and drying himself and would then emerge as a whiteman, to the admiration of all. But tragedy struck: his suitcase was stolen. He then tried to tell the people the truth of what happened to him in New Zealand, the land of the whiteman – he had fallen in love with a white woman, but she had betrayed him with a lover and he had beaten both of them, for which he was deported to Samoa. But the people did not want to listen to him: they beat him to a pulp for 'He had betrayed their hopes and dreams which they had wanted him to live out for them.'[48]

So is the novel telling us that the white woman is dangerous and must be avoided like the plague? As we have seen, the relationships Catullus has with white women in London must be seen in terms of his fantasy world. But not all the relationships. There is nothing dangerous about Bridget, the Irish wife of Erasmus. Note the significance of her name: St. Bridget is an earth-goddess who became a saint under Catholicism. Bridget helps Erasmus survive in London. He has a pean to white women in London, linking them to the land:

> It' like this. Britain' got two great survivin' assets an' only two, as far as I' concern'. One is the ancient law o' the lan' an' the other is the womenfolk. An' when I tell you that I back the women the whole way every time, I know wha' I' sayin'. Salt o' the eart', countryman. (pp. 112/3)

While Catullus's act of intercourse with Dulcie on the plinth of Nelson's column might look like sexual revenge against the colonizer, in fact Dulcie is one of the dulcet women helping him survive. After Dulcie paints a picture of the two of them nude, a picture of two real people, he thinks of her in contrast to the women he met in New York:

> Dulcie was a lovely understated slice of London bed-sitter ghetto life, shabby, irreducible, enduring, charming, natively intelligent, sexually unfathomable, marvellous. (p. 55)

Dulcie is upset that he is spending so much time with Lilith. When Dulcie makes love to Catullus, she is trying to save him:

> The room clung to their bodies. Dulcie's skin was milky. He was
> black leather. Their perspiration would dry like glue. They were
> together and apart, and Lilith was waiting, none the wiser. Words
> ceased. Dulcie's meaning began to articulate itself. The true spirit of
> metropolitan cities was more easily apprehended through the silence
> of their generous women. Generosity was a snatched hour in a
> private room.
> (p. 165)

Dulcie pleads with Catullus to be taken to Jamaica, but he
believes he cannot take her home, any more than he can take
Olga. Was there not at least another way of taking Dulcie home,
in his consciousness? It is of importance that she is one of the
members of the small group that receives the news about what has
happened to Catullus back home. Would the other women have
cared?

We cannot leave the novel without some comment on the
homosexuality. Are we to make something of the fact that
Catullus meets a group of white homosexuals and decides to
interview them on the T.B.U., where he has his sexual fantasy
about the woman taking recording levels? Or that the person in
charge of the program, a West Indian stuck in England, has both
the arrogance and the lack of gumption to do anything dangerous
on the T.B.U.? Or that the homosexuals are sympathetic figures
with an understanding of what it is like for colonials to be
exploited by the mother country? Or that the black prostitute
thinks Catullus is gay and he allows her to think so? The novel
does not emphasize the idea that Catullus may be suppressing his
homosexuality like Johnnie Sobert, but we do not forget that one
of the things colonialism does is take away the manhood of the
males. There are few fathers, and therefore father-figures, in
Salkey's novels. There is a corresponding confusion about sexual
identities. Not much is made of this in *The Adventures of Catullus
Kelly*: but the homosexual Englishmen, by their very presence,
warn Catullus about the exploitation he is going to face from the
predatory women he gets involved with, a warning he chooses to
ignore.[49]

But then, Catullus was an adventurer. He had gone to England
to get the missing pieces of the puzzle. It is unfortunate for him
that it led to a breakdown of his mind: but breakdown was
inevitable for without it, there could be no rebuilding. Catullus

does have an advantage, after all: he has studied English literature, and with just a reshuffling of the pieces, he can find in English literature the evidence to understand the mother country. The most obvious example is the fiction of Joseph Conrad. But we can look at other works too. For example, Pip in Dickens's *Great Expectations* discovers that he has been turned into a gentleman by a convict in Australia. Thus we can see Catullus as a pioneer comparable to Salih's Mustafa Sa'eed. But Salkey's novel is different from Salih's. There is no double-narration in Salkey's work. Catullus has not met someone who can narrate his story in Salih's novel, nor has he met someone who can arrange all his diary entries into a meaningful pattern as in Armah's *Why Are We So Blest?* This is a job *we the readers* must do. We must get out of the nightmare ourselves. We do not get out of the fantasy by embracing another.

* * *

'Playing *Anancy* to the last, eh?'[50]

By now, we know that Salkey deals with the relationship of home to exile, that exile itself can take different forms. In his poem 'I Never Left' from *Away*, the poet says: 'Yes, I am one of those who left the island; but I am also/one of those few/who remained behind;/I never left.'[51] The reason why the poet never left is he *had* to follow the paths created by colonial forces, to go where the extracted capital was taken. In contrast: 'Just consider, for a moment, the style of some of those who stayed./Dry land tourists! Inner émigrés!/North Americans deferred!/Incredible mirror images!/Shouldn't they have gone abroad,/instead of staying put/and being so far removed/from the native truth?'[52] Thus the epigraph to *Come Home, Malcolm Heartland* is a quotation from an interview with Alejo Carpentier: 'A yearning for escape is, in fact,/a search to find oneself; which is,/when all is said and done, a return/to oneself.'

Malcolm Heartland is in the tradition of Salkey protagonists who have deliberately gone abroad in a quest to end exile. Malcolm was a radical in England during the time of the Black Power movement: unlike Catullus, he had stayed on in England and gotten involved in the movements there. But now he has decided to go back home to Jamaica. The novel begins with a question asked by a Caribbean journalist: 'What made you decide to return home after living for so many years, here, in London?' Hasn't London become home while he lived there all these years? The reporter wants to know:

> they also say that you're afraid of what you call the failure and nothingness of the struggle. Intellectuals hate failure, public failure. You all gathered in London in the early fifties, mainly for metropolitan approval and recognition. The approval 'thing' is finished now, and so is the recognition 'bit'. Malcolm, Stokely, Rap, the Panthers and the others broke the back of that. The young Brothers, here, stepped good and hard on the pieces. That's left the intellectuals without aim and purpose. So it's home where the grass is greener and the old embarrassment at a minimum.
> (p. 15)

Malcolm's reply is a question: 'What am I to say about that?' The reporter asks whether he agrees; Malcolm replies, 'Seems extreme. Overstated. Dramatic.' When the reporter continues probing, Malcolm says that he is going back for his own reasons. The reporter retorts, 'Playing *Anancy* to the last, eh?' 'That, too, if you like,' replies Malcolm. 'And for your editor and your interested readers perhaps.' (p. 15) Once again, Salkey is giving us an Anancy clue. The novel is going to behave differently from the reporter who knows all the answers. To emphasize the point, we read on page 38 that Malcolm 'felt like Anancy'.

Malcolm has been through it all: there are no surprises left, it seems. He too is from the middle class; he has two degrees in English literature and a degree in law which he obtained in England, though he has not practised because this is a very difficult thing for a black man to do in England – he has taught and has been involved in the Black Power movement. He appears to have no hang-ups about white women: his lover is a black Guyanese nurse. He is ironic, sophisticated, experienced. He is more mature and seasoned than Johnnie Sobert and Catullus Kelly. When the attractive Claude asks him, 'Has it been very difficult for you to think and act "black is beautiful"?' he replies, 'Black's been overloaded, as a colour, from way back, for all of us, everywhere. A re-evaluation is long overdue.' (pp. 35/6) When she probes further,

Is it difficult for you, living away from home, as you are, to make love, easily, naturally, to one of your own Black women?'

his thoughts are as follows:

Living among a vast majority of White women in London had not influenced Malcolm's sexual budgetary considerations, in any way; in his view, his friendship with Honora neither supported the theory of his having cowardly settled for Black love over White, nor, in his own estimation, should it suggest that his was an immigrant's preference for the better and more beautiful of the two loves. The simple and unremarkable truth was that Honora had, consistently, made it easy for him to continue the fruitlessness of his and her own wayward hoping. It had become a prolonged hit and miss relationship in exile, which, to an outsider, would seem open-ended and futile but which had its peculiar compensation. It had distilled itself into a blend of freedom and dissipation.
(pp. 36/7)

He replies,

I don't find it difficult to make love to one of my own women in London. If that were so, I'd imagine it would take the kind of self-loathing I don't honestly think I suffer from. Do you see what I'm trying to say?

This is not the kind of slickness we associate with Johnnie or Catullus. This is balanced, qualified, subtle, self-questioning. So it would seem that Malcolm is ready to go back home. And he has no nostalgia towards home either.[53] When Thomas Cyrus, a Jamaican, tries to talk him out of returning home because 'You' ol' home town's in you'head . . . the new boys are in, with a vengeance,' Malcolm thinks of

the imitation of the North American executive image in the civil service and in the business sectors of the society and among the bright, younger members of the two political parties in the Island. Much of it had seemed to him, judging from the reports he had had from old friends passing through London on their way to conferences on trade, aid and International monetary considerations, in Brussels, Paris, Bonn and Geneva, to be the usual acting out of the new rôles of the bustling, over-earnest executives from the client states of the Third World.
(p. 20)

Malcolm is aware of the new game being played out with new actors and a new stage but with old directors and producers. So he seems to be ready.

But as Malcolm attends a speech at Hyde Park, he is attracted to a woman, Claude, short for Claudette. She takes him home saying she wants to talk, not to have sex. Later she takes him to see Calvino, her political guru, who comes from Bermuda, he says. Calvino has all the correct radical images in place: large oil paintings by Cuban, Haitian and Nigerian artists, art objects of the revolutionary struggles in Mozambique, Angola and Guinea-Bissau, vanguard posters, stapled reports and mementoes of visits to Havana, Prague, Peking and Los Angeles. Calvino's first question is, 'What's your political philosophy, brother?' (p. 74) When Claude says Malcolm is returning home after twenty years in London, Calvino says, 'And you're going back to make the revolution? No point in returning unless you intend to make the revolution, baby.' (p. 75) There follows a game between Calvino and Malcolm: the former talks of the revolution while the latter talks of power-structures. 'The real power's elsewhere,' says Malcolm.

> It's predictably White, Anglo-American, neo-colonial and absentee, all over again, and with more than a few native middle-class custodians to see to it that things, at home, function properly, profitably, in somebody else's interest, for somebody else's profit. (p. 77)

From the perspective of the nineties, it may seem evident that Calvino's language gives him away as someone not to be taken seriously. But we have to project ourselves back two decades to see just how seductive that kind of language was. For example, look at how it hypnotizes a serious literary critic, Jonah Raskin, whom I quoted in the introduction. Raskin ends his book as follows:

> *The Mythology of Imperialism* was finished in Algiers in November 1970. With a group of American revolutionaries, I had gone to see Tim Leary and Eldridge Cleaver. From Algiers the fall of the American Empire seemed more necessary, more imminent. Here we were children of America bound in our struggle for life and love, reaching out to join with the revolutionaries of the Third World,

with the exiles from our land. In Algiers our drive for liberation
from the jails of America, and from the mind controls of the state,
accelerated. The underlying assumption here is that the principal
contradiction in the world is between the revolutionary peoples of
Africa, Asia and Latin America and the imperial powers. That is
why in this book Ho, Che, Mao, Debray and Fidel are specters
haunting Conrad, Lawrence, Cary, Forster and Kipling. They have
opened the doors for our own liberation; they have ignited the
cultural revolution which will burn away the rags of Amerika and set
the stage for a new world-wide commune of free and loving brothers
and sisters.[54]

This could be Calvino speaking. Malcolm is not satisfied with
Calvino's answer to his questions about theory. Malcolm says to
Claude, when Calvino leaves the room,

> It feels false. In fact, it strikes me as a weird case of self-
> dramatization somehow . . . It all seems so emblematic, spuriously
> symbolic, a kind of London political carnival escapism, really,
> Claude. Sham, actually. That's it, sham.
> (p. 79)

Malcolm decides to be 'self-interestedly cautious'. Calvino says
that some of 'us' got 'the call to struggle' by hearing it 'coming
loud and hard from the States,' others in different ways 'just
listened to their tiny, Black consciences, saying, "Come on,
home!" He asks, 'How was it with you, Malcolm? Tell it straight,
now, man.' (p. 81) Malcolm replies cautiously,

> There wasn't exactly a voice in my case . . . I've had enough of
> London, and by the looks of things, race and politics, I mean,
> Britain's had enough of me, too. Anyway, I've been away, too long.
> I want to go home.

We see the two different definitions of 'home' here: the psychic
home, the ending of alienation, and the return to the physical
home from which one came. At the heart of the situation lies a
complex history:

> He and thousands of others had escaped from the Caribbean to
> London. He, Malcolm, had been more fortunate and better prepared
> than most of the immigrant-workers and students, in being able to
> survive the hazards of the crossing from a colonial setting to a

slippery, many-layered metropolitan one. He had absorbed, in part, the trauma of the acclimatization to the new society. But even he could not admit that, with all his social advantages, he had gained anything of value from his efforts to achieve an ordinary life-style away from Kingston. And by that, he was admitting that it was impossible for him to realize his basic humanity, his plain, living, everyday personality outside his island home. So, now, he was escaping, again, searching for himself, and trying to return into the only state of consciousness out of which he could call himself a Jamaican, a Black man, in a world, economically, socially, politically and technologically, hostile to him, both as an individual and as a member of a group, marked by its cultural dependence and political powerlessness. How was that ever going to be made clear to Calvino and Claude? he asked himself, in despair . . . He was using the word 'return' very privately.

(pp. 82/3)

Claude and Calvino do not want Malcolm to leave: they want him to join them. Claude had seduced Malcolm to bring him into the fold – she was a recruiting agent. As he discovers with some anger, she is not averse to having sex with Thomas for, she says,

A cunt's a cunt, for most women; it's absolutely demystified; we give it, when we want and sometimes when we're not even inclined: we're glad, even flattered, when we get to know how you look at it, and there are times when we exploit you, because of that. But we don't carry cunt around on an altar, in the way you tote your prick about on a gun-carriage in some sort of atavistic ritual.

(p. 152)

By this time, Malcolm has discovered that Thomas was working with the group. At a Black Power meeting at the Centre to be addressed on FRELIMO by Calvino, he receives a note from Gussie (who had a Nigerian father and a Scots mother) which reads, 'Claude is not who you think she is. Calvino is a bigger surprise. Tom is in it too.' And he has added a postscript, heavily underlined:

You not going to believe what I have to tell you. I know that. I will get in touch a little later at Calvino. I know you will be there. Do not look for me in the flat.

(p. 122)

Before the lecture begins, Malcolm meets a black American

wearing the fashionable 'wagon-wheel Afro' of the time who says,

> They aren't leaders, baby; they're phonies; they're no good. I know
> them, in the States; I can spot them, here, too.
> (p. 134)

By now, we cannot tell the difference between phonies and those
telling the truth because they seem to use the same words,
articulate the same ideals and have the same fashion. While the
black American demythifies Calvino and other Brixton leaders,
we wonder if she is not herself a romantic. She says she is going to

> Tanzania where the scene's real. Like real people? Like reality? Like
> *Ujamaa*, like the Arusha Declaration, like the Tanzan [sic] Railway,
> like Tanzanian Socialism! That's where it's at, brother. Not in
> Brixton, with shit talkers like Calvino . . . Tell him to get his black
> Bermudian arse to Tanzania and struggle against the kulaks in the
> rural areas, like round Lake Victoria, up the slopes of Kilimanjaro,
> in Iringa hill country, the same kulaks who're deep into profiteering
> farming, with coffee, cotton, tea, and Calvino will beg heavy time off
> from the class struggle to sit and talk shit in Dar. That's how
> Calvino rips off on the revolution, brother. What does he know
> about *Frelimo*? But he's going to talk his guts out about it, in a
> minute. Shit!
> (p. 118)

'Kulaks' in Tanzania? Is that a Kiswahili word? It was a word
brought from outside by radicals romanticizing Tanzania – like
any Westerner seeking paradise, she is listing Lake Victoria, the
slopes of Kilimangjaro, and Iringa hill country.

When the lecture begins, so does a police raid. Malcolm notices
a man opening the door for the police and then hiding, a man we
are to see later, Clovis. Malcolm sees Calvino escaping instead of
staying where the action is (in contrast to Castro fighting at the
frontline during the Bay of Pigs invasion, a photo of which
Calvino has in his room). So Malcolm wants to hear what Gussie
has to say. But Gussie does not turn up at Calvino's: he comes
later to Malcolm's flat with a woman named Rhiannon who
seems to control him and to observe everything with 'cold
and piercing eyes.' Gussie tells a sceptical Malcolm that Calvino
and company are spies: they want him (Malcolm) to join them
because they need the backing of his barrister brain and his

intellectualism. The woman, Rhiannon, says that Calvino is a spy for the Portuguese government (this being before the coup in Portugal and the independence of the Portuguese African territories). Claude, she says, is working for the White Rhodesian set-up in London with a direct line to Special Branch in Salisbury (p. 168). And Tom is a very hard-working contact-man in London and Paris for the security cell in South Africa 'whose special Southern and Central African bureau of investigation operates in Johannesburg' (p. 169). By leaving, Gussie and Rhiannon say, Malcolm will miss out on the fact that the most secret of secret agents are roaming London, attending all the radical meetings and dazzling the audiences with their fire for change. When the token black person falls from grace, Rhiannon says coldly, since he treasures his role in the White market, he is easily enlisted by any White racist since he has always discriminated against fellow blacks. Malcolm still does not believe; Rhiannon makes statements he pays no attention to: 'please don't say we didn't warn you . . . You mightn't be around when the lid blows . . . you innocent, bad!' (pp. 171/2)

Back at Calvino's place, Malcolm still sees Calvino and Claude as 'brazen actors in their own brand of fantasy' (p. 176). Malcolm mentions that Gussie and Rhiannon have visited him: Calvino makes negative comments on both. 'Who're you working for, Claude?' asks Malcolm. 'We're all part of the struggle,' Calvino says, adding that his scene is tri-continental (p. 178). Malcolm sees them as

> metropolitan playthings, small-cut figures, bobbing up and down on a string being pulled at a distance. They were no less dangerous for that!
> (p. 179)

Thomas announces that they have decided to give Malcolm a farewell party. They invite Honora as well. She confesses her infidelity to Malcolm, but he basically does not care; this gives him the excuse to leave with no strings attached. He knows that Tom has visited Honora again; he has also found out that Tom is a member of the group and the seduction of Honora was planned. Everyone is at the farewell party. When he still refuses to change his mind, they say, with a sinister ring, that he knows too much, enough to burn them all. Malcolm thinks that Gussie's the mastermind and that Honora is part of the group as he had seen her getting into one of their cars. Rhiannon says,

> I think you're a waste of time, frankly. I also think you're dangerous. Most fools are. We've been foolish, too, in going as far with you. Calvino knows how critical I've been concerning the whole silly operation in getting you in. I do think there's something you ought to know, right now: you definitely won't be allowed to play the fool behind our backs.
> (p. 196)

Malcolm replies, 'You're the most sinister of the lot.' Still, he chances saying,

> You're a tight, little group of self-regarding amateurs, aren't you, playing at resistance politics, playing at something or other?

Honora is alarmed:

> 'If he says he'll join you, will he be able to go back, as he wants to?'

Finally, Calvino says,

> Brother Malcolm knows what we're up to. He's seen that little light that we actually thought we had covered over nice and dark. We know he knows. We *all* know he knows, damn it!
> (p. 201)

But we the readers, do not know: yet we believe that Malcolm does.

Clovis, the barman at the Centre with whom Malcolm had a discussion before the farewell party, comes to see him off, saying he was hoping for a chat with him. Malcolm says he is welcome to come along in the taxi to the docks. Malcolm finishes everything. Clovis laughs admiringly, saying, 'So, you got everythin' covered copasetic?'

> Then he pointed to the corner on his right. 'Bet you anythin' you didn't check the cupboard drawer? Is the only t'ing that shut in the room; everythin' else you leave open.'
>   As Malcolm turned and bent over to open the drawer, Clovis sprang forward and drove the long blade of his bread knife into Malcolm's back. He stabbed him four times, and backed away.

> Malcolm fell, clutching the knob of the drawer and bringing the
> cupboard crashing down across his chest.
> (p. 205)

'The woman who pay me to do this say to tell you that is only
fantasy catch you; is nothin' else,' says Clovis. 'I don't know wha'
she mean, but that's the message.' 'Why, Clovis?' Malcolm
stammers as blood pours out of his mouth. 'Who's the woman?'
Clovis replies that he didn't see her: she phoned him and arranged
to pay him. 'Is a job for me,' he says. 'The firs' big piece o' money I
pick up, since I come. I don't ask no question.' It is clear that it
was 'the most sinister of the lot,' Rhiannon, and that Honora will
be killed too. As Malcolm dies, his 'eyes were fixed on the ceiling.
His mouth was open. His fists were clenched.'

Until the last but one page, not only Malcolm believes that he is
leaving England and returning to Jamaica: we the readers do too.
We are almost bored by what seems to be a pointless game of
accusations and counter-accusations, of who is an agent and who
is a double-agent, such that, like Malcolm, *we let our guard down.*
The end comes so suddenly that we are left stunned: it takes just a
page for Malcolm to get killed. Our expectations are frustrated:
he only goes home in the sense of dying. What did the self-aware
Malcolm miss that led to his death? And what did *we* miss?

We have to retrace our steps. There are things we did miss, just
like Malcolm. One of them is the early feeling by Honora that
Malcolm had a 'cruel inattentiveness', that he "had been neither a
responsible companion nor a caretaker; he had merely been a
casual user.' Her body 'had been unimpressive to Malcolm,' he
had treated it as though it would always be there, 'enslaved by his
uncaring ownership.' He 'took it violently, and mainly because of
continuing bursts of aching need, and very seldom out of soulful
affection and love.' (p. 29) So there is a chink in Malcolm's
psychic armor. After his first experience with Claude, Malcolm is
told by Honora about Tom. She says, 'you must have wanted
what happened between Tom and me to happen, so you could get
your release.' (p. 62) When it is clear he is leaving, she says, 'It
would've been different with a white woman, I suppose.' (p. 62)
She continues,

> Every one of you, every single Black man, in this blasted country . . .

prefers a White woman to one of his own. He might treat her just as he would to a Black woman, just like shit, but the White woman always gets the preference. And for ten years, now, I've been stopping you from getting what you've always wanted.
(p. 63)

Could such an accusation be true of such a self-aware, ironic, educated person as Malcolm? When Claude is with him the first time, she asks him,

Are you attracted to white women, really hung up on them, particularly so, but find that you're too guilt-ridden because of it to do anything about it sexually?

His reply is, 'No hang-ups . . . No guilt, either.' Does it mean that *just because he says so, it is so*? The following are his thoughts when he sees Claude sleeping on his bed:

Her white peasant cotton blouse, speckled with small embroidered floral clusters, was beautiful. But the blouse was white. His hands froze. His fingers curled inwards. Like the retracted claws of an unsure predator his fists hung over Claude's breasts. They seemed white, too. They were those of some other woman, not Claude's, more an intruder's. They were white. He couldn't touch them. The two mounds of flesh, because of their new reality and because of his self-imposed discrimination, were strikingly forbidden.
(pp. 54/5)

Honora and Claude are right: he does have a hang-up about white women. That was why he was attracted to Claude in the first place – he thought she was white. It was only later that she told him that she considers herself black because although her father was English, her mother was Barbadian. Fanon says in 'The Man of Color and the White Woman': 'When my restless hands caress those white breasts, they grasp white civilization and dignity and make them mine.'[55] Malcolm had noticed Claude at Hyde Park corner when he was jostled by her. He thought she was an overseas student or an *au pair*. After he led her away from the crowd surrounding the speaker, he is so convinced that he is cool and aware that he does not notice that

She went along with him without protesting and with a smile of cool

success which could have meant that she had accomplished a tricky
job almost without effort.
(p. 32)

The only explanation for why he does not leave 'the revo-
lutionaries' since he says they are fantasists is that he wants to
keep possessing Claude sexually, as we see from his hurt feelings
when she has sex with Tom. His attraction to white women comes
from his colonial history. Because of this, he does not see how
much of an earth mother Honora has been, like Bridget in the
previous novel. Erasmus recognizes that his psychic and physical
survival depends on Bridget – a name that suggests 'bridge' – but
Malcolm does not make any such discovery about Honora.
Salkey's poem, 'Georgetown Gal', celebrates her: 'Georgetown
Gal,/Guyana cawn know/the magic them got/in dat sweet head
o yours!'[56] Honora knows that because for the Caribbean people,
'everything belonged to those who lived elsewhere,' very few
people at home 'wished hard enough to possess what was theirs,
work at it, and so love it for itself' and 'Malcolm's own will to love
was just as fragmented.' (pp. 27/8) The necessary will to love had
been shattered centuries ago and had not yet healed itself and
reshaped its power, she thinks. Malcolm has only suppressed the
problem.

There is also the critical question of how he misjudged Clovis.
Close to the end, he talks for the first time to Clovis, who
expresses the disappointment of the colonial finding the reality in
the mother country quite different from the propaganda:

> This is a tough country . . . When I did ups an' leave home, I did
> have a wrong picture o' the place, man. We really out o' date bad
> concernin' the set-up, over 'ere, you know. We still seein' it like it
> was in a school book, you understan'? Not so it go a *rass*!
> (p. 183)

As for Malcolm, Clovis says,

> *You is a dreamer. An' you know wha' 'appen to dreamers in this
> daylight worl'? They get kill off in them sleep, in the middle o' the
> sun-hot.*
> (p. 185, my italics)

When Malcolm asks him the classic radical question – whether he
won't try to change the situation – he says not even with the

Israelis as cover because the Rock is not going to change, for two reasons. First, every leader is going to betray the people; perhaps this is the people's fault because they always want messiahs. Secondly, the Jamaicans are not going to take the example of any other country that has had a revolution; whenever there are signs that there is going to be a revolution, it turns out not to be true. 'Rock change my natural ways,' he says.

> 'I hard as *rass*, now. I come like the Rock 'self. I not notice anymore. I have I an' I only. I don't care 'bout anyone else. Is I an' I, from now on. Sof' conscience gone. Is pure rockstone I make out o', you see me, 'ere.
> (p. 187)

Malcolm recognizes Clovis's 'spiritual desolation' but he does not accept his statement, 'I lookin', money, now. Anywhere I can get it, I goin' to take it.' (p. 189) Instead, Malcolm is a romantic intellectual, for all his scepticism, as we see from the contrast between Clovis's direct speech and Malcolm's convoluted and qualified thoughts about it:

> He appreciated how cruelly the corrective policies of some of the least self-seeking politicians were thwarted, and how expediently the others welcomed the restriction of their client-status, reaping the large, personal benefits of the widespread dishonesty and treachery, so uniquely, historically built into the situation, as they continued their futile neo-colonial game of independence without revolution. *Clovis hadn't stated his wish for a socialist alternative, but Malcolm was sure that was near enough to the form of change he would be prepared to seek.* His story had implied it, Malcolm pressed himself to believe. Clovis's unspoken hurt and dismay demanded it. He, too, would return to a just society, and help to develop it with his labour and his dreams, if the revolution would make it his and everybody else's in the Island. Malcolm was almost certain that that kind of rearranged ownership would make sense to Clovis and the rest of the dispossessed. In the meantime, Clovis would survive in London by virtue of his highly individualistic personality and his ability to work hard for his own personal gain. *He was one of thousands of unrecognized and deferred heroes among the Black immigrant workers in the country.*
> (pp. 191/2, my italics)

Malcolm's misjudgement of Clovis is fatal. Just before stabbing him, Clovis talked about assassinations throughout history. He was giving Malcolm every warning possible but Malcolm was missing them. Malcolm was working for the workers and peasants of his country and against his own crass class-interests, yet it was a member of the oppressed class that killed him, and only for money. Tragically, the warning this novel was giving was not taken in real life: four years after it was published, Walter Rodney was assassinated in Guyana, the hit man being a member of the working class, the class Rodney was working for. The assassin was able to get close to the idealist because he was trusted, and he did it for money. Years later, Salkey got an Anancy revenge against the person who masterminded the assassination through *The One*.[57]

There seems to be a third reason why Malcolm is assassinated, a more shadowy one. Was he killed because he found out that the radical group working in London was fake, that it consisted of the kind of self-dramatizing actors the Third World is always throwing up? Did they kill him because he would tell others about their being fake? Possibly. But why did he conclude that Rhiannon was the most dangerous one of all? Why did she and Gussie tell him that the others were double-agents in the pay of South Africa, Rhodesia, etc.? Behind the self-dramatization of the group is the control of other forces that are using the group to defuse radicalism. A black Canadian of Jamaican origin told me that *The Man* knew that a revolution was coming so he decided to turn up the heat in the sixties and early seventies and make the signs appear earlier than they otherwise would have done. *He* controlled the leadership that sprang up, using a lot of phonies and *agents provocateurs*, and thus defused the whole thing. What is being suggested in the novel is that while the group is self-dramatizing, and while it needs some intelligent and qualified thinkers like Malcolm to give it credibility, behind it is a force seeking to defuse radicalism altogether: and it is this that Malcolm almost but not quite comes to suspect through Rhiannon. '[The One] set up a baffle system that hide him while you still seeing him!' says Sister Buxton in *The One*.[58] We need an explanation for how Calvino owns such a large house if he is merely acting. Why did he stand aside while the police raid took place? Was he expecting it? Had he prepared it?

Just as Malcolm does not really *see* Honora, he does not trust his insight into Rhiannon until too late. Many people have noted that West Indians sound like the Welsh. For example, in *Escape to an Autumn Pavement*, Dick asks Johnnie, 'Where did you get that Welsh accent, Mr Sobert?' (p. 15) Salkey turns it around; when Rhiannon turns up at Malcolm's door with Gussie, Malcolm detected not only a Welsh intonation in her lyrical slickness but also something of a damped down Jamaican accent. (p. 167) When the British colonized the islands, several of the people sent out to run them were Scots, Irish or Welsh: colonials from 'home'. Rhiannon is an important figure from Celtic mythology. Patrick K. Ford says,

> Adventures in the Otherworld are common enough in romance, but in medieval Celtic literature they play a large role. It is often difficult to distinguish between the Other World and the world of ordinary mortals, and movement between the two is effected with little or no difficulty.[59]

Salkey wrote to me on July 31, 1985,

> Oh, about Rhiannon: I took it straight from *The Mabinogin*, that Welsh folk classic. She had three birds who could sing the dead to life, and three living to death. Rhiannon brings life to her companion and she is somewhat responsible for Malcolm's tragic end.

However, I think there is a more relevant interpretation of Rhiannon. In 'Pwyll, Prince of Dyfed', Rhiannon is accused of killing her child and is sentenced, in the words of Ford, to tell her story 'to those she thought might not know it, and to offer to carry strangers up to the court on her back.' While the accusation is false, Ford's comment on her is most important:

> The characterization of Rhiannon is strong and sure; she is assertive and dominant, often domineering. It is clear from her first entrance that she will accomplish her ends despite the ineptness of her intended mate.[60]

This is the character of Salkey's Rhiannon. She is guilty of killing her 'child'. Malcolm is sharp enough to see through the play-acting of the group: as a radical intellectual, he understands a great deal of historical forces. But precisely because he is an intellectual, he misses out on the dirty side of colonial rule, the skullduggery, the blood and grime. One of the recent accounts of this dirt is Philip Agee's *On the Run*.[61] Agee was a C.I.A. agent who became convinced the Agency was undermining democracy and aiding right-wing régimes in Latin America so he quit and began to tell all. Thomas Powers reviewed the new book:

> Did Mr Agee's activity hurt the agency? You bet it hurt. The best evidence of how much can be found in his careful account of C.I.A. efforts to convince him he had been neither forgiven nor forgotten – following him on his travels, spreading rumours about his alleged connection with the K.G.B. and D.G.I. [the intelligence service of Cuba], surrounding him with agents, tapping his telephone and even providing him with an elaborately wired typewriter in order to monitor what he was putting down on paper. Most difficult of all was a two-year period in the mid-1970's, when the agency, with high-level help, managed to bar him from residence in Britain, France, Italy and the Netherlands, apparently hoping to hound him until he was forced to take up residence in the Soviet block, where his true allegiance (from the agency's point of view) would no longer be in doubt . . . Tough as that period was, Mr Agee suspects still darker plots, a phony drug bust in Spain perhaps, or even an attempt to kill him. He may be right; a Federal judge refused to release secret documents describing 'illegal acts' targeted on Mr Agee on the grounds of national security.[62]

Powers says it was the United States' Constitution that protected Mr Agee: he implies that Agee might not have survived had he been a defector from Israel, the Soviet Union or France. Yet the United States has toughened up so that if Agee now recalls more secret operations, he may have to content himself 'writing novels'. Ah yes: but what kind of novels? David Morrell writes exciting novels about western intelligence agents, their twists, turns and covers, for example *Blood Oath* and *The Brotherhood of the Rose*.[63] But what kind of fictional protection would a real agent or somebody who knows too much need?

So Malcolm has lived, and died, in a very complex world. And yet he could have had some power over that world if he had understood what lay within. Jung says,

> The so-called civilized man has forgotten the trickster. He remembers him only figuratively and metaphorically when, irritated by his own ineptitude, he speaks of fate playing tricks on him or of things being bewitched. He never suspects that his own hidden and apparently harmless shadow has qualities whose dangerousness

exceeds his wildest dreams. As soon as people get together in masses and submerge the individual, the shadow is mobilized, and, as history shows, may even be personified and incarnated.

The disastrous idea that everything comes to the human soul from outside and that it is born a tabula rasa is responsible for the erroneous belief that under normal circumstances the individual is in perfect order . . . we can see why the myth of the trickster was preserved and developed: like many other myths, it was supposed to have a therapuetic effect. It holds the earlier low intellectual and moral level before the eyes of the more highly developed individual, so that he shall not forget how things looked yesterday. We like to imagine that something which we do not understand does not help us in any way. But that is not always so.[64]

Malcolm is 'civilized' through his class, education and experience in the metropolitan center: yet what lies underneath? R.D.E. Burton tells us in his essay, 'Derek Walcott and the Medusa of History':

The nightmarish quality of the West Indian historical experience would not require emphasis unless as Walcott, Lamming and others have lamented, West Indians were not themselves so prone to forget or ignore it: the genocidal destruction of the original inhabitants, the enforced diaspora of millions of Africans and their reduction to chattel slavery, the yoking of the islands to European (and, later, American) economic and strategic design, emancipation unaccompanied by the major social transformation that would alone have made paper freedom a reality, the indenture of East Indian and Chinese labourers, enduring racial and social cleavages, the eventual acquisition of political independence without genuine economic autonomy, the ostentatious prosperity of the few, the poverty and resentment of the many, a dismal chronicle of exile, exploitation and frustrated expectation. From the moment of their 'discovery' onwards, the West Indies have been less subjects than objects of history. In the mythology of imperialism (a mythology which, characteristically, perhaps, a majority of West Indians have made their own), it is the European who is the creator and bearer of history and a major element of colonial ideology is to deny the colonized an autonomous past and, by denying them this past, to deny them a present – and a future. Thus in the West Indies the European appears less as discoverer or even conqueror than as *creator ex nihilo*, drawing the islands from earlier dark nonentity by a species of divine *fiat*. He eliminated the indigenous population, imports the crop – sugar – and founds the socio-economic institution – the plantation – which together dominate the West Indies to this day and repeoples the islands with an un-ending supply of deracinated Africans for whom the Middle Passage is an existential death from which they are reborn to the living hell of the New World. Even the slave's freedom appears less as an acquistion of the slave than as the gift of the master, just as, a century later, the 'gift' of political independence confirms – or, at least, seems to confirm – the dependency relationship.[65]

To awaken from the nightmarish experience of history, the artist has to administer shock treatment because it is not enough to provide the correct historical and economic knowledge, necessary as this is. Salkey shows us why you cannot go home just yet by presenting in his poem, 'Dry River Bed', the story of someone who does:

'his expectations/were plain:/family,/eyecorner familiarity,/ back-home-self,/or so he thought.' . . . the villagers clawed at him/and what little he'd brought back;/they picked him clean/as a eucalyptus . . . he quickly saw/that home was a dry river bed;/he knew he'd have to run away, again,/or stay and be clawed to death/by the eagle/hovering over the village;/nothing had changed.'[66]

So Malcolm is deceiving himself when he thinks he can go home again. Not only in spite of but also because of his education, which is a liberal Western one, Malcolm does not see what he is getting into. His education makes him believe that you only need to speak the truth and the walls of Jericho will come tumbling down, on the assumption that the educated person sees the truth instead of a Potemkin version of reality. He did not know how dangerous the play-actors were, and he did not see that he could be destroyed by Clovis, significantly named after a Frankish king. The truth can even be used by 'the other side'. Clovis says that when Malcolm gets home,

And there'll be the li'l ol' State Department and the Peace Corps and the C.I.A., and the Black puppets and the middle-class stooges and our Caribbean love of constitutionalism and a thousand and one reasons why you'll never make the fucking revolution, and I know it, bro'.
(pp. 92/3)

Malcolm is like the protagonist in Ishmael Reed's poem, 'Dualism', sub-titled 'in ralph ellison's invisible man':

i am outside of
history. I wish
i had some peanuts, it
looks hungry there in
its cage

i am inside of
history. its
hungrier than i
thot[67]

The protagonist in Reed's poem underestimates history, standing outside it, as he thinks, and wanting to feed it peanuts. But he is swallowed up by history, for it is hungrier than he thought. (We shall see in the chapter on Reed that by spelling the word 'thot', Reed makes a second interpretation possible as well.) By not realizing that he is swallowed up by history, by giving it the peanuts of analytical and radical thought, by thinking kindly of those who have been oppressed, Malcolm exchanges one island for another:

He was locked out of the society he had chosen for his exile: a double lock-out, in his case, both at home and abroad.
(p. 56)

As we read the title of the novel, we tend to pay more attention to 'Malcolm Heartland' than the first part, in both rhythm and meaning. We see the name as symbolic: 'Malcolm' for 'Malcolm X' and 'Heartland' for the heartland of the country, the history, the culture. But Claude deflates this meaning by saying, 'I found your surname symbolically interesting. Both names, in fact.' (p. 49) *We are being told that the protagonist is not all that important in the meaning of the text.* In *Come Home, Malcolm Heartland*, it is not the protagonist but *the text* that plays Anancy to the last.

Salkey's long poem, *Jamaica*, explores and celebrates Jamaica's real history. It begins with the sub-head, 'I into history, now'. It says of a group of young women, 'You did know/say/that none o' them/know how much history/under them skin,/coil up inside, there so,/like baby hold back from born.'[68] After exploring and retrieving that history, the poem ends:

culture come when you buck up
on you'self
It start when you' body make a shadow
on the lan',
an' you know say
that you standin' up into mirror
underneat' you.

I say to meself,
'Is how the *mento* music go?'

You say,
'Is how the river flow?'
or, 'How the sea does lay down so?'

I done wit' you.
I into history, now.
Is the lan' I want
an' is the lan'
I out to get.

Salkey says that the ultimate aim of the responsible intellectual, whom he calls a worker-intellectual,

> should be broadly educational: that is, that worker *must* assume the role of a committed teacher, recorder, critic, analyst, explicator, and above all, a close learning-companion and servant of the people and of the culture as a whole.[69]

But what will the writer do if the people will not be educated? The writer gets them fictionally to take an aesthetic ride which reaches a dead-end, as in my radio-play, 'X', where the conductor shouts, 'Terminus!' I said 'TERMINUS!'[70] They will then have to retrace their steps and see where and how they let themselves be taken. Only after that will they be able to jump ship and begin their own journey into history.

Chapter II

Breaking Out of the Island:
The Novels of Francis Ebejer

Presumably because I myself am an islander,
the concept of islands, of islands within islands,
seem to recur in my work.

– Francis Ebejer[1]

Malta is different from Jamaica. The 118th edition of *The Statesman's Year-Book* states about Malta's history:

> Malta was held in turn by Phoenicians, Carthaginians and Romans, and was conquered by Arabs in 870. From 1090 it was joined to Sicily until 1530, when it was handed over to the Knights of St. John, who ruled until dispersed by Napoleon in 1798. The Maltese rose in rebellion against the French and the island was subsequently blockaded by the British aided by the Maltese from 1798 to 1800. The Maltese people freely requested the protection of the British Crown in 1802 on condition that their rights and privileges be preserved. The islands were finally annexed to the British Crown by the Treaty of Paris in 1814.
>
> On 15 April 1942, in recognition of the steadfastness and fortitude of the people of Malta during the Second World War, King George VI awarded the George Cross to the island ... The area of Malta is 246 sq. km (94.9 sq. miles); Gozo, 67 sq. km (25.9 sq. miles); Comino, 3 sq. km (1.1 sq. miles); total area, 316 sq. km (121.9 sq. miles). Population census 27 Nov. 1967, 314, 216 ... Chief town and port, Valletta ... Malta became independent on 21 Sept. 1964 and became a republic within the Commonwealth on 13 Dec. 1974.[2]

Compare this with the same volume's entry on Jamaica:

> Jamaica was discovered by Columbus in 1494, and was occupied by
> the Spaniards between 1509 and 1655, when the island was captured
> by the English; their possession was confirmed by the Treaty of
> Madrid, 1670. Self-government was introduced in 1944 and gradually
> extended until Jamaica achieved complete independence within the
> Commonwealth on 6 Aug. 1962. The area of Jamaica is 4,243.6 sq.
> miles (10,991 sq. km). The population at the census of 7 April 1970
> was 1,861,300 distributed on the basis of the 14 parishes of the island
> . . . Kingston and St. Andrew, 550,100 . . . St. Thomas, 71,400.[3]

Malta is physically close to Europe and to Africa while Jamaica is
close to the United States. Malta was not a slave society and the
indigenous people were not wiped out by the conquerors so the
'original' language survives in competition with imposed European ones. But the similarities are greater than the differences.
Both countries have had the experience of many conquerors from
Europe, both are meeting points of many cultures, and both
contain island people. Joe Friggieri could be talking about Salkey
when comparing a character from Ebejer's third novel with one
from *Il-Gaggia* (The Cage) by Frans Gammut in 'Disillusionment
after Independence in Maltese Literature':

> Whereas Ebejer's Joseph escapes *inwards*, as it were, right back to
> the womb of the land, seeking complete fusion with his country,
> Fredu Gambin escapes *outwards* – he leaves Malta and swears never
> to come back to her shores. These two extremes represent the
> contemporary Maltese writer's dilemma. This escape – inwards or
> outwards – is symptomatic of the tension experienced on many levels
> by the generations of young Maltese, now perhaps more than ever
> before.[4]

Ebejer's first two novels were written before his country acquired
independence: his later works deal with the problems that come
after Independence.

* * *

> The Sirocco – it kneads your breath and cloys it. Strange wind the
> Sirocco – you're neither here nor there; you're neither of the earth
> nor of the sky. It gives you that feeling . . .
> It made the sawdust on the floor damp and cloggy, so that when
> she walked over to the old beggar at the door, the stuff stuck in
> sodden clumps to the bottom of her shoes.

This could have easily come from Salkey's *A Quality of Violence*: it begins with a force from nature, a force connected with the people; in other words, it is not only that the people are part of nature and are influenced by the environment but that the force of nature becomes a symbol or metaphor or indication of some deeper force at work among the people. But it begins Francis Ebejer's first novel, *A Wreath For the Innocents*, first published in 1958 and reissued in 1981 as *A Wreath of Maltese Innocents*.[5]

On one level, the novel is a love story. Lieutenant John Xiberras de Balyard is the son of one of the upper-class families of Malta. His mother is European, so he is the closest connection to Europe that the country has. It is even within the blood that this ruling élite is connected to the European ruling class. John falls in love with Lucija, the daughter of a wine shop owner and therefore a girl who is very close to the people of the land. But just as John is not merely of the upper class of Malta, being a mixture of the Maltese upper-class and Europe, so too Lucija is not merely of the peasantry: her father had fallen in love with and married a woman from the upper classes. Far from making him sympathetic to his daughter's love, though, this makes him determined to break off the relationship because his wife's family had cast her out. His hatred of her family is a class one:

> If only the damned girl would stop and try to understand what it meant to be born at the lower end of the social scale. It was all very well for people to preach equality. Those at the bottom wanted to be equal, but what about those on top? And yet, strange as it might seem, it was largely those on top who came out with all the fine speeches about the so-called Christian spirit.
>
> Christian spirit! Toni felt a contraction in his chest, for a moment as painful as that in his stomach. Their Christian spirit!
>
> Toni had heard that in some countries things were not so bad, that class-hatred was outdated – a thing of the iniquitous past, somebody had told him. He did not know if that were true or not. But it certainly was not true where his own country was concerned. There were many things that needed changing completely here, he thought ferociously.
>
> And the time will come, he said to himself, as he felt the red-hot twinges again. Soon we shall have our own Labour Government. Then we shall see: soon there will be a bloody hell of a change!
> (pp. 22/3)

The family of Xiberras de Balyard does not want John to be involved with a girl of the lower class. His mother is determined to break up the relationship. His father is not all that concerned since he has become indifferent to the outside world after discovering his wife's self-sufficiency:

> Because of this and the consonent difference in temperament
> between him and his wife he had been able to create a life of his own,
> upstairs in his room, first, with the origins and history of the Knights
> of St. John, and then, with his collection of cigar-bands. He had
> demanded nothing more from life.
>   In the old days he had been passionate with her and it had upset
> him when he had reached so quickly the basic frigid element in her.
> When they had taken to occupying separate beds, he had known a
> few months of bitterness and frustration. But that, too, had passed.
> His innate love of solitude had reshaped his life from a pattern of
> desire and passion to one of slow, comfortable existence, in which
> the only demands he made were on himself.
> (p. 41)

The frigid element in her is not just that of an individual woman: it is a basic frigidity in the relationship of the Europeanized upper-class to Malta. The relationship is uncreative: worse, it is a slow death, although the Maltese upper-classes will not admit it for doing so will mean having to break out into new and frightening territory. The frustration of the relationship could be seen in Freudian terms: the Count's hobby is collecting cigar bands, not cigars. He is unprepared for the story his wife tells him about the son but agrees that something must be done:

> Blood which had been nurtured and cherished through countless
> generations, blood which had been kept pure and untainted through
> God knew how many vicissitudes was too sacred a covenant to be
> allowed to be sullied in one unguarded moment.
> (pp. 42/3)

The father, trying to preserve class, speaks just like the wealthy white man to his daughter in Albert Wendt's *Sons for the Return Home*, and for the same reason: she wants to marry a person across the class/racial barrier.[6] One might argue that it is not race that is the issue in Ebejer's novel, but in Malta, class does include an element of race. Trying his best to persuade his son to marry a

Charlotte or Catherine or Brigida, the father says something that comes out differently from what he intended:

> 'Once,' the Count began hesitantly, 'before I met your mother, that is, do you know that type of woman I wished most of all to marry? Sometimes the thought of it nearly drove me mad, and at night, before I slept, it was a torment. I would go into the village and look at the peasant girls, and say to myself: I shall marry one of them one day. You see, it was a . . . a desire for their strong bodies, their earthly limbs, their faces full of character. I . . . I found myself comparing them with the women I knew, the aristocratic young ladies, and it wasn't to the peasant girls' disadvantage.'
>
> He paused, gearing his thoughts to the main purpose. 'I yearned for something my family had been starved of for generations. It was as if fancy food had begun to sicken me and I hungered for wholemeal. I was miserable with longing – and ill, literally ill! I remember it quite plainly, and how at that time, too, I suffered from the most terrible pains in my chest. One day, in the fields, I succumbed; I took one of these women to me. She was everything I had craved for. I will never be ill from starvation again, I told myself . . .
>
> (p. 87)

This is very much like what happens in a short story by Lucio Rodrigues. Set before the Liberation of Goa in 1961, 'It Happens' shows the yearning for a boy of the upper class for a peasant girl, in terms of nature, the land, and life as against the appeal of Europe:

> And in the silence his body communed with hers in the language of touch, motion, taste, smell; feelingly, searchingly, insinuatingly, vibrating the skin into ripples of delight. The green garden of her virginal body blossomed at his touch and like a fond gardener he felt the beauty of the *abolim* of her lips, the roses of her cheeks, the full-blown dahlias of her breasts, the white lotus of her belly, the lily stalks of her arms and thighs, the aralia and the dark flower of her groin.
>
> And his pilgrim lips and fingers wandered over the maps of her body, circling up giddy heights and burrowing into warm hollows, round smooth curves and over hard edges, dreaming over long undulating lawns, trippling over familiar paths, and slowly, sacredly exploring the dark secret shrine where dwells the mystery of Kama.
>
> And as he explored, blood panted fiercely in his veins, rushing tumultously into the main stream, and his limbs leapt with the leaping tide, and from the bent bow of his body flew the flaming

> arrow of desire, yearning for its target, penetrating like a
> ploughshare into earth, till the gathering storm within him burst like
> the monsoon rains, watering the seed, filling, flooding, spending
> itself, and leaving in its wake a strange quiet, a peace, a repose of
> tired, fulfilled limbs.[7]

In Rodrigues's story, the girl gets pregnant, as does Lucija in
Ebejer's novel, and the family sends the son off to Europe
(Portugal to be exact). In a more complex bit of maneuvering,
John's family also arranges to send him to Europe. John's father,
in continuing his story, says that all desire for the girl had left him,
and then he realized why: there was a clash of bloods, his being a
type unmixed and centuries old. He was ill for a long time, and he
could not get well until his system had rid itself of the pollution.
John draws a different moral:

> unless our blood gets . . . polluted, as you so colourfully described it,
> we'll remain the sorriest species of mankind . . . We're scared of new
> beginnings, and, even more, of clean, fresh air.
> (p. 88)

The priest, Dun Saver, sees the relationship between John and
Lucija as a means of finally ending class hatred and is happy that
God has chosen him to nurture and guide this young love. (p. 47)
So he blesses the relationship and wants to officiate the marriage.
But like Lucija and John, Dun Saver has underestimated class
forces plus the fact that history is labyrinthinian and some people
in the upper class know how to use this fact. Conspiracies are part
of history, and who would understand this better than a Bishop of
the Catholic Church? And who would better know how to use
cunning to achieve the ends of the ruling class? When John's
mother fails with his father, who slowly turns to his son's side, she
goes to his uncle, Monsignor Assalon Xiberras, who had worked
in the Vatican during the war. When the Monsignor first sets eyes
on Lucija, he has a feeling of pride because all the Xiberras
women have been beautiful; but he resists her and the attractive-
ness of a world in which all were truly equal. Instead, he reminds
himself, 'the Family was a vocation, too! *And* a sacred one' (p.
102). Class exists within the Church, even while the Church creates
the image of being impartial. The Monsignor sends for Dun Saver
and tells him, in his oblique way, to use the power of confession to

break up the love of Lucija and John, to declare that it is a sin. The priest is spiritually destroyed. He tries to do as he is told: but Lucija walks out of the confessional. He later dies. Lucija seems to have succeeded in her rebellion.

Yet things are not so simple. Yes, John and Lucija are in love, but is it a love that comes from knowledge or from innocence? Notice the exchange between Lucija and Dun Saver:

> 'You do love the young man, do you not?'
> 'I do, oh, I do. I can't live without him!'
> (p. 46)

This is sentimental, a sentimentality that comes from not knowing. Quite early in the novel, when she looks at herself in the mirror,

> She looked then at her face, and she was fully conscious for the first time of her youth and beauty. Yet she could not rid herself of the feeling that it was a stranger who was looking back at her from the mirror: a beautiful, totally mysterious stranger.
> (p. 12)

This Lucija is not ready.

John comes to the wine-shop while her father is in hospital. A man says,

> It's the second time this week that bitch has closed up on us . . . I lay you five to one she's whoring about somewhere while her father . . .

John hits the man (p. 90). A fight starts. Lucija comes back and shouts at the people to leave John alone. Finally a policeman turns up. The incident gets publicity:

> The newspapers gave the incident considerable space and political colouring.
> The Left-wing papers made much of it, a special editorial in one referring to it as 'the kind of degenerate practice, only too typical of a degenerate class, which the Workers' Movement was determined to stamp out once and for all, together with colonialism and the retrogressive trappings of its fellow-travellers.
> Right-wing newspapers were just as vehement in their denunciations, one paper calling the incident 'a base contrivance by some *agent provocateur* or other worthy of the wickedness of

Rasputin, and no doubt, engineered in the secret conclaves of
international socialism and atheism.'
  Coming as it did in the middle of one of the bitterest political
campaigns ever known on the Island, with the people divided over
vital issues at a time when the British colonial occupation was on its
way out after over a hundred and fifty years, the incident was almost
blown up into a major political issue.
(p. 92)

Both political groups are locked into fixed positions and do not
want to see the reality or the possibility of interaction between the
classes. We see what John and Lucija are up against. Their
innocence will make them transgress the rules: yet the rules are
there and their innocence will also make them fail.

The Countess is distressed by the incident and goes to see the
Monsignor. He uses all his power to break up the couple. He
manipulates a priest into getting Lucija's father to sign papers so
that she will be locked away in an asylum and looked after by
nuns. Later, he manipulates John into going to Europe for a
while. He succeeds: but not for the reasons he thought he would.

Lucija is pregnant. John does not know, but his mother does
and she goes to visit the convent. She and Lucija are strangely
drawn to each other:

Lucija watched her almost against her will: she could not help
admiring her. She marvelled at the finely-chiselled face, the exquisite
smallness of her figure the subdued elegance of her clothes, the
silvery hair beneath a hat the like of which she had not seen before;
and the blue eyes, the fine skin, the delicate chin. She seemed in
many ways different from the others; she stood distinctively apart.
  That's how I would like to look when I am her age, thought
Lucija.
(p. 212)

Lucija never knows who she is. The Countess is moved to touch
her face and say softly, 'I hope you will be happy, my dear.' By
now, John's father has accepted his son's lover and is looking
forward to a grandchild. But Lucija loses the baby. She is sharing
the room with two other women, Carmen and a white woman
named Marija. One night, Carmen, scared by the lightning, came
to her bed for warmth. This turned Marija into a fury and she beat
up Lucija, who woke up in hospital, having lost the baby. Lucija

had not known that the two women were lovers. But actually, it is
not so much that Marija is responsible for the loss of the baby as
that Lucija had willed it. While out of the convent for a while, she
had found a way of getting to the travel agency where John
worked, only to find that he had gone to Europe:

> When she dreamed of him, she awoke refreshed. In her mind, John
> had been no further away from her than the other side of the high
> garden wall which separated her from the world outside.
>   Now, she stretched the numbed powers of her imagination to their
> limit, searching for him. Often she did not find him. She had never
> been abroad. She knew little of life outside the Island. It was a cold,
> heart-breaking search over unknown ground . . .
>   In such periods of defencelessness, the doubts came, one blinding,
> vicious stab of doubts after another, obscenely hurtful. Nausea
> reached her. When that happened, she almost hated the being in her
> belly and wished to God she were free of it.
> (p. 230)

Lucija has the limitation of her class: she has not been to Europe,
she has not had the chance to go outside the island, so she cannot
even imagine what the outside is like. *Her imagination is trapped
by the island.* This is where John committed an error. As the
outside world was part of the experience of his class, he could not
imagine it not being part of the imagination of the lower classes.
And for this error, he loses Lucija and the product of their love.
On his return from Europe, before he goes to the convent to claim
Lucija, his mother knows what is going to happen. She knows
now that she is a stranger to her own son, that things will never be
the same again, and that she has brought this on herself. And

> She almost wished now the girl had died with her baby. That way,
> she would not be alive now and ready to disown him when he went
> to her.
> (p. 247)

She feels anguish at her folly:

> Why had she not let him take the girl at the very start? Was Family
> really all that important? How *real* was it?

She wishes Lucija would be weak and give in to him – but the girl is like her in her strong will. When John comes to her, she will not weaken in her resolve:

> What mattered now was the memory of Marija's hammering blows on her body, and that moment when she had awakened to grey, curving shapes, an awful whiteness and the relief that it was all over at last – the spell had been broken, however high the price, the sacrifice, had been.
> (p. 250)

What spell had been broken? What whiteness? Just as in Omotoso's *The Edifice*, whiteness, the whiteness of European rule, has gone deeper into the psyche than people realize. It has affected all the classes. Even though Lucija was genuinely in love with John, it was a love mixed up with the desire for whiteness, something she had not recognized for she did not know her own image in the mirror. Now she knows herself. When John says his car is outside, she says, 'I am not coming with you, John . . . I have decided to remain here.' (p. 251) She feels sorry for him and decides she will not tell him the secret of the child. She is right that things are over:

> She saw the effort he was desperately making to rekindle a fire that was no longer burning except for a few sparks now and then.

The end echoes the Bible:

> 'It is finished?' he said in a low voice.
>   'Finished.'
> (p. 252)

John now realizes what Lucija had known: he had come to her not out of passion but out of the old Xiberras sense of duty. He comes to a realization about his class:

> Pollution! He now realized that pollution could work both ways – not just sullying the Noble House of the Xiberras de Balyard. The Family, too, had done more than its share of polluting!
> (p. 253)

Lucija now has self-awareness. She recalls the words of a beggar woman who had said to her,

> What was once full will be empty . . . But the strangeness will not
> grieve you; it will not give you despair, but courage . . . You will feel
> contentment when everything is gone . . . It will be like the priest's
> absolution and a peace.
> (p. 257)

Even if she could not break out, she knows future Lucijas will. She
had said 'no' at the time when it counted, and she has had the
experience of love with a man from the upper class, an experience
that will remain with her. Equally, the experience of Lucija will
remain with John. So who has lost out?

The mother has. The father has too because in his weakness, he
was not able to impose his will on the family: he had come to
accept the idea of Lucija as daughter-in-law and her child as
grandchild but nothing came of it. The Monsignor has lost out the
most of all: instead of feeling triumph, he feels tired and worn out,
like a spent candle. The fact that he had protected the family
seems hollow to him. He had not expected that John would look
'so devoid of interest, so unconcerned – so unhurt' and that 'the
woman would elect to lead the life of the cloister' (pp. 258/9). The
Monsignor had not imagined a member of the lower class having
a life and imagination of her own. He is denied even the burst of
energy he would get from feeling he has successfully manipulated
everything. Things and people are out of his control. He considers
unburdening himself to the Archbishop and giving up the
priesthood. But he pulls back: he will throw himself into his work
and thus he loses the insight he has gained, no longer seeing the
potential in the ordinary people. He passes by a group of workers
destroying the old structures but he is going to resist

> threats to old-standing tradition – a sacred cause. Too much sudden
> progress, too liberal. Tendencies to secularize life in the country.
> Won't do! Socialism. Modernism. There was a direct threat.

Ebejer said in an unpublished interview with Adrian Stivala,

> I felt at the time that, if ever there was emancipation from
> colonialism, that emanicipation should belong to the Maltese
> woman.
>   So I started with Lucija, a working girl, caught up inside a
> particular socio-economical, psychological, political and religious
> milieu from which she tries to break out. The novel traces Lucija's

development right up to the point when she at last could say NO. For all that, she fails largely, it was still too soon; but the word of self-asssertion has been irrevocably uttered, and acted upon, and at least for the book's Monsignor Assalon Xiberras: 'For a second, it occured to him that he was looking at the first of a new breed of Maltese woman.'[8]

Actually, Lucija says 'No' several times, each time a greater act of the will than the one before. She says 'No' to her father, a male in a patriarchal society and a class-conscious worker; 'No' to Dun Saver when he wants to force her into confession during which he can tell her, on the instructions of the Monsignor, that she is committing a sin; and finally 'No' to John. In the second 'No,' she has rejected the power of the Church because she knows what is right, although she does not know the full complexity of the Church. The memory of her true love and sexual relationship with a member of the upper class will remain with her all her life so her last 'No', which comes out of experience and self-knowledge, is the most important of all. She rejects admittance into the upper class because that is not what she wants. Ebejer says in an interview with Daniel Massa,

> The search carried out by my heroes/heroines is an inner search out of the island – a kind of metaphorical, spiritual, psychological search not a physical [one] . . . the sea represents a mystical wall which the islanders' psychology cannot penetrate.[9]

Lucija's imagination could not cross the seas to be with John in Europe; but paradoxically, when she chooses to be enclosed inside walls, she has found her freedom, as much as it is possible to get at this time.

A comment is required about the symbolism of sexuality in the novel. Ebejer says to a Torinese student studying his novels for a doctorate, 'I can truthfully say that alone in our countryside I often get a genuine sexual urge – for the earth.'[10] Thus the following description of the Monsignor is negative:

> He had never had any real vocation for the priesthood and could easily have made a success of himself in some other career. However, three factors had helped him decide to embrace Holy Orders: his scholastic brillance, *his near total lack of desire for women*, and a long-standing Xiberras tradition whereby each generation had

produced at least one Monsignor of the Church.
(pp. 52/3, my italics)

It is significiant that the women Marija (which means 'Mary') who kills Lucija's baby is very white. That is the end of the appeal of whiteness for Lucija. She does not hate Marija, but the nuns keep her away so that she is denied the balm of apology and forgiveness until she (Marija) goes mad. In her fate, we can see a little of what happens to the Count, the Countess and the Monsignor: they are denied any catharsis. Just by being who she is, Lucija has begun the process of change, even in the life of the Monsignor. As he had planned his battle, for the first time in his life, the Monsignor, 'used to having mountains come to him, had elected to go himself to the mountain' (p. 170). As for Lucija:

'I am not going to give in so easily this time,' Lucija resolved grimly. 'I must know everything; there are so many things that are incomprehensible to me – things that I dread because they are hidden.'
(p. 200)

It is precisely because things were hidden that they had to be brought to the surface.

* * *

'You must pray for her,' the boy said. 'You gave my sister a beautiful body but her soul is dark. You forgot to care for her soul.'
    Bertu said without moving his head, 'It is the way her mother was made too. There's no understanding her.'
    A sigh escaped the boy and he leant closer to her father and caressed with his fingers the old man's cheek.
    'She does not pray at night,' he said. 'She never prays. The Lord's wrath is upon us unless she mends her ways.[11]

In *Evil of the King Cockroach*, re-published in 1968 as *Wild Spell of Summer*, Ebejer once again uses a woman as a symbol or metaphor: but he does it differently from before. Rosie is a woman of her time, a young Maltese woman of the fifties coming into her own and yet not having enough self-knowledge at the beginning. She is seen differently by the people around her. Her pallid, very Christian brother Georg – strictly, her half-brother, born of the same father but a different mother – sees her as an incestuously dangerous sensual woman:

> Now she is doing something to her face, he thought. Clink of cosmetics jar on glass-topped surface came to him vividly. He heard her sigh . . .
> Hastily he tried to pray.
> But there were no sounds. He clapped his hands to his ears, but his eyes remained strained beyond the wall on which the wooden-framed, glassless Virgin was hung.
> He could still hear sounds from the next room. He could almost see her . . .
> He fell on his knees by the bed and covered his head with his hands and the rosary swung against the skin of his face, this way and that, sending queer shivers through him. He remained like this while he heard her undress.
> (p. 37)

Georg sees her as desirable and therefore evil. It is not so much that he is a Christian saint, as his father believes, as that 'his frail body is the arena in which pagnism and Christianity fight each other', as Ebejer said in a letter to me dated August 30, 1985. Rosie strengthens those pagan elements within Georg that he cannot suppress: so he projects blame onto her.

Everybody around Rosie sees her as desirable. The novel begins with Paul, a young boy from the noveau riche upper middle class who wants her. Rosie says, 'You students like playing with my kind for a while, then marry someone else in your class.' (p. 18) She does not give in to him: she lets him kiss her and then pushes him away. At this point, Rosie does not know what she wants. As long as we see her from the outside, as almost everyone does, we are able to see her as somebody special – desirable, evil, a temptress, etc.

Does Rosie not want Paul because she is frigid in a clinical sense? That is a tempting conclusion, particularly because when Paul's father, Zaren Micallef, who rose up from peasant origins, tries to seduce/rape her in his luxuriously carpeted office, she says twice, 'I am a virigin.' (p. 182) Yet to conclude that she is frigid is as false as to draw the opposite conclusion, the one most of the men draw, that she is promiscuous. Micallef says, his lips to her breasts, 'I like the sense of other men's lips and hands on your flesh.' (p. 182) Earlier, when the adolescent and unripe Paul has failed to make any headway with her,

> his glumness spread, slowly, like the slow dying of speech. She had
> been amused. The light striking straight across the sides of his face
> from behind made his pimples look like a photograph of the moon
> she had once seen.
>
> If he wants to make love to me tonight, she thought, I shall let him.
> (p. 56)

Why does she decide she will let him make love to her, then? The
answer is that she does not know what she wants because she does
not know who she is.

Thus whenever she makes up her mind to do something, she
goes ahead to do it in an obsessive way, then she suddenly changes
her mind and drops it. For example, she was angry with her father
for rejecting the offer by Micallef to buy out their cheesecake
business for £400 (£4,000 in the later edition). She nags him as
much as his second wife had done because she (the wife) wanted to
escape the confines of the shop and go out into the glittering
world. Finally, her father agrees to sell and goes with her to
Micallef's house. Micallef plays power games and says they must
have misheard his offer: he had offered £300 (£3,000 in the later
edition). Nevertheless, it appears that Bertu and Rosie will accept
the offer, particularly because Bertu can no longer go into the
basement to make cheesecakes: he feels the king cockroach that
watches him down there contains the spirit of his dead wife and
the exorcism by Dun Mattew had failed. But because Rosie feels
challenged by Micallef, she decides they should not sell and she
will make the cheesecakes herself despite the heat.

Rosie does not know what she wants because she does not
know who she is: she carries within her something that comes
from pre-Catholic Malta, the something that Christianity fought
against and characterized as the devil:

> When she had left her father, the devil was in her. Suddenly she had
> thought of leaving the house for ever. As she turned into Kingsway,
> the lights and the massing of people seemed to whip the devil inside
> her into a frenzy. She felt it deep in her chest and in her thighs,
> coursing through her and clutching at her throat so that when she
> had suddenly come face to face with Paul outside Cordina's Café she
> could not speak with the pain of this thing in her body.
> (p. 57)

The name 'Paul' is no accident. The apostle/convert Paul had been shipwrecked on Gozo. He had suppressed one side of himself to embrace the other. Ebejer's Paul has pimples on one side of his face, which bleed, particularly when Rosie slaps him. He too is 'two-faced': he does not know how to become a complex being except that he keeps after Rosie, knowing she contains what he needs. At least he has more possibilities than Georg, who is plagued by thoughts of sensuality, without any color except that of death. He denies the attraction of the sensual life Rosie represents. At the end, he pushes Rosie down the steps into the basement and she is almost killed. Then Bertu realizes that he (Georg) had done the same thing to his mother Clara.

Everybody seems to be trapped, the entrapment being externalized by the way they see the king cockroach. Paul sees the cockroach in terms of his failure to seduce/rape Rosie:

> She struggled fiercely but he held her firmly, straddling her soft, slippery body, squeezing it between his knees and thighs . . .
> Until, in one instant, he felt nothing but the thing on his forehead. All his maddened faculties converged on it and to him it was bigger than his mad desire to die. He rolled away from her right across the floor and clawed his forehead with his hands, whimpering. He stumbled to his feet, holding his face. He heard his own sobs. Then the girl, as if from a long way off, said calmly, 'it's only a cockroach.'
> (p. 110)

Nobody can kill the cockroach, which is of a tough species that has survived unchanged from pre-historic times. But when Rosie is pushed down the stairs by Georg, the cockroach comes to feed on Rosie's blood on the floor. The priest picks her up and tells Bertu to kill the cockroach. Meanwhile, a stranger comes in and takes Rosie from the priest. Bertu then brings his foot down on the cockroach:

> When he removed his foot, the imprint of his sandal in the red was clear and in it was half the severed body with the antennae waving wildly until gradually they drooped and stopped.
> (p. 202)

When Bertu wants Rosie to live, he takes action and discovers the cockroach was only a cockroach.

When Rosie is at death's door, the people realize that she is only a mortal, not the siren that so many of the men, including the priest, thought she was. The priest was obsessed by the fact that he could once have been a missionary in India, doing good to the suffering people out there: but he had lacked the courage to go out. Now, as he helps Rosie, he sees that there are people here to help too:

> He held up both hands to the light of the waiting-room and looked at her blood on them. He looked at it in silence. He thought in awe. Even as she lay in my arms that I discovered Rosie was a child; she lay in my arms, just like any disease-ridden child in India.
> (p. 197)

The priest saw himself as a developed European needing to save the poor Indians out there: now he sees the underdevelopment within.

The stranger who walked in to save Rosie is actually no stranger: she had first met him on a bus while she was getting away from Valetta. The bus driver was driving fast to keep ahead of another bus. Seeing that an old woman passenger was terrified, Rosie had told the driver to slow down, which he had done, losing the race and the passengers he would have got if he had got there first. The old woman was the driver's mother. As they sit having coffee, Rosie thinks of the young conductor who had refused to tell the driver to slow down, 'Up there in the bus . . . I could have killed him, he made me so mad, but now – he was little more than a child.' (p. 133) And she feels 'as if something taut inside her had yielded.' Through Grezzju and his mother, Rosie finds out about the person she is looking for, Wenzu, a farmer who 'sees deep into things'. Grezzju says 'They say he is friends with Lucifru', but the mother says that she had consulted Wenzu when expecting Grezzju because the baby moved so much she was frightened of losing him. She does consult Wenzu. He bounces her unstated problem back at her: his last sentence is, 'sometimes, for a little second, one is God.' (p. 145)

Through Grezzju and his mother, Rosie had begun to know the land, the fruits, the seasons:

> 'The harvest will be soon. That smells nice, too. And the grapes – they are all purple and bursting to be picked and eaten. Have you

ever smelled grapes when they're ripe on the vine?'

'No. How do they smell?'

'How can I tell you? You must smell them yourself. Let me take you.'

'No, no,' she said.

'And there's nothing better than the peaches on the trees, too, and the plums and the apricots. Sometimes, when the moon is full like tonight and it's summer, like now, I sleep there in the field. Out in the open. And it cleans me of the diesel and the smell of your town.'

'You have a field and yet you do not work on it,' she said, open-eyed with surprise.

(pp. 138/9)

Rosie returns from Wenzu to Grezzju, wanting to stay with him and work the field and all it contains; she sees him as

the symbol of the boy she hated so unreasonably but with all her heart – he with his pimples and the money with which he had taunted her so that she had wept all night.

(p. 146)

She could not get him out of her system at that point so she had to go back. So Grezzju comes for her when she needs him and is ready. And he brings her back to life on the farm.

Rosie could be saved because she did not have her mother's greed and materialism. She had a potential for reconnection to the land. She lacked self-knowledge at the beginning but she had energy and the willingness to break out. If the bus goes too fast, unlike the more traditional mother, she can use her good sense to tell the driver to slow down. She can be sensuously in love not with Paul but with Grezzju, the person who is both close to the land and who drives a bus by which she can move. But first Rosie must be freed from the mythifying of the men around her for they can otherwise trap her into roles that are not of her creation.

* * *

The theme of the return to the land is worked out further in Ebejer's third novel, *In The Eye of The Sun*.[12] The Author's Note gives us a clue to the focus of the text: 'All human characters in this book are imaginary. The land is real.'

Joseph is of peasant origin. He was a brilliant medical student but a few months before graduation, he drops out of university. This is inexplicable to everyone, including himself: all he knows is that he is psychically dying and must get to the roots to live. His sister thinks there is a curse on the family. His university professor thinks he has had a temporary lapse and will return. So does the professor's white-skinned daughter, Yvonne, who was in love with him. Joseph's old teacher from primary school days is also upset and tries to talk him into going back. He says,

> 'Never had I entertained higher hopes for anybody else in my long career,' . . . 'It's a rare thing, and incredibly beautiful, is it not, for a son of the land to reach the academic heights you had reached, Joseph.'
> (p. 71)

The exchange assumes a great importance for it shows both what the teacher is aspiring to as a colonial and what Joseph feels is killing him. I quote at length:

> 'The white women,' the old one went on. 'The great white women of the world's greatest works . . .'
> Joseph had stopped playing with the whistle and it lay in his hand, fingers pressed tightly to it.
> Now he turned to the schoolmaster.
> 'The white women,' he said slowly. 'Ah yes, after a time I discovered they were not to be found in reality, and what of them did exist was a travesty of what you . . . of what I had first imagined.'
> He heard the schoolmaster move.
> 'What are you saying!' the schoolmaster said. 'Unlike me, you've been out in the world. Surely, there, beyond the village confines, you must have discovered them, a few of them, one at least, exactly as the great masters had depicted them . . .'
> 'I saw them only in my dreams. When I thought I had found them, they were not the ones.'
> Plaintively, tick of teeth on pipe-stem, 'Are you perhaps insinuating that the great masters did not know what they were writing about?'
> Cruelly he replied, 'you and I just did not understand the masters, nor the white women.'
> 'You are out of your mind. Do you mean to say that the white women of the masters did not exist – with their rich, brocaded dresses, their shining hair diamond-studded, their exquisite

mannerisms, their cultivated poise, the rare beauty of their mind and spirit, their brilliance and intelligence, their culture?

Joseph sighed . . .

An indescribable urge to hurt rose in Joseph. He was fully conscious of the disillusionment he was going to throw on this man who had all his life dreamt in terms of the great poetry of life behind the secluded high walls of the city's great houses . . .

'The masters' white women were not as we had imagined them, *mast*.'

'There is no doubt they were.'

Joseph leaned off the wall. 'They weren't.' He stopped and picked up a handful of soil. 'It was the brown body, as brown as this, the masters extolled,' he almost shouted savagely.

He heard the schoolmaster's gasp, saw the shape of his head like something dwindling into his chest leaving only the yellow, dull glint of his baldness.

Joseph flung the soil violently against the cistern wall. 'The brocaded dresses, you say,' he said harshly. 'Their cultivated poise, their mind, their spirit! . . . Sickening! I say it was the body that was brown under the skin and smelled of earth and weed, the body draped by the most ordinary material, the thighs that shook as primitively as a partner's in mating, the breasts burning with a fire no cultivated poise or exquisite mannerism could kindle . . . that is what inspired the masters, earth itself, all the lasting things civilized society is intent on destroying . . . Not just the skin, their mind, their spirit, as you . .. as you, schoolmaster, as you would have me . . .' He stopped, groping for breath . . .

'Peasants,' he said, the word sounding like a gurgle, expressionless.

'What but the peasant in them,' said Joseph, 'could have captured and expressed the supreme elemental force from which stems, too, the inspiration of a poet?'

'But Beatrice, Laura . . .' The schoolmaster's voice faltered in the dark.

'It was their brown spirits that enraptured Dante and Petrarch,' Joseph said quietly. 'Can there be more doubt about that? However white their skin might have been, it was the transcendental earth in it that captivated them, loosened the life-stream that gushed forth into the magnificent poetry we, the two of us, schoolmaster, used to relish so much.'

'Brown spirit! Earth!' The schoolmaster stood up with the very force of his objection. 'We are trying to leave all that behind, my boy. To lift ourselves from it and all its connotations. Transcend its baseness, its vileness, its pettiness.'

(pp. 73/5)

The white woman, as in *The Adventures of Catullus Kelly*, is the symbol of, the danger to and the bait for the colonial who seeks to climb out of his colonial inferiority. In Chuck Berry's 'Too Much Monkey Business' – recorded by Elvis Presley in 1968 just after he completed shooting *Stay Away, Joe*, a movie about the bourgeois dreams of the Third World – reference is made to the blonde-haired woman who wants to get the narrator hooked, make him settle down and write a book – a book which will not reflect the truth of Third World man.[13] In Ayi Kwei Armah's *Fragments* and *Why Are We So Blest?*, the protagonists discover that through education, they are the humans making the crossing to the world of the gods and thus both cut off from and used to betray their people. The teacher and Joseph do not have such knowledge because they have not been off the island. For the teacher, the ideal was to break away from the soil, to climb into the world of the white women of literature; for Joseph, the white women were represented in real life by the white-skinned daughter of his professor. When Joseph is close to the goal, he realizes it has all been a lie. He is dying psychically and wants to get back to life by running away from the lie. But everywhere he turns, he finds people who want what he is rejecting, who assume that he has gone crazy or has a curse on him, that he will eventually return to the university. Everybody wants to climb into that rarefied world. Even the peasant woman in whose house he is staying – which was his house when he was young – appears to be sympathetic only because she wants her daughter to be the first person from the village to become a doctor.

Joseph's desire to return to the land is actually a deeper desire than he knows. When he gets to his old house,

> He was like one gaining time. He raised his eyes and felt the house present in him like a clamour gradually getting louder even in its quiet and in the reddening light that was slowly engulfing it . . . he felt incredibly old, came back after centuries of empty, wandering existence.
> (p. 57)

There is something dead in his spirit, as in the case of D.H. Lawrence's protagonist in *The Woman Who Rode Away*: but Joseph wants to find a solution, not offer himself as a sacrifice.[14] Books have been killing him. When Karla says that it is a great sin he is committing, he says, 'You speak like your books – all rules and maxims, rigid, without imagination.' (p. 80) He doesn't yet know what he wants, though: 'When he was close to her, his gaze wandered all over the room as if searching for something.' (p. 81) His attempt to reconnect with the land is not simple because there are things buried in his past that he is hoping to discover, which is why he has returned to the house.

Joseph's movement back to life takes several stages. One of them is dealing with the white women. Before returning to his old home in Dingli, he had tried working as an assistant nightwatchman. Yvonne had visited him there. He found that although he felt her breasts, he was unable to make love to her until he went out and came back with hands that were brown with soil:

> He held them before him for a moment like a blind man, for he was not really understanding anything: except for blinding darts from the flaming sword that pointed out his future, everything seemed unreal. He leaned over her and passed his hands, brown with soil, over her neck, slowly over her breasts. The whiteness was gone in an instant and when he put his face and mouth to her again, its scent too . . . The grit from the soil got between his teeth and he marvelled at the brownness of her skin.
>
> Then desire overwhelmed Joseph at last . . .
> (pp. 19/20)

So we are not surprised when he is drawn to the brown Karla. When he is in her room, 'he forgot everything else but the nearness of her, the brown smell of her' (p. 93). Then,

> What mattered was that she could look like this, and his eyes savouring her loveliness, and his whole being taking in the smell of the soil that was in her veins, as if each vein had a breath, and each breath as sweet-smelling as all the summer dawns he had known.

Yet when he presses his lips to hers,

> There rose, in one big tumult in his ears, all the thousand shrieking, head-piercing voices and raucous thumpings of an enemy inside him, but, unheeding, he kept his lips to the girl's mouth.

This enemy is the 'white women': just identifying them intellectually does not solve the problem. Later, when he is in Karla's room at night to make to make love to her, when she is naked in bed, she says she loves him more than her life and to be near him, she won't go to the university. He insists she should go. Why does he insist when he is running away from the university? He releases her and dresses. 'You love the other one,' she says. He denies it: but the denial rings hollow. The problem goes deep, and the exorcism will have to be more profound.

The problem is tied up with his childhood and his relationship to his father and to his maternal aunt, Zija Assunta, who had a hump. He remembered that he would always be consoled by his aunt from his father's harsh treatment. His father made him wear shoes, read books, etc. His aunt would protect him, saying,

> boy, you're tired, that's what you are. Don't mind what he says. Rest from those books, you're tired.
> (p. 27)

And then, 'Some of the soil on her hands falls in tiny flakes upon his lap and face.' (p. 27) So in his conscious mind, he recalls his aunt as an antagonist to his father, a means of resting from the tyranny. Another way of escaping from his father was to climb to the top of the house: he had put up a stake on the roof so that he could throw a rope round it and haul himself up when his father had forbidden him to climb to the top using the ladder. The stake was still there: he helped Karla climb.

One day, Karla had a severe headache and there is no aspirin in the house. Her mother uses a home remedy, which he recognizes: he says his aunt used to do the same thing for him. Karla's mother says she remembers the aunt:

> In two years, so many things happened in your family; first your mother went, then your father, then she, this Assunta.
> (p. 129)

The mother had apparently killed herself. The woman continues,

> Your father should have married Assunta after your mother died . . . She was like a mother to you. He should have married her. It broke her heart.
> (p. 130)

He says slowly, 'They could never marry.' The woman replies,

> Hark at you. But your father, God rest his soul, did he know what

> he wanted? They say in the village first he wanted Assunta, then
> went and took your mother. God punished him by giving him a mad
> wife.
> (p. 130)

She says that if Assunta had not gone sick a long time ago and
grown a hump, his father would have taken her: but he only loved
her without the hump. After Joseph's mother died, she says,
Assunta wanted to marry the father: 'When he died she broke her
heart and died, too, like everyone else.' Joseph does not believe
her. 'Don't I know well enough that she hated him!' Joseph leaves
the place. He begins to go through a breakdown: that is, a
breaking down of his fixed values. He returns to his childhood
days, falling ill in the process, so much so that the peasant woman

> lifted one of her breasts and placed its thick, dark point between
> his lips. His sigh was such as a child would make, and his shud-
> dering . . .
> (p. 139)

The rest of the novel is dream-like. It rains. Joseph sees Karla's
drops of blood mixed with rain-drops. The farmer thinks she is
dead on the stake. Joseph suddenly says, 'I wished a stake like
that right through my father's heart.' While the mother accuses
him of killing the girl, he says he could have killed his father: he
had made the stake pointed because he had wanted to drive it
through his father's heart. Now he knows. And then he would
have gone to Zija Assunta to say, 'He'll trouble us no more; I hate
him; you hate him. Say you hate him, hate him. Say you hate him
. . .' (p. 145). Joseph continues his return to 'the womb': he escapes
to a deep cave, where, in a daze, he sees an incident from the past:
a German pilot was shot down, and Zija Assunta found him in the
cave. The young Joseph watches her

> rip with one backward sweep of her arm the blue-grey trousers, sees
> the man's nakedness, the blood, Zija's gun, hard and cold, pressed to
> the groin . . . the sudden noise, the smoke, the twisting, flailing . . .
> squirming . . . all's still . . . shuddering . . . all's now still . . .
> (p. 154)

Three days later Joseph is found lying downwards in his aunt's
grave, the stone lifted to one side, earth scattered everywhere, the

old, rotted coffin lid broken in many places, his face lying on the damp soil pressed on a few dusty black shreds of dress. Yvonne in Sliema and Karla in hospital – she is not dead – 'received the news of Joseph's death very nearly within the same hour' (p. 158).

So what does it all mean?

Ebejer was asked in an unpublished interview whether the psychoanalytical basis is modern. 'I should say it is modern,' he replied.

> The central theme is Freudian (Oedipus complex, but here applied to an aunt who after all is a mother figure, his mother being almost out of the picture). In the manner of dreams (through flashbacks) it is Jungian. Joseph's search is for roots that might explain his extraordinary feelings. When he comes to the truth, he dies (it kills him).[15]

But it is not enough to explain the relationship to the aunt/mother in Freudian terms. It is not only that he discovers when he has 'killed' Karla that he had made the stake pointed because he had wanted to kill his father. There are layers of discovery for him to make. Karla, his love, has realized that he cannot shake off the other woman, the white woman. She is willing to give up the university to be close to him, but he wants her to go, to do the very thing he hates his father for doing to him. She was at an impasse: and so she had thrown herself on the stake to kill herself. Her blood unlocks in Joseph's mind and memory the knowledge that he had wanted to kill his father. He had thought there was refuge in his aunt/mother. He cannot stand the discovery that his aunt loved his father and wanted to marry him. That must mean that she acquiesced in his oppression: being forced to read books and to wear shoes, cutting himself off from the feel of the earth. The blood of Karla unlocks other things. Earlier, he had tasted the blood of a rabbit while with the nightwatchman, which had brought back a similar experience when he was young. The blood of Karla leads to an escape into the cave, which brings back the blood of the killing of the German pilot, of his aunt's frustrated destruction of his manhood. It is Joseph's manhood that has similarly been destroyed, and it is his aunt/mother, not his father, who has done it. As Okot p'Bitek's Lawino says, 'all our young men/Were finished in the forest,/Their manhood was finished/In the class-rooms,/Their testicles/Were smashed/With large books!'[16]

Like the narrator of Salih's *Season of Migration to the North*, Joseph has tried to get away from the cold of European books and the white women by returning to the folk and the soil and the sun. But there is no simple escape. Joseph has to connect up with not only the land and the sun and the peasantry but also the very opposite: the white world, the white women, and the complexity of the world. All these elements are within him. He 'kills' a peasant woman, Karla, just as he had tried to 'kill' a white woman before that, covering Yvonne with dirt and later rejecting her to such a degree that her father's sudden death seems to be out of frustration at his 'failure'.

Can the land be combined with the books? Can the white women be combined with the brown women? Integration can only come after disintegration. Although Joseph cannot find the way, others coming after can do so because of him. Ebejer says of Joseph in an early description of the novel,

> His Freudian search for the brown flesh/brown earth carries with it
> the symbiosis of trauma which is translated into concrete events and
> incidents. Here although the opter-out is a man, as against the two
> heroines of the first two novels, it is, again, the feminine side of
> Joseph that is trying to come out. It is in the fact that he
> acknowledges this side of his nature (many don't and thus remain
> half-men) that makes him a whole man.[17]

* * *

In The Eye of the Sun goes as far inwards as possible. Now it is necessary to go out. *Come Again in Spring* has a twenty-four-year-old narrator who is telling his story in the United States, first in San Francisco and near the end in New Orleans.[18] We do not know his name at first but later discover it is Miguel Sanchez-Guerrero, who comes not from Malta but from the Canary Islands. What is the difference between him and a protagonist from Malta? Malta is a meeting point between Europe and Africa and the Mediterranean. The Canary Islands are European, belonging to Spain. The protagonist can maintain the illusion that he is European, even while the Third World beckons in that Africa confronts the Islands on the East, because his ancestors came from Spain. But he has fled Europe to America:

Ah! Europe.

Europe must be years behind, deaf, blind, mute, crippled, arthritic, anaemic, syphilitic, moronic, juiceless, impotent, senile, a menstrual rag on the face of the earth, a prurient blotch on God's cheek. Europe is something you sometimes miss. Europe is a couple of sleepless nights in a row. You even let yourself weep a little, then stop and think: *It isn't worth it, think what a lucky son-of-a-bitch you are now.*

(p. 6)

He has come to America to find the best of Europe. This is why he is attracted to Shirley, a married woman with whom he is having a frustrating affair:

Shirley is five-foot-six. In bed she hardly ever moans, but fixes her eyes upon my face all the time. I play a little game sometimes. I shut my eyes, then suddenly open them again to see if she's still watching me. She is. Shirley is intent, quietly intent. She's aware all the time. When it's over, she rises noiselessly and leaves the bed. After throwing me a coy smile, she goes to fix me a highball. (And that's the *true* climax!)

(p. 5)

So Shirley, clearly from Shirley Temple, represents to him the innocent America he is trying to reach out to in his flight from decadent Europe. But he has not got through to her yet:

She humbles me, I want to crawl. She irritates me, I want to hit her. Each time she adds more folds to the veil behind which she hides.

(p. 10)

It is so frustrating that through running away from Europe, he also has a desire to go back

To the sewers, repositories of all our plagues, all our famines, all our sores, all the ravages at the hands of barbarian hordes. To the dankest and most mysterious of all the corridors of our princely courts where intrigue shot murder redder than blood and blacker than night into the breasts of kings and courtiers, and thus empires came into being and empires sank out of sight.

There I'd know myself again.

(p. 10)

But it is Shirley he loves

and have loved from the moment I lightly touched her face over a
cauldronful of tortured, screaming crabs at Fisherman's Wharf, San
Francisco, U.S.A. In this, the winter of *my* discontent.
(p. 10)

However, two factors make it very difficult for him to find this
innocent America. One of them is external: the whole world is in
America, as we can see from the people who live in this apartment
building. The landlady is German (with a French grandfather),
his roommate is Turkish, and a friend, Harvey Owala, is Kenyan.
In contrast to Miguel's obsession with America, Harvey says,

Kenya will one day be great, greater even than Ghana can ever hope
to be . . . However, a purge of some of our fellow Africans is
inescapable before Utopia is attained. Europe is dead, and its soul
now inhabits Idi Amin. We must not repeat its mistakes if you
follow me.
(p. 15)

(If that sounds like a mysterious statement about Amin, is is
probably because Amin was helped into power by certain
Western forces.[19])

The second factor is internal. Miguel feels guilty about what
has happened to 'Pablo'. We do not know at the beginning who
Pablo is: as Miguel tells his story, we have in italics his internal
dialogue with Pablo. Mixed up with this is the fact that Miguel
knows he is fragmented and has to search all over the place to find
the pieces, as the narrator does in *Season of Migration to the
North*:

it's like someone took something from us and hid it, and we don't
like it. Or may be we broke whatever it was ourselves and hid the
pieces, and now they're important, and we've forgotten where we hid
them, and our souls keep begging for those lost pieces to be found
and be put together again, and it drives us all crazy.
(p. 37)

In this respect, though his world is much wider, Miguel is like
Joseph. He too hankers to reconnect with the earth. He says, 'One
day I'll go back to Tenerife and meet a nice, pure girl from one of
the villages, marry her and be blessed with fat, brown children.'
(p. 25) But he has miles to go: and in any case he is probably

idealizing the girl from his village, just as he has idealized Shirley.

His first 'talk' with Pablo has to do with his haunted feeling of betrayal, of having let him die of a bullet in the heart and not returning:

> I might even have warned you it was too dangerous, in fact pointless, to plot against them. They're so strong. They have their own resources and those of powerful friends. Dear, stupid, dead Pablo, you thought you'd change the world, didn't you? Did you know they were shooting at me, too? . . . Pablo, this woman is like you is like me is like you is like the woman. You must understand. She might make this place home for me. For when you died, Tenerife was no longer my home, not one corner of Santa Cruz, not one cave in Las Canarias.
> (p. 20)

The speech to Pablo has been triggered off by the description of Shirley as America:

> Shirley at the wheel of the Oldsmobile: long, slender fingers; large, deep, blue eyes; hair brushed tightly back; skin like white wine; forehead like mine; small-breasted, long-bodied, flat-tummied; firm, slim wrists . . .
> (p. 19)

So the action is always slipping from the external world into the internal, Miguel's subconscious, and he always sees the external world in internal, symbolic terms. Shirley is not just America but is Pablo and America. Owala is not just an individual from Kenya but is an African is Africa. Selchuk is not merely a Turk from Cyprus but is a European who is an Asian. All this is happening on the American landscape.

In an unpublished description of his novels, Ebejer says,

> In *Come Again in Spring*, I resuscitated Joseph from his tomb in the village cemetery and reincarnated him in Spain. The world around him is still old and decadent, so he must fly to wider fields. The U.S.A. What, back to colonialism? The odd type of colonialism that is the U.S.A? In other words, Miguel (*pace* Joseph) is wanting to find the answer way back in colonial days, only this time it's not British but American. Trouble is that he takes his old skin with him, and it is in that skin largely that he roams about American streets, trying to find the answer, almost the same one his counterpart Joseph had

sought in Malta.[20]

Yet Miguel is Joseph and Miguel is not Joseph. Joseph is at the crossroads so he decides to go back and down. He is unable to come back up. But Miguel is closer to Europe and America than Joseph is and can maintain the illusion that he is European. He has a much more sophisticated, European consciousness than Joseph, a Maltese peasant. At any rate, his use of language is very sophisticated, so much that the novel reads like an American novel with its 'hip' language, cross-cutting, humor, speed of action, and listing of apparently contradictory things. Sometimes, the novel reads like an extract from Reed's *Flight to Canada*:

> 'I can go and get another,' I say, not too sure. But I snap my fingers saying it. (I'm good at that. I guess the habit started among people when slavery ended and, though the whips were hidden away for the sake of civilization, people just couldn't give up the beloved sound.) (p. 77)

But though attracted to America, Miguel knows that 'You don't really matter, because you're nothing but a tiny gallstone inside the big belly of the United States of America.' (p. 65) (This is the image of the United States as whale from Melville and George Orwell's essay on Henry Miller.) Miguel does not belong at this point but wants to love America, wants America to love him; he wants to find America, and for him it is the women who are the symbols of America. Shirley is *the* symbol: but one day he comes across another version of America. Owala had been badly beaten by a black American; his daughter comes to make amends. Miguel says of her:

> She is smart all right, and clever. Now Owala is pretty clever, too, but not smart the way she is. She's American smart, and she's black, and I have a feeling she's damning America because America likes her smartness, even encourages it. But she doesn't want to be smart simply because she's American, and because America, with its latter-day, super-duper guilt complex, encourages her, but because she wants to be herself and smart by herself, and for nobody else. So she damns America.
> (p. 75)

Her name is Mildred. She becomes Owala's lover, but he shares her with Sammy, the Turk, who is normally faithful to his wife back home. They tell Miguel they want to share her with him. Mildred becomes one of the tests Miguel feels he must face, the test that is going to bring everything together, including his betrayal of Pablo and finally his feeling that either he betrayed God or God does not care about him. But he has no sexual desire for Mildred: in fact, he is more attracted to Mildred's (black) girlfriend. He says,

> I keep seeing Mildred. She's here. I can see her, all of her.
> But I say to myself, somewhere in the back of my mind, I say this to myself: '*I'm not really seeing her*. I'm seeing God instead.'
> (p. 135)

He makes her do all kinds of things: walk around naked, crawl on her hands and knees, and 'Get up on that sofa. Your legs up the back and your head hanging down.' (p. 139) She seems to faint:

> Suddenly I go crazy. I put my arms around her, heave, and place her the right way up on the sofa. While she's like that, I pass my hands over God's black flesh and start stripping Him of the little that's left to strip Him.
> I tell him, 'Okay, see if You don't care now, God of my fathers.'
> I clutch hard the sides of His waist and He's firm and shiny and black. For a time I just stare at Him with my empty sockets. Then I kneel down before Him. I grasp both His knees and draw His legs apart, and they open up like they've been wanting all the time to do just that.
> I make ready to place myself between His thighs. I mean, screwing God all the way up. I'm about to enter, be sucked up into His Royal Indifference for ever and aye, when suddenly the knees snap shut, throwing me off balance.
> I look up and can't see His grin anymore. It's gone off completely. There's nothing. Just an ordinary, little girl asleep. There isn't even a face to grin with. He cares so much He's hidden His face. And the tic on His cheeks. That's what He has gone and done.
> I want to jump and yell with joy. And that's what I do. 'He cares. *Dios*, He cares.'
> (p. 140)

Mildred is scared because she does not know what is going on. Reed says in 'Remembering Josephine Baker', first published in December 1976 and included in *Shrovetide in Old New Orleans*,

'There was the joke making the rounds recently about someone having witnessed God and remarking, "She's black."'[21] But Miguel knows that God cares – a black God, a female God cares – and that there therefore is a meaning to his life. Mildred also represents the suppressed Africa in Miguel: he had moved a great distance West, to America, and to the American West, instead of moving a short way East, to Africa. Harvey Owala has been responsible for bringing Africa to his mind. So he is ready for the next stage: going back to the source of what the world considers to be American culture, New Orleans, the place where jazz originated, where European culture met African culture, albeit on not quite just terms. And he gets a call from Shirley inviting him to go with her to New Orleans.

Now Miguel is ready to embrace Shirley, away from her (unseen) husband. The voice of Pablo now comes in clearly: Pablo, whom he has linked to Shirley because the excessively innocent image he has projected onto her always brings Pablo's voice up from the depths. Miguel has a boil on his ass that was treated roughly by Annette, the landlady. As he is about to make love to Shirley in New Orleans, she notices the boil and says she will go downstairs to find help. Then,

> Pablo is standing behind me, and he suddenly pinches my boil and after I've yelled with the pain, he leans over me, drops a kiss on the top of my head and says . . .

We interrupt Pablo's statement for station identification. A constant refrain in the New Orleans section is 'Me, I'm just someone who's gradually going mad in New Orleans' (e.g. on p. 167). In what way is he going mad? His mind is undergoing a breakdown. He has been wearing a mask, he has been running away from Europe, which means he has been running away from himself. He is unable to possess the desirable Shirley until New Orleans: but when he thinks he is ready, his boil (i.e. his internal sickness) is inflamed and ready for lancing, and as he walks around, he meets his past. For example, he goes to the French Quarter, as all visitors to New Orleans do. 'Why do they call it the French Quarter?' he thinks.

> French are the little bits and pieces of architecture ironwork stuck,
> quite unnecessarily I think, to houses the like of which I've known
> all my life. It's the spirit of the homeland of my ancestors that I
> inhale constantly, walking these streets.
> (p. 163)

He is not wrong: the French buildings had burned down and been
rebuilt by the Spanish.

We return now to Pablo. At last Pablo speaks to Miguel: and
speaks of betrayal. Miguel betrayed Pablo to the police. He even
betrayed Pablo with a kiss. He was a Judas who did not attempt to
return the thirty pieces of silver, who did not hang himself but
fled, seeking not expiation but innocence:

> How you ran, Miguel! And in court, how moving were your
> protestations of ignorance and how touched the judges were by your
> description of your great love for me, Miguel. Miguel! Ah, Miguel,
> she's like me is like you is like me is like her is like you is like me.
>
> By all means give my birth and my breath and my blood and my
> flesh, all the heat and cold of my passion, and my youth that never
> aged, but you must know and understand her and not pretend you
> don't as you did me. Miguel, ah, Miguel, don't give her to the
> soldiers because you're afraid, afraid, afraid, afraid . . .
> (p. 160)

Miguel is afraid of the changes coming over Europe, which he sees
in terms of the Soviet Union and communism. He had a
discussion with a lawyer on the plane to New Orleans and told
him that Americans tend to think they are immune to communism
whereas they are hungering for a religion, which communism is.
The lawyer did not believe him. Miguel gives up, sounding like an
American right-winger:

> why should I bother about Communists in the State Department or
> sitting furtively and pleasant-faced on Boards of Education? There
> are bigger things than Communist infiltration, the C.I.A., Sierra
> Clubs, campus subcultures, space exploration, détente or the next
> grain fix to Russia.
> (p. 169)

Miguel has been less able to accept the notion of changes coming
from within, from people like Pablo.

Whereas Miguel thinks he is going to get Shirley, he meets an

Argentine woman sitting all alone in the lobby. Her name is Señorita Mercedes Argueta and this is her first visit to the States. She tells Miguel she was never married but once, a long time ago, she fell in love with a schoolteacher like her, who died. His name was Salvador. 'Señor,' she says, 'you look sympathetic. I do not want to burden you with my woes.' (p. 185) She has never been to Europe: but she is Europe in America. When Miguel pours her a drink, 'Half way through, she puts the glass down with an old-world movement of hand and wrist which is very beautiful to see.' (p. 186) Now both begin to 'go mad', just as Miguel has been saying he is also going blind: she becomes Shirley to him – and since Shirley has become Pablo, she becomes Pablo – while he becomes Salvador. She says,

> Nothing would be sufficient but my entire body, for it is completely yours. For when you went, you left me with a great part of it which I have looked upon through the years as yours and yours alone, and now it must be yours completely and in the truest sense. Let it be yours, Salvador. My Salvador.
> (p. 188)

We must interpret what is happening. Chapter 14 is delirious: with insanity or with recognition? It begins,

> Let it be said that I was blind. Mad and blind. Let it be said that of all my conscious actions this was the least so. Let anything be said, anything. I'm without defense. I have no apology to offer. I am what I am and I did what I did.
> (p. 189)

They make love for ten minutes:

> In those ten minutes, I loved Shirley as it wasn't in my power to love her before. In those ten minutes Shirley was love and home.
>   Ten minutes, in which my madness was suddenly diverted and I discovered the entire secret world of love, tenderness and compassion for the first time and, I fear, the last.
> (p. 189)

Without realizing it, he gets caught up in a parade, actually a jazz funeral, with 'Shirley'. Who is the funeral for? It turns out to be for 'Shirley'. He takes her to his room in the hotel, she starts to undress, and she jumps out of the window. In those ten earlier minutes of love-making, they knew each other completely the way they would have known each other if they had had years together. The interior comment at this point is, 'You're safe. You're safe from the soldiers, "palomita". They've had their hostage. You're safe.' (p. 194) Does this mean that this time, he has saved Pablo, or that he has found another hostage to take Pablo's place? That once again, he has been responsible for another person's death? I think it is the last of these because he reflects (the story being told after the event):

> Don't kiss me, *palomita*, don't kiss these betraying lips, the uncertain heart. Don't lay your hand on this hand that betrays and profanes and infinitely corrupts, even while it loves insanely. I love you and yet I can offer you nothing but sadness and distress and pain and disillusion and betrayal, the soldiers half-way through or, at the end of it all, death inside a bullet hole in a shirt filling with blood.
> (p. 194)

Miguel realizes that there is no escape from Europe, from himself. And it is significant that while he was seeking to possess the 'innocent' Shirley – who was not really innocent, as we recall from the image of the screaming crabs – he instead possesses Mercedes from Argentina, from the country in Latin America where a large number of the people claim they are Europeans on the Latin American continent. Miguel discovers he cannot dodge Europe, for Europe has polluted the rest of the world, thanks to its voyages of colonization:

> Europe, this is your sea, this is your land breeze.
> I'm coming back to you, you old whore. Aren't you pleased? I know there'll be no end to your chiding, your blasphemies, your anger, your senile, impotent, helpless, hopeless diatribes. You'll yet break my back, with work, with false hopes, with agonizing memories. For you're lousy with memories, aren't you? What's left for you to remember? And you'll see to it that I remember, too. You'll see to that.
> (p. 195)

The conclusion is, 'Eagles don't fly in these parts anymore.' The eagle of the United States, perhaps.

Not only in the range of its characters and in the places it deals with but also in the use of language, of short paragraphs, of ragtime pacing such that the reader must keep the story going in his mind while the player pauses, the novel is like an American novel.[22] It has ranged as widely as possible in contrast to the novel about Joseph, which burrowed inwards. Miguel had fled from himself, seeking innocence, only to discover the contradictions and the guilt were within him: not only was he the colonized but he was also in some senses the colonizer. He had betrayed his friend Pablo, who had tried to carry out a people's revolution against European domination, because he was afraid, afraid of breaking the chains with Europe. The Canary Islands are considered to be part of Spain though they should belong much more to Africa. Miguel had then fled to America, seeking an innocent Europe there: but he had discovered there could be no true innocence after the crime. He was never able to possess Shirley. He was pursued by the guilt that was within his own skin. So he courageously decides to come back. With this kind of information, he will now be able to look inwards. He is in a better position to do this than Joseph because he is not cutting himself off from the rest of the world, he is not escaping any more.

* * *

'HIS NEW POWERFUL MALTA NOVEL OF FASCIST LOVE LUST AND INTRIGUE AND THE BRUTAL NAZI SIEGE OF THE ISLANDS,' reads the blurb to Francis Ebejer, *Requiem for a Malta Fascist*, sub-titled: or *The Interrogation*.[23]
Ernle Bradford says in the Foreword,

> one is for the first time looking beneath the skin, and experiencing *as a Maltese* what it was like to grow up in those turbulent years before the War when the Mussolini cult was making strides across the Mediterranean. The atmosphere is brilliantly conveyed, the political rivalries and tensions, culminating in the War itself – when all the barriers are down, and those who have espoused one cause are revealed, and those who have chosen the other side (or taken none at all) are called upon to justify their convictions.
> This is a political novel in the best sense of the word, for politics are a reflection of human passions. It is also a great deal more. While it has a Stendhalian breadth, which gives it the dimension of

actuality, Ebejer also displays an immense sensitivity toward the minute beings who are caught up in the tidal wave of power-politics and War.

Bradford's is an excellent comment on the breadth of Ebejer's novel, but there is more to the novel than that. Malta is not merely an island: it is the crossroads of history and several cultures:

He gestured classically. 'Just look about you. Granted we here in Malta have been ruled over the centuries by practically everybody who happened to pass this way: Phoenicians, Greeks, Romans, Arabs, Normans, Angevins, Swabians, Castilians, Knights, French ... but surely we're grown-up enough to stop the British from using us to play their games of Empire with. They've been here since 1800. We've given them our land and harbours for their armies, for their ships and now for their aircraft, too, and all for a mere pittance. What else for? For our own lasting benefit? I'll just give you one guess ... After no less than a hundred and twenty years, they give us a self-governing Constitution in Twenty-One only to revoke it periodically on the flimsiest of excuses. Now something's happening, a hope is springing up only a few miles across the sea in the land of our Italian brothers. Apart from that, can you deny that it's only Mussolini who can stop the Communists this side of Europe? He understands this sea and its civilization. The British are all out for appeasing Russia. Besides, culturally, artistically, intellectually, we're Latin.' He stopped with a satisfied air and his usual seductive grin.

I wanted to disagree violently with him. I wanted to remark even at the risk of extreme pedantry: 'Why just Latin, if you want that argument? Why not Semitic, too, when our linguistic roots and derivatives stand at the ratio of twenty-five per cent Latin to seventy-five Semitic?'

Taking advantage of the pause to jerk my depleted political knowledge into some sort of action, I said quietly, 'Aren't you also ignoring the very fact and reality of the Labour movement? It's there, you know, and it's been rising and spreading quietly since 1920. Straight from the grass-roots, and there it's only indigenous culture that counts ultimately – not Latin, not Anglo-Saxon, or any other from north or south or east or west you might care to name. Besides, I hope you're not wilfully trying to forget that the majority of us look upon the British not as rulers but as friends and protectors. We called in Nelson in 1800 when Napoleon's thugs were being nasty to us.'

'Protectors from whom – now, at this very moment?'

'Your Mare Nostrum people,' I replied calmly, but sick to death inside and desperately striving for the right answers.

(pp. 64/5)

If one's whole history has consisted of invasions and settlements by 'outsiders', what does this make of the indigenous people? Who are they? What role do they play in their own history?[24] No wonder a Maltese could be attracted to a simple answer. Lorenz, the narrator, talks of his attraction to Paul, a pro-Italian fascist:

> For the first time in my life I had experienced friendship, lasting, necessary. He reminded me of things I wanted to remember. He made me forget things I wanted to forget. And now politics had begun to take him away from me, drive a wedge between us. We argued all the time . . . At the time, I wasn't anti- or pro–anything or anybody, certainly not where Franco was concerned. But I was against, violently, jealously, anything that could disrupt, in fact or fantasy, our friendship. Anti–the village, yes. Above all, anti-Kos. Oh, yes, anti-Kos.
> (p. 41)

Kos is the narrator's cousin. We are introduced to Cousin Kos in Part One, entitled 'Twenties' (Part Two is 'Thirties', Part Three 'Forties', and Part Four 'Postscript Now'). The novel sets up the chief problem in the way the first part is narrated. It deals with the childhood days of Lorenz, consisting of sharp but unclear incidents, comments and sayings, unclear because they are in the language of the days before the narrator had acquired a structure of understanding experience. The novel begins as follows:

> Cousin Kos flew the kite off the roof of Uncle Polly's house where he always lived. When the wind rose, he pulled it in again. Cousin Kos would stay on the roof a whole day of Spring and most of winter and autumn. In summer he built a little hut on the roof with some planks and a few of my aunt's sheets. When he got a bit older, they strengthened the wooden walls and sometimes locked him in.
>
>   It was a high time for us watching Cousin Kos flying his kites and calling to them in his own strange language. When there was no wind, he leant his elbows on the roof-ledge and gazed down at us in the street.
>
>   Sometimes he waved to us, then walked off out of sight to re-appear soon after with a bucket of washing-water which he at once emptied over our heads. He never failed to miss me. I used to think it was me he was really aiming at. We would get mad and sling a couple of stones, but we never tried to enter my uncle's house to go for him.
>
>   Sometimes, too, a few pigeons from a neighbour's loft would

perch next to Cousin Kos. He would stroke their backs and talk to
them, then shove them in the behind and send them flying off again.

He laughed again then, and he laughed loudest and most
mockingly when we were playing. He was always calling my name,
though never clearly as he had an impediment. He would call Enz
for Lorenz . . .

Thus in the beginning was Kos.
(pp. 3/4)

Lorenz's relationship to Kos contains clues to his hidden self. His
aunt says, poking his sides,

As you are beautiful, fit son for the devil, so is our Kos beautiful,
but inside him, like the angels. As God made him ugly outside for a
purpose, so inside you, you are ugly, needing some of our Kos's
beauty that is inside him. You rascal! You wastrel!
(p. 19)

In reply to Lorenz's statement that he cannot make out what Kos
is babbling about, his uncle says,

Pray to the Almighty that one day you might understand what your
cousin Kos says. It is of matters pertaining to minds broken in two
divisions or more and the truth, the whole truth about oneself that
one must inevitably face before one dies. In that wholeness, some of
it good and some of it bad, lie integrity, true knowledge and a full
rich life, even if in many parts of it your heart will break many times
over.
(p. 19)

But since we do not know yet what the narrator has done wrong,
we tend to overlook these statements: perhaps they are special
pleading.

The story becomes coherent in Parts II, III and IV: Lorenz is
older and has developed a structure for his story and his way of
seeing the world. Yet as he tells the story, curious things keep
popping up:

And she had stayed in my mind – with the hut girl, the fair one.
Ester was dark, like Lina of the past. That projection of the past I
wanted to cling to. But not Kos. Kos was a memory I hoped I could
do without. (p. 39)

I looked up again at the lighted window high above the columns.
It was the only sign of life. For one stark, blinding moment, I almost

imagined seeing Kos's face looking down at me from it, as from the dreaded past. Yet, when I looked again, the window seemed as empty as the streets, its brightness that of a cold, dead eye turned on an even deader city. (p. 47)

Paul was in the fascist group. I was in the opposing one. The shouting was deafening. The police were rushed a few times by both sides but they held their ground.

It was nearly eleven at night when the crowds began to give way. *Karozzini* rattled up and off again with people making for home. Motor-cars headed out towards Floriana at full throttle. The police began to relax. The shouts had ended. The more timid among the audience at the night's opera emerged from the Opera House and scurried off to seek their carriages and cars.

I had walked up with the crowd, sick in my stomach, wishing to meet Paul, yet dreading it. I watched the portals of the Opera House close, looked up at the high window that seemed eternally open and lighted, half-expecting to see Kos sitting, grinning evilly, on its sill; then at the spot where an eternity ago, it seemed a Turandot poster had symbolized for me all that could destroy my little but precious world of friendship, love and loyalty. (pp. 75/6)

Elena wore a veil with her hat. Through the delicate half-mask, her face bore the whiteness of porcelain. I stood by her side, smoking compulsively.

A crowd had gathered beyond the police barriers the length of the quay away from us near the church of Our Lady of Liese. Some jeering began. '*Assassini taljani*,' 'Kiss Il Duce's arse for us.' 'Just you dare come back and see what we'll do to you.' For one mind-shattering moment, I imagined seeing Kos's face in the crowd. I fought hard a feeling of vertigo. I looked again, half wishing, half dreading to prove my eyes right. But no Kos, no Kos at all! Insuperable relief . . .
(p. 139)

What is clear from the above extracts is that Lorenz does not understand himself, that he has suppressed elements in himself and that these elements are haunting him in the form of Kos. How much can he understand of the story he is telling, his story, if there are things in him which are projected onto the world he is dealing with? What kind of a story does he tell if what is happening lies beyond his consciousness?

Not that the storyline is unimportant. Since the colonial experience denied the colonized peoples any knowledge of their past, history and culture, the novelist has to be historian, storyteller, mythmaker, psychologist, explorer, healer, etc.

Lorenz describes what happens as the Second World War

affects Malta. Malta is caught up in conflicts of class and differences of ideology on an international plane. Lorenz likes the British while Paul sees that the English are colonizers first and liberals second. Paul is attracted to Mussolini's fascism because Malta has a strong Italian component. The narrator is horrified by fascism: but he loves Paul. Through Paul, Lorenz gets friendly with Count and Countess Matveich, anti-communist refugees from Europe (he from Russia). Later, Elena becomes Lorenz's first lover: at the same time, he is friendly with Ester, who is Jewish. How can someone be friendly with both a Jew and a fascist? What is the nature of his liberalism? Can one separate friendship from political beliefs? What does he really feel about Ester?

Now Ester here . . . I could really go for her. She clearly possessed everything that could satisfy a man's carnality. In his mad, spiteful way, Paul had asked me whether I had poked properly inside her. I had often wondered how attracted he was to her. Perhaps he was, and hid the fact from me. From himself too?

I had never as much as squeezed Ester's breasts, or tried to pass my hand over her legs and thighs. Kissed her, yes, once or twice. And with real fondness. I had never really wished to possess her.

At the same time, deep down I was afraid that sex with her might damage, or at least severely curtail, the very ideal and practice of our unique friendship. And that I prized too much!

Yet now here I was, with almost perverse single-mindedness firmly determined in putting myself and this very special friendship to the test when there wasn't really any earthly reason why I should.

We were alone and at the highest point in that area. I focussed my glance on all those parts of her that would inflame my carnality, boost my courage and finally induce me to lie close to her body, make love to her, hold Ester to me. It might solve for me a few problems which I only vaguely knew existed. Sacrificed would be the best friendship that I had ever had!

I let her talk on, recounting tales about the policeguard. I wasn't listening anymore. My hand had gone to her leg, caressing it around the ankle, then up to her knee. She had not yet tried to stop me. She might even have not noticed my advances while she spoke animatedly. Considerably emboldened, I raised my hand further up and laid it firmly on one of her breasts. Her voice broke off. I was suddenly afraid that she might scream, jump to her feet and run away. I thought of the nymph Arethusa fleeing from the opportuning Alpheius. But nothing of the sort happened. She resumed talking. Her face had taken on a little more colouring than usual, that was all.

> Steadfastly pursuing my plan, empty of any desire, but glowing with fondness of her, I pushed her gently backwards until I was lying on top of her, muttering her name to her lips.
>
> Yet, paradoxically, fearful that she might in fact yield.
>
> She said against my cheek, 'Where's Paul these days? Paul and you, I like you so much. I really miss him . . . How is Paul?'
>
> It was then that, sensing Ester's vibrant thrill at her own mention of our friend's name, I at last gladly drew back from her and set free the supreme image that I had been holding locked up inside myself. (pp. 70/1)

Lorenz knows that there is a falseness to his attempt to seduce Ester. There is something he has blocked from himself. Hence he talks too much and is relieved when she mentions Paul's name. We shall say more later about why he is not sexually attracted to Ester, although he wants to be. We notice at this point, though, that he is less interested in Ester than in Paul.

Lorenz has many discussions with Paul, trying to draw him away from fascism. When a bomb blows up Ester's house, killing her father and permanently maiming her, he blames Paul and his fascist friends. He eventually phones police inspector Cefai, disguising his voice by putting a handkerchief over the receiver, and lets him know where the fascists have hidden weapons. Cefai captures the weapons and some of the fascists. Count Matveich and Paul are jailed; Matveich is later deported. Cefai does not know who the informer is, but he keeps calling Lorenz in, accusing him of being a fascist since he associated with fascists.

Paul later escapes from prison as a result of a bomb dropped by the European fascists. He hides out with Elena. He and Lorenz begin to fight. This is the second time they fight over a woman. The first fight had come about because Paul had called Lorenz a 'dirty Jew-lover' and said, 'Your Ester, what do you hope to get from her? . . . her body? Or have you probed inside it already?' (p. 67) Lorenz begins the fight, which ends,

> I had seconds of insight. There was no hate, anger yes. I couldn't make out what sort of anger. It only seemed to dissolve when I looked up and saw his eyes above me.
>
> I was sure we were both dead, turned to stone, welded together for eternity. I held my racking breath back to listen to his breathing. We both sobbed, turned to stone and joined together as if for all time.

The fight ends with the exchange being a loving one: Lorenz loves

Paul. The second time, the fight comes about because Lorenz is insulting Elena. He has discovered that she has been making money by prostituting herself to British officers. He says sarcastically that she may be able to use her influence to get Cefai out of their hair. Paul shouts at Lorenz to stop the insults:

> 'You could to it in one hour. Or does it take less with these fat, old men?'
>
> An explosion of sun rendering me unconscious for a second. Sun leaping off the slabbed floor and bashing me down again over a chair. Sun, Paul . . . We fought. Like old times, but this time there was real rage in me, a battering, heedless strength in him. We straddled each other alternately, struck hard. Elena's face – or was it Ester's, or both? – a blurred distortion within shifting spaces of me and him. We grabbed each other by the throat when hitting became nerveless and weak.
>
> I don't know whether it was Elena's screaming at us to stop, or our own breathing through black, naked mouths . . . Then my breath came faster, still painfully, even if freer at last. And it was Elena screaming. She couldn't stop screaming, she went on and on. Over Paul on the floor. Then she stopped screaming, but she remained over Paul, touching his face, and Paul remained on the floor. His eyes the widest, the most beautiful blue and the most seeing that I had ever seen them.
>
> (p. 197)

Paul is dead. Elena disposes of her body. When she returns:

> 'Come and lie down,' she whispered.
>
> I settled down beside her. On her bed. On the bed on which we had laid out Paul. She started undressing me, quietly, with no hurry, no fuss, soothing me. She directed my hands to her bare body. She was very warm and as soft and quiet as I used to know her.
>
> She held me to her and spoke to me.
>
> 'Don't go looking for him too far. I'll help you. I can't bear to see you like this. And when Paul is so near.' My body like ice, and the dry, tearless emptiness beginning to engulf me . . . she clutched my hand and squeezed it hard against her belly.
>
> 'Look for Paul here,' she said.
>
> Then I understood.
>
> And I loved Paul. Through this woman, strained to him inside this woman, time and time again, more strongly after each time, with all my longing . . . the stream of all my years.
>
> This woman and I, lost to everything else but the others, burning flesh, tabernacle, between us, muttered and moaned his name

endlessly each into the other's mouth.
(pp. 200/1)

Lorenz is in love with a fascist. This was why Inspector Cefai was harassing him. But Lorenz is an anti-fascist! Yet look at his actions. He betrays the fascists to Cefai. The Count is deported and Lorenz becomes his wife's lover. True, Lorenz opposes the fascism of his friends, but he betrays his friends, and it is real betrayal, even if done in the name of anti-fascism. He betrays Dr. Deguara, the doctor who had saved his life, who is executed.

Near the end of Chapter Three, Cefai tells Lorenz, 'Son, you're riddled with albumenuria. How you can, in your physical condition, satisfy a woman like the Countess beats me.' (p. 175) Albumen is white: Lorenz is riddled with the disease of whiteness. (An interesting comparison with Salkey's second novel: Sobert says, 'Till the whole world is covered with albumen!' on page 106.) He is obsessed with Elena because she is a Countess from Europe and (therefore) white. He is not passionate towards Ester because she is dark. The first 'beautiful girl' he saw when he was young had 'yellow hair' (p. 5). Paul is white and has blue eyes. Yet in contrast, the naked Kos is white and the first girl he kisses, his first 'girl-woman', though having a pale face, has 'dark hair' (p. 31). His hidden obsession, which overwhelms the opposite tendency, in his desire for whiteness. We have seen it earlier: it is the desire of the colonized for the whiteness of the colonizer, of Europe, of civilization. Lorenz is of peasant origin. He is fleeing the village, as represented to some extent by Kos.

After Elena has Paul's baby, there is a battle for the child, which intensifies after she (Elena) dies in an air raid. Ester brings the boy up and then escapes with him to the young state-coming-into-being of Israel. Lorenz follows to try to get the child back, but is caught by the Israelis and interrogated. The interrogation is gruelling:

> Did you think Elena loved you?
> Were you afraid Paul might fall in love with Elena, she being such an enchanting seductress, it seems?
> Is that why you went to bed with her in the first place?
> Were you anti-fascist out of personal conviction or . . .?
> (p. 223)

The questions get tougher:

> When did you start neglecting Paul?
> Why did you start neglecting Paul?
> What made you decide it would be a good thing if Elena slept with
> Paul?
> You wanted him to sleep with Elena, didn't you?
> Didn't you?
> (p. 230)

The second segment of the interrogation above startles us. We did not know that Lorenz had schemed to have Paul make love to Elena: we only knew they had been making love when Elena pointed to her pregnancy after getting rid of Paul's body. Lorenz had blocked this out of his story and his consciousness. Why did he do it? *Newsweek* has something interesting to tell us:

> As Liz ghoulishly tells it, the only reason she and Eddie Fisher got married was that she was Mike Todd's widow. 'Fisher adored Mike, and we resurrected him. That's all we had in common, and that's sick. Boy, did I realize how sick it was.'[25]

The Israelis deport Lorenz. Near the end, he receives a letter from Ester that she saw him, arranged for him to be arrested and sent away, and has brought up Paul's son, who has now become a doctor. So a fascist's son is brought up as an Israeli by a Jewish mother, the very woman who was mutilated by the actions of the fascists. This does not mean that the new Israeli is taking on the role of the fascists by bringing up the son of a fascist – or that Israel behaves like a fascist state – but that Ester redeems the crime of the fascists by redeeming the child of the fascists. She does not run away from ugliness, and she prevents Lorenz from running towards what he sees as beauty, namely, the son of Paul and Elena. She ensures that Lorenz returns home. In contrast, Lorenz's betrayal of the fascists is real betrayal; to underscore this, Paul's mother, a peasant woman, dies in an air raid because she has refused to leave the building, saying the rosary and waiting forever for her son. Suppressed violence came to the surface in Lorenz when he fought and killed Paul. So what we have is a narrator who has hidden his deepest impulses from himself. What are they? Who is he?

Let us turn for help to someone Ebejer mentions frequently in his interviews: Jung. Note the following statements by Jung in relation to the story of Lorenz:

(1) There are certain events of which we have not consciously taken note; they have remained, so to speak, below the threshold of consciousness. They have happened, but they have been absorbed subliminally, without our conscious knowledge. We can become aware of such happenings only in a moment of intuition or by a process of profound thought that leads to a later realization that they must have happened; and though we may have originally ignored their emotional and vital importance, it later wells up from the unconscious as a sort of after-thought . . .

It was the study of dreams that first enabled psychologists to investigate the unconscious aspect of conscious psychic events.

It is on such evidence that psychologists assume the existence of an unconscious psyche – though many scientists and philosophers deny its existence. They argue naively that such an assumption implies the existence of two 'subjects,' or (to put it in a common phrase) two personalities within the same individual. But this is exactly what it does imply – quite correctly. And it is one of the curses of modern man that many people suffer from the divided personality. It is by no means a pathological symptom; it is a normal fact that can be observed at any time and everywhere. It is not merely the neurotic whose right hand does not know what the left hand is doing. This predicament is a symptom of a general unconsciousness that is the undeniable common inheritance of all mankind.

Man has developed consciousness slowly and laboriously, in a process that took untold ages to reach the civilized state (which is arbitrarily dated from the invention of script in about 4000 B.C.). And this evolution is far from complete, for large areas of the human mind are still shrouded in darkness. What we call the 'psyche' is by no means identical with our consciousness and its contents.[26]

(2) A patient of mine dreamed of a drunken and disheveled vulgar woman. In the dream, it seemed that this woman was his wife, though in real life his wife was totally different. On the surface, therefore, the dream was shockingly untrue, and the patient immediately rejected it as dream nonsense . . . His dream was actually saying to him: 'You are in some respects behaving like a degenerate female,' and thus gave him an appropriate shock . . . Consciousness naturally resists anything unconscious and unknown.

(pp. 14/17)

(3) These instinctive phenomena – one may not, incidentally, always recognize them for what they are, for their character is symbolic

> – play a vital part in what I have called the compensating function of dreams.
>
>   For the sake of mental stability and even physiological health, the unconscious and the conscious must be integrally connected and thus move on parallel lines. If they are split apart or 'dissociated,' psychological disturbance follows. In this respect, dream symbols are the essential message carriers from the instinctive to the rational parts of the human kind, and their interpretation enriches the poverty of consciousness so that it learns to understand again the forgotten language of the instincts. (p. 37)
>
> (4) The recollection of infantile memories and the reproduction of archetypal ways of psychic behavior can create a wider horizon and a greater extension of consciousness – on condition that one succeeds in assimilating and integrating in the conscious mind the lost and regained contents. Since they are not neutral, their assimilation will modify the personality, just as they themselves will have to undergo certain alterations. In this part of what is called 'the individuation process' . . . the interpretation of symbols plays an important practical role. For the symbols are natural attempts to reconcile and reunite opposites within the psyche.
> (p. 90)

Jung talks about dreams while what we have before us is a text that is a novel. However, the narrator refers frequently to dreams, visions and hallucinations:

> I was eighteen, but I had long learnt to gauge all my feelings and experiences against the ideal of that day long ago when, out of a ramshackle farmhouse deep in a valley, a *vision* of a girl happened before my eyes, shutting me in from all the horrors of my waking life, the nightly *dreaming*, terrors of Kos and his doings and the things he drew out of people that made me feel an unwanted stranger among them.
>
>   Paul, Ester and I fitted my old and beautiful *dream* so perfectly.
> (p. 61, my italics)

> I thought of arms and ammunition hidden in a secret chapel in a deep, dark valley. *Nightmares* of dead and dying people. One particular *nightmare* that dwarfed all others – *a vision* of Paul's face, mutilated, eyeless. Paul dead.
> (p. 102, my italics)

> I was admitting Elena into the magic circle of my *dreams*.
> (p. 105, my italics)

We noted earlier all the times he suddenly sees Kos. Lorenz is actually an incomplete being and his unconscious is throwing out images to point out his need for self-knowledge, real balance and wholeness. His chief problem is his innocence. The word 'innocent' appears frequently in this novel, as in other novels by Ebejer. But what kind of innocence is this? Look at Lorenz's actions. Following a moment of unacknowledged eroticism between him and Paul, Paul shows him the arms his group has hidden in a chapel. This is done in a moment of trust: and Lorenz reveals the arms and therefore betrays the group. It seems that he has done this to keep Paul from being taken from him. Yet when Paul asks him if he was the betrayer, he denies it convincingly. He begins an affair with Elena. She supports him during the war. He never asks her when she gets her money and her supplies or who her 'influential friends' are. Yet when he finds her kissing a loathsome British officer, he calls her a 'whore'. Her reply is, 'What a child you are, Lorenz.' (p. 184) He betrays Dr. Deguera, the doctor who saved him. No wonder, although he is ostensibly talking about the Italian and the German fascists, he is actually referring to himself when he says, 'Fascism had two faces, one more terrible than the other' (p. 157) and says on the next page, 'Fascism had two faces and I was hardened to both.' So when he calls Elena a 'whore', the word applies to himself.

His innocence, then, is a complex matter. First of all, it arises from simplicity: as a colonial, as a peasant, he does not have knowledge of his world and ultimately of himself. He does not know or recognize what his deeper, ugly impulses are, clothing them in the liberalism that comes with the British and the English language. When he does ugly things, he hides the ugliness from himself and from us. Like Salih's narrator in *Season of Migration to the North*, he suppresses and is therefore unaware of the violence in himself, covering himself over with the raiment of balance, unlike his cousin Kos, whose nakedness haunts him. The violence bursts out with drastic consequences. So when he calls Elena a 'fascist bitch' and Paul 'fascist scum' (pp. 113 and 117), the two people he desires most, he is not being truthful. No wonder the novel abounds with images of blindness and partial-sightedness. Ester loses one eye and has to wear a black patch. Lorenz says, 'But I couldn't see too clearly. Not just the sun. My eyes had begun to give me trouble.' (pp. 194/5) Hence there is significance in the fact that since Malta is a Catholic country, stray bombs destroy part of the annexe of St Paul's Parish Church and A one-armed crucifix still hung over a pulverized altar.' (p. 188)

To find wholeness, Lorenz has to abandon his innocence. Significantly, the chapter containing the interrogation, Chapter Seventeen of Part III, comes just after he at last goes home to the village and meets his mother, who, 'When she saw who it was, she collapsed on a chair, tossed her apron over her face and head and began to sob wildly.' (p. 221) His stepfather had died just before the War and one of his brothers had emigrated to Canada. 'Where's Cousin Kos?' he asks his mother. She rises to her feet, perhaps sensing the 'unbearable screaming' inside him, and takes him to the roof:

> I looked and noticed at once the thick, wooden cage that was as large as a room, neatly and securely roofed over with planks and matting. Inside it was Kos, sitting on a low stool, legs crossed, turning the pages of a large picture-book. He was half-turned to us.
>
> He had grown as I had grown, but there was no mistaking the disfigured face, the squashed shoulders, the mean body. He had also aged as I had aged. His grey hair and my grey hair. His profile, my profile. With the disfigurements. His visible, mine . . .
> (p. 222)

At the end, Lorenz is out of the cage: he is living with Kos and 'Now, too, he can pronounce my complete name and not just half of it.' (p. 242)

Requiem for a Malta Fascist is a national novel, a novel Malta needed, dreamt about, made Ebejer write. He says in the Author's Note:

> I wrote just over three-fourths of this novel between the years 1968 and 1969. During the ensuing period those friends who read what I had written continually urged me to complete it. Both my personal life and literary career had veered off to other spheres and other interests and it was not until 1976 that I picked up the story again and gave it its inevitable conclusion.
>
> The majority of the episodes and circumstances relating to the political atmosphere of the time and the protracted bombing of the Maltese islands by the Axis powers are drawn from my own personal memory of actual events.

But it is not a national novel in a direct way. Keith Wilson quotes a large chunk from page 241 of the novel and comments as follows:

> Any distance between the author and narrator seems to have been
> entirely lost here and the novel is left with a few tired counters being
> desultorily flicked around by an Ebejer thinly disguised as a Lorenz.
> *It is difficult to know how to deal critically* with such a descent into
> bombast at what is such a crucial part of the novel for the validifying
> of its central character's whole experience. The imaginative
> distortions that rhetoric of this kind imposes on the novel at its more
> propagandist moments indicate something of the difficulty of the
> writer who conceives of himself as in part the voice of his nation and
> who thereby runs the risk of assuming an overwhelming burden.
>   When, *to all international intents and purposes*, that voice is the
> only one, it may not be surprising that it is given to screeching a
> little. The screech is heard in the perceived need to give potted
> summaries of wartime Maltese history . . .[27]
> (my italics)

Wilson misses the point. Of course the protagonist gives us
Malta's history: that is one of the functions of the Third World
novelist, and it is credible that a teacher (which Lorenz is) would
know the history of Malta and be able to summarize it. The point
is the relation of the narrator to that history. Lorenz expresses not
confidence but sceptism in the last paragraph quoted by Wilson, a
paragraph about which he is negative but which I find indicates
Lorenz's recognition of having to embrace his complexities,
including Kos: 'And yet I, imprisoned as I am in my own
existential dimension, cannot reconcile myself completely to any
of this.' David Rubadiri does something similar in *No Bride Price*.
The protagonist, Lombe, is as innocent as Lorenz. He does not
really notice anything going on around him and he has a balanced
way of talking. When a coup takes place in the country, he
suddenly knows all the reasons why the coup took place. When I
first read the novel, I thought this was a flaw on the part of
Rubadiri: how could someone who did not know anything about
the political forces the day before the coup know everything the
day after and articulate things for us in such a clear way? But that
was just the point: Rubadiri was showing us that the protagonist
still did not know: he had only acquired the style of knowing. And
this is what I saw happen in real life in Uganda after Idi Amin's
coup three years later.[28] Wilson goes off the track by not paying

attention to what Riggan calls the unreliable first-person narrator.

The issue of *World Literature Written in English* that contains Wilson's article also contains a review of the novel which is much more understanding of what Ebejer is really doing. Stephen Bayliss says,

> *Requiem for a Malta Fascist; or, the Interrogation*, is disarmingly simple and readable, and it is not until it draws towards the simple and 'satisfying' conclusion that the problems begin to arise for the reader. Lorenz, who is the narrator and protagonist, clearly feels fulfilment and resolution at the end, but for the reader, no such easy comfort is achieved . . .
>
> The tale Lorenz tells is set in his native Malta, spanning the years of the rise and fall of European fascism, and follows his emotional and political involvement with and estrangement from his world. This in itself may seem straightforward and clichéd enough, but the style Ebejer adopts seems to add an almost dream world dimension to the work . . .
>
> This in many novels points to a conflict between the demands of the literary reality in its need for resolution and the demands of the real and largely arbitrary world presented; but in *Requiem*, Ebejer introduces an aspect of the tale which at once explains the imposition of the form on the reality. This aspect is highlighted in the alternative title for the book: *The Interrogation*.
>
> The 'Postscript Now' chapter, set in the 1920s, has Lorenz looking back upon the period of his life which is the novel. This period both climaxes and deflates in his interrogation by the Israelis who, just prior to the formation of their state, intern him as a spy. Throughout the book Lorenz has referred again and again to his interrogators and how they were surprised or fascinated by different aspects of his life, and it is only at the end that the reader realizes what effect they have had on the ordering and interpretation Lorenz has made of his life.
>
> As a literary technique, the interrogation as a bottleneck through which the whole tale must pass is a masterpiece. Lorenz has lived through a rough period in Malta; he finds himself forced to argue and rationalize his life to those who would kill him; and now, many years later, he writes his story down. Thus, Ebejer clearly sets reality adrift by distancing his protagonists from it. The repetitive and pressured recounting of events, feelings and relationships to the inquisitors defines to Lorenz his life, not the events themselves.
>
> In consequence, the rationalization, the acceptance and the calm at the end, while creating a sense of light and balanced structure for the novel, becomes at once brittle and endangered to the 'superior' reader. The novel's form is satisfied, but any sense of its being a

closed system is lost. One feels at the end that Lorenz has not been writing his story to those who may read his book, but rather trying to explain himself to his interrogators in a way they never give him a chance to. The novel itself becomes Lorenz's final act of trying to order and come to terms with himself. The confusion of his interrogation has given way to answers and he must explain.[29]

I agree with a great deal of what Bayliss says. Yes, there is the question of the 'superior' reader missing the point. Yes, the novel becomes Lorenz's final act of trying to order and come to terms with himself. I would say, though, that *the Israeli interrogators trigger off Lorenz's own internal interrogators in the telling of his story* such that he asks questions that the Israelis could have not asked. For example, 'What made you decide it would be a good thing if Elena slept with Paul?' The Israelis would not have got as far as asking such a question: they would have not have had the material, nor would they have been interested. Ebejer wrote to me, 'Here I wanted the form to suit the theme, and I wanted the reader to question himself in the process.' We are now in a position to see that the first chapter was a later recounting of striking images from Lorenz's youth. It is significant that after the chapter containing the interrogation, Lorenz comes to terms with Kos. The external war, then, is connected with the inner one that Lorenz has gone through.

At the end, Lorenz goes back to the country and lives with his cousin Kos. He takes Kos out of the cage, and Kos can at last pronounce his full name, 'LORENZ'.

* * *

A shipwrecked sailor was struggling in the water. The shore was near, but his strength was almost spent.

Then suddenly there was a friendly presence in the water, a strong, sleek body that buoyed him up, escorted him to shallow water, saves his life . . .

When a dolphin mother gives birth, her baby is expelled underwater. The first act following birth is critical: to lift the freshly born youngster up to the surface for its first breath. So powerful is this motherly instinct that other struggling animals have been pushed to the surface instinctively by female dolphins.

How marvellous and beautiful! The instinct to protect the next generation drives some automatic motor response in the dolphin and in many other species.

This is not the beginning of Ebejer's *Leap of Malta Dolphins*[30]: it is an undated letter sent out by Jacques-Yves Cousteau in June 1987. It continues:

> Certain reefs that teemed with fish only ten years ago are now almost lifeless. The ocean bottom has been raped by trawlers. Priceless wetlands have been destroyed by landfills. And everywhere are sticky globs of oil, plastic refuse, and unseen clouds of poisonous effluents.
>
> Is all now lost? I do not believe it. If I did, I would not be writing to you today. I passionately believe that the perceptive few who have the opportunity to see the ultimate disaster ahead must band together now to warn the slumbering many. (Is it not always thus?) Such corrective measures as exist must be put into effect immediately. Pioneering research and exploration to help us better understand the sea and its creatures must be undertaken without delay . . .
>
> Our wastes cannot be 'thrown away.' We dump pollutants seemingly out of sight in the rivers and sea, but they eventually come back to us and our children with devastating impact – through the food we eat, the water we drink, and the air we breathe.[31]

Compare this to the Author's Note to *Leap of Malta Dolphins*:

> This is a work of fiction. I suppose the Maltese Islands should have been among the last places to choose as a setting for this story. Ecology so far is hardly a problem there; rather, it has been the Republic of Malta that, in the United Nations, first raised and encouraged interest in the protection of the sea bed. Apart from that, the efforts of the government and citizens of Malta to preserve and protect the Islands' numerous monuments and historical sites, dating from pre-Neolithic times right up to the last colonial occupation have been officially acclaimed by UNESCO. I can think of no other Mediterranean island with such a record.
>
> However, it was precisely this awareness of and active concern for the environment on the part of Malta that prompted me to write this novel in the first place. That was in the first place: for the rest, it has been the people involved in the story itself, with their interrelationships and motives and motivations, both the true and the false, who took up the initial stirrings of the theme and transformed them into resonances of love and lust, charity and greed, modulated to the ageless lust to destroy or to conserve, be it themselves or their environment, or both.

A note about environment and ecology? Keith Wilson says that the first half of the Author's Note is 'this strange mixture of curtesy and speech to Malta' and that 'Ebejer concludes by making a similar act of deference to his own characters,' after which he says of the last sentence,

> Again the careless abstractions, again the slightly hieratical stance and cadence, and again the risk that the novel itself will collapse under the weight of the authorial voice as it emerges from the throats of the characters.

He quotes a speech by the character Sarid and assumes it to be the authorial voice. Wilson's conclusion betrays a colonial arrogance:

> The omnipresence of a strident authorial voice in Ebejer's work, apparent both in disguised monologues like the above and in obtrusively choreographed symbolism . . . is perhaps a sign of the self-consciousness of the artist in an isolated community that has never been sure of what place – as commentator, as prophet, as church/government spokesman, as church/government critic – the artist should have. A country that has so often acted as temporary home to foreign writers, Malta has never been particularly attentive to its own, and at a time of national resurgence the position of the writer who uses the ex-colonial language is additionally anomalous. A tendency to hector and to take on the pose of daring innovator in such a context is natural. It is also a pity, because if Ebejer could develop the negative capability that would allow him to turn himself into his characters and forsake the egotistical sublimity that turns all his characters into him, he would be the writer who genuinely gives the Maltese experience to an international community.[32]

So the function of a Third World artist is to give the experience of his own community to an international community, like a country selling its raw material and labor to an aloof mother country? Is it necessarily anomalous to use the imposed colonial language? People do use it, and the writer makes it his own. Besides, Ebejer writes plays in Maltese so he is more of a bi-cultural writer, as he has said.[33] Wilson is unable to understand the novel because of his assumptions – who possesses 'the egotistical sublimity'? – which are revealed in the fact that he provides a *straight* summary of the plot on pages 476/7, completely missing the ambiguity, ambivalence and irony Ebejer talks about in relation to this novel in the interview with Daniel Massa which follows the Wilson article.[34]

Leap of Malta Dolphins begins as follows:

> For the greater part of the night, sleep would not come. The very few
> times it did, it was fitful, like dark patches in a too-bright area, made
> more blinding and uncomfortable after each dozing off. He had
> thought he would sleep well after making love to Lenarda. But that
> had never been the case . . .
> At four in the morning, he got out of bed, shaved, and put on his
> thick, brown gun-suit. He brewed some coffee, which he drank at
> once. Then he took his gun and went down to his car. Outside, there
> was not yet the slightest hint of dawn. The air was keen, the silence
> widespread. The boats in the bay looked like bystanders gone to
> sleep.
> (p. 3)

This is Marcell. He had made love to his wife, but she responded,
as always, with revulsion. Why? He does not ask. We first see her
from the outside, when she wakes up in an empty bed. Then there
is a touch of eroticism in the description:

> [The sun] crept over the floor, up on her lap, and over her blouse,
> heightening the aureoled contours of her breasts.
> (p. 6)

We are attracted to Lenarda by that line and by the line that
follows: 'Her hair leapt in dark flames with the young sun's eager
reflections from the lazing bay below.' We are not surprised, then,
that not only Marcell but also a whole range of characters turn
out to be obsessed with her. When she walks down to the
restaurant of Karmenu, Marcell's brother,

> Karmenu watched her his heart in his mouth. Her extraordinary
> beauty. Her presence in his restaurant. Alone with him . . . in
> moments like this, Karmenu traveled far and wide in his mind, all
> images clear and throbbing in a warm, sensuous light.
> (p. 6)

Shortly after, Georg, a young student, walks in. His father had
been a friend of Karmenu's: they had emigrated to Canada
together but had returned because they could not stand the cold
and the loneliness. The father had died of pneumonia, leaving
behind his invalid wife and his son. Karmenu talks about the tons
of frozen meat from Australia that were washed away the

previous night, so he has no meat for his restaurant. Thus we are introduced to the connection between Malta and the rest of the world. We are prepared for

> the loud din of modern machines, the cranking, the winching, the steady clangor, the thud of heavy wooden beams striking the water for the first new jetty of the proposed Free Port at Dolphin's Leap.
> (p. 9)

In reply to a question by Massa whether this is a specific village, Ebejer says,

> I gave it a fictitious name, Qabzet id-Delfin, which is translated as Leap of Dolphins . . . Dolphins' Leap is the name of the village.[35]

We see the significance of the name from the statement by Cousteau quoted earlier. An old fisherman says in reply to Marcell's comment that the fishermen had the shore to themselves when he was small,

> Ah, that's finished; as are the dolphins . . . This sea used to swarm with them; inside the bay itself, can you imagine? Leaping and playing about and we fed them and we got sort of friendly. You'll see hardly any now: they don't dare, I suppose; they've been scared off. I think they're sad, wherever they are now.
> (p. 74)

Marcell has left Lenarda to think, to decide how to deal with his obsession, and to hunt. He had married above his station and Lenarda had been cut off without a penny from her family. His brother constantly quarrels with him about it, particularly because Marcell lets her have all the freedom to move around. He is out of doors when dawn breaks:

> The dawn had broken over Marcell in a slow unveiling of dark corners, mysterious earth sounds and smells, and strange, unearthly shapes.
> (p. 17)

This description of nature also indicates that Marcell contains 'dark corners, mysterious earth sounds, strange, unearthly shapes'. Marcell makes a resolution: he will spare every other bird and wait for an eagle. And the eagle came:

> He fired both barrels instantaneously. The bird hung for a moment in midflight as if nailed to the sky by the tips of its wings, then plunged to the earth, a couple of fields away from where he was standing.
> (p. 18)

When he goes to pick up the eagle, two dogs appear and run off with it. He follows in angry pursuit:

> Nothing on earth was more important to him than that eagle and his share in its existence. It was not simply now, at this point of death, but before, too, in all its mysterious journeyings and secret preyings, through those very same days and nights of his own existence with the beautiful Lenarda.
> (p. 19)

The dogs lead him to completely isolated countryside up the mountain. He reaches the top and sees the cottage. The dogs are squatting inside the gate, the eagle between them. As he moves forward, one of the dogs plucks up the bird and disappears inside the house.

It is the home of an old man, Sarid. The accident was no accident. The old man says, 'I have often dreamt about such a meeting, haven't you?' (p. 20) Marcell has not seen Sarid since he was twenty-one. In reply to questions about his life, Marcell says his life is a failure. He has been unemployed – he is a lecturer – for three months and his relationship with his wife is a failure too. 'Should you continue to suffer there?' asks Sarid. Marcell replies, 'I don't know. I'm all confused.' He then pleads, 'Help me. You're so wise, Sarid.' (p. 22) There was a connection between the two, that of student to teacher/guru/mentor, which had been broken after an accident resulting in Sarid's blindness. He tells Sarid about his marriage:

> Then, two years ago, I met my wife. My beautiful wife, Sarid. Intelligent, rich family, great big house in which her mother lives up at Naxxar.
> (p. 24)

'Did you marry her for that?' Sarid asks:

> Marcell stepped forward until he was standing in front of the old
> man, who had not once moved from his position on the edge of the
> bed, looking sightlessly at the wall, past Marcell, as if past some
> memories, straight into others. A midday arrow of light from the
> window fell harshly upon the white head so that one side of the face
> was illumined, the other completely in shadow.
>   'I think I married her to forget you.'
> (p. 25)

From the rapid dialogue, and from the description of Sarid, we
are left, to use the favorite cliché of American reporters, with
more questions than answers. Did Marcell marry Lenarda to
forget Sarid, or is it that he is so much under the spell of Sarid that
Sarid's will overwhelms his? Marcell has mythified Lenarda: she
represents something he desires desperately. Looking for a way to
break from the hold of Lenarda, he is ready to accept Sarid's will.

   Sarid lives near a neolithic temple. He suggests they take a
walk. Marcell tries to help Sarid along the first few steps. Sarid
chuckles. 'I know my little domain like the back of my hand,' he
says, adding, without being aware of the irony, 'That is, like the
back of my hand before I went blind.' (p. 25) Sarid takes Marcell
into one of the spaces that had once enclosed a praying chamber.
'The mammoth walls still showed the pittings in the stone with
which ancient men had decorated this house of their multiple
gods.' (p. 26) Sarid helps Marcell experience the land and even the
beginning of Maltese time and the spirit of the land. Finally, Sarid
says, 'All you can see before you, Marcell is your heritage, want it
or not, as it is mine.' He charges Marcell with a new responsibility:

> I'm old and powerless. There's very little I can do. But this land is
> dying. You can help give it life again.
> (p. 27)

The responsibility is spelled out in a long speech:

> 'Your happiness,' Sarid said at once. The words seemed to tumble
> from his lips. 'I sense it deep inside you. Conquer it, destroy it by
> what lies before you in the sun, this sick corner of our land, and by
> virtue of all that I have ever taught you. What is happening to it is
> evil, as what's rendering you unhappy is evil. Conquering the one to
> reclaim beauty, you would destroy the other, the horrible weight you
> carry about with you and which has lain upon my own heart ever
> since we met this morning. Then you'll be free as air again, the

Marcell I once knew. You must be free. If only for me to rediscover you.' . . .

It was as if they were his own words Sarid was uttering. And his own lips speaking them.

'Even if I cannot see, I feel with all my senses what is happening down there.' Sarid's voice was gentle, immeasurably sad. 'From up here on this sacred spot, where the hand of man has not intervened for centuries, I'm quite aware of the profane rush for moneyed progress and uncouth civilization along pernicious ways leading only to the ugliest passions. The gradual and noisy destruction of the very earth our fathers toiled upon and loved. There, in that bay, our first ancestors clambered out of their rough boats. And from there, too, they labored hard to carry the precious soil up io the top of this hill, where soon enough they built this temple, not simply as an expression of their sentiments to their gods, but, too, as an indelible mark of their patrimony over this countryside.

We're standing in the center of it. And we must be its guardians, if no one else will. Down there, in the old settlement of our neolithic ancestors, the men from Tyre and Sidon came in their long boats with the painted Phoenician eye, and after them, the Carthagenians, the Romans themselves and so many others. And among them were wise men. They made of that harbor a gentle kind of homecoming, and this temple they used as their own temple, thus preserving everything from the ravages of time and mechanical man.

And the sea itself . . . what a gift it is! It hugs our shores forever pressing on, clamoring for our attention, that we may recognize all that it is offering us – if only we would listen properly – a wealth of sustenance right through all the ages of this planet. Instead, man persists in ignoring its insistent message of redemption. Rather, he goes on polluting it, desecrating it, flinging its wonderful gifts back in its face.' He turned to Marcell.

'The people of the harbor and the town below, your town, Marcell, must not continue along their new, mistaken ways, changing the customs of centuries-old life in that corner of the island, poisoning the finest fishing grounds around, destroying the streets, the valley and the hillsides – divinely guarded treasure troves of wisdom – with machines. A Free Port would be a tragedy. They should try and find somewhere else, if they are so determined to construct one. Raise your voice with mine. Stand strong and resolute in a way that I, time-ravaged as I am, cannot be.' He laid a hand on Marcell's shoulder. 'This should, henceforth, be your entire concern. It is your real destiny, Marcell – believe me when I say that. It should also spell the end of your personal agony . . .'
(pp. 28/9)

Fired with purpose, Marcell notices Dirjana, the daughter of Sarid's servant, Mansweta, and smells 'the warm freshness of her brown skin', which is in contrast to the whiteness of Lenarda. He returns home, where he tells Karmenu that he wants the eagle stuffed. A quarrel begins over Lenarda. Karmenu says,

> She gets into her clothes, and then she comes here, and every man's hitching his eyes on her. I tell you, my brother, every man stops to look at her. Where did she go; where did she go? How the hell do I know? I'm not her keeper. But you are, I guess, for you sleep with her. Or perhaps that's all you do. Sleep.
> (p. 34)

Marcell's manhood is hurt and he pushes his brother in the chest, sending him toppling over the vegetables. He goes to his room to think. When Lenarda returns, Marcell says he has to go out: 'And from that moment on, Marcell thought he had stopped loving and desiring his wife.' (p. 39)

Marcell goes to visit his mother-in-law, Clorinde. 'I feel it is my duty to tell you . . . that I shall no longer be a true husband to Lenarda,' he says to her. She concludes it must be because of sex. She decides to show him Lenarda's and her sister Karmelina's room.

> My workmen were doing something to a wall in their old room when this door was discovered. Imagine, Marcell, a secret door in my own house! I'd always known, of course, that this house is terribly ancient.
> (p. 47)

He enters the secret room in anticipation and this is what he sees:

> Photographs lay scattered in a crazy improbable pattern all over the floor of the turret. There were dozens of them, from small snapshots to postcard and even larger sizes. From the simplest to the most sophisticated, the most faded to the expensive ones that had carried their age well. A thin layer of dust lay on nearly all of them. Bending over to scrutinize them more closely, he at once caught sight of the mutilations. Criss-crossing lines of sharp-edged scratches disfigured them all. On one of the largest, right across the chest of the man in the photograph, a childishly obscene drawing was scrawled as if with the bitten end of a stick dipped in red ink or paint. Not a few looked as if they had been crushed inside a fist, then smoothed and flattened out again, the figures horribly disfigured but still recognizable. Large

and small, together they looked like the map of a continent only a
nightmare could conjure up.
(p. 50)

On his return downstairs, he hears from Clorinde that she has
only dusted the photos but otherwise left them untouched all
these years. She does not know who did it, Karmelina or Lenarda.
Karmelina had died of scarlet fever at the age of fifteen. On his
way out, Clorinde says, 'I still refuse to see her [Lenarda].' It
appears that she resents Lenarda for being alive while Karmelina
is dead and blames her for that death. 'When are you going to
forget Karmelina?' Marcell mutters. 'Stop loving a ghost.' Yet
that is his own problem, though he thinks he has exorcised it by
agreeing to do what Sarid has bid him.

Marcell begins the process of fighting the free-port scheme by
getting the people to rediscover their own self-worth. There is a
great deal of resentment of him at first because he was educated
and ought to know to behave better. He moves among the people
as an ordinary person, without fine dress or airs. Moving among
the fishermen, talking to them, facing jeering from young children
who think he has gone mad, Marcell begins the process of
restoring the self-respect of the people, like bringing a dead sea
back to life:

> Then slowly, imperceptibly, day after day, nets and other fishing
> gear started to appear on the new quay. The more enterprising from
> among the fishermen began to extend their land activities past the
> men's lavatory. Workmen, digging up the street for the laying of
> fuel-oil pipes for the tankers of the future port, found themselves
> exercising extra care not to trip over nets lying about, or damage all
> kinds of fishing tackle with their heavy tools.
>   The encroachment was so slow, so unobtrusive, and so apparently
> unintentional that at first no one in the village seemed to notice.
> (pp. 145/6)

One person who did notice was Sa Tereza Kate, perched on her
high balcony and using her binoculars. We shall say more about
her later. The person who is most upset about the village coming
back to life is Sur Bert, who believes in 'progress' and who stands
to make a huge profit from the construction work for the free port
as well as from the port itself. Like a lot of other people, Sur Bert
believes that Marcell has been acting the way he has because of his

frustration over his wife. This is so, but not perhaps in quite the way the people think for Lenarda remains a mystery to him.

He goes back to visit Clorinde and to visit the room with the photos. 'What are you running from, Marcell,' Clorinde asks insistently:

> 'I'm so glad you came to me.' [Clorinde said.]
>   'You still hate Lenarda.' [Marcell said.]
>   'Don't let her harm you.'
>   'The canker is here too,' he said, raising his voice a little. Lenarda may even have brought it with her to the village from right here.' . . .
>   'Seal it up again, Clorinde.'
>   'What!'
>   'The room. Destroy the photographs. Their evil . . . I can almost sense it, it's alive.'
>   'After my death perhaps . . . I, too, hear voices speaking to me, Marcell.' (pp. 118/9)
>   'How I have sacrificed! Karmelina need never have died. I cannot bear the thought of the tyranny and shock of her young, doomed days with Lenarda.'
>   'I'm sacrificing happiness, career,' he said, 'separated as I am from the community, even if it's tainted.'
>   'Make love to her again. Break her!'
> (p. 120) .

What Helena Kosek says of Josef Škvorecký's style in his novel *The Cowards* applies to Ebejer here:

> The brief, terse sentences . . . [through] their telegraphic brevity . . . simultaneously awaken the reader's imagination and urge him to read between the lines, to follow, as it were, the subtext of the novel.[36]

Like everyone else, Clorinde has mythified Lenarda and wants revenge against her through sex. Marcell spends the night at Naxxar. He has to look at the photos again. He is prepared for the photos by a portrait he sees of an ancestor of Lenarda's:

> He looked long and hard at the portrait, seeing in it shades and images of Lenarda, especially around the eyes, in the soft yet firm line of the mouth made up in the cosmetic fashion of that period. (p. 122)

It is 4 a.m. Marcell emerges from a disturbed sleep and goes into the room, putting the light switch on. One bulb, low-powered, comes on. I quote the whole scene since it contains a key to the mystery:

The whole room with its contents seemed to rush violently up at him on wave after wave of muted screams. Gazing down at the strange, dust-gathering museum on the floor, he allowed his mind to probe right through and far beyond it – to all the dead years he found difficulty in imagining, much less knowing, now. Lenarda as a child: He saw nothing but shadows. Lenarda growing up inside her family: again impenetrable shadows. Lenarda and Karmelina together: black night. Karmelina, the little saint her mother had enshrined inside every particle of dust in this old, brooding house . . .

Cautiously at first, then determinedly, he stooped and picked up one of the larger photographs. On his first visit to this room of mystery, he had not really examined any of them very closely except to determine the fact that they were mostly of Lenarda's father. He blew on the photograph and dusted it with the palm of his hand. Swarthily handsome, black mustached, slightly overjowled face, evidently in younger days . . .the man smiled from under a Panama hat. Foliage lay behind him and a corner of the swan pond, showing the front half of a swan certainly long dead now. The child's savage pencil mark dissected the figure. Starting from the leg it went right up to the chest and part of the face.

Carefully he replaced the photograph in its original position on the floor. Stretching a hand farther out over the pile, he picked up another. Again the vicious tear. And now, too, the tiny, stabbed holes over the face and stomach.

There were two figures on the next photograph he picked up. Marcell looked closely at it. The father was in the foreground, as usual, the second figure, much blurred but clearly a man, a little too far for the camera lens. The wild grill of lines across him was clearly intended for him and was not merely a haphazard continuation of other lines on the father's figure.

Marcell was about to replace the photograph on the floor when something about the bearing of the second man held his attention. He lifted the photograph closer to the light and scrutinized every section of the mysterious figure, maddened as he was by the elusiveness of someone known but so far unrecognized. And at that every moment, in the deep stillness, the blurred, mysterious figure took on a voice and form right by Marcell's side.

'It is me. Perhaps you have not sufficiently recognized me.'

Marcell turned sharply round and saw the old gardener in the doorway.

The old man came in quietly, closed the door, which he had

noiselessly opened, and, in a hushed, reverential voice, said, 'I hope I
didn't frighten you, *sinjur.*'
(pp. 123/4)

The gardener says that the person who slashed the figures on the
photos was Karmelina:

> 'But you never saw her doing it.' His voice was a little harder, almost
> accusing.
> 'I did not,' said the old man at once. 'Even so, was there any
> need?' he continued. 'But *is-sinjurina* Lenarda, ah, she was gay and
> loved us all. *How she loved us.*'
> 'Are there any more of you here?'
> 'Alas, yes.' The old man pointed. 'There and there, and there, too,
> beneath the window.'
> Marcell picked up the indicated pictures one by one. The father
> was in all of them, clear and in the foreground, with the gardener
> remaining a shadowy figure at the back. *Both had received the same
> treatment from the child's weapon.*
> He said, 'Madam maintains it was Lenarda.'
> 'Madam speaks from the heart, and her heart is always for
> Karmelina. She died, Karmelina died.'
> (p. 125, my italics)

The dialogue continues. Marcell asks whether Karmelina died of
scarlet fever. Although the gardener's answer is ambiguous, it
appears so. Marcell asks whether the room was disinfected, closed
for weeks, and the mattress burned:

> 'I don't remember things like that. Perhaps yes, as you say, and
> perhaps no.'
> 'But you must remember.'
> The old gardener drew himself back, *his servile manner gone for an
> instant.* 'I don't remember,' he said firmly.
> 'Why should she hate you?'
> 'Perhaps because she hated all men.'
> 'Who? Lenarda?'
> 'No, no, *not beautiful Lenarda.* Karmelina.'
> 'All men?'
> 'Starting with her father, alas. He was a beautiful man, my master.
> Like a god, handsome. Sometimes he beat me with his own hands.
> Once he even said he would kill me one day. He never did, as you
> can see, though I'd have deserved it, I suppose. Now I'm old and
> tired and soon I'll depart to join him. It broke my heart when he
> died. *He took Lenarda wherever he went. He wanted to take*

Karmelina, too, but Karmelina was always for her mother. I think it
made my master very sad. *Dead Karmelina was always running to
madam.* She used to cry for her even when she was no longer a little
child. And so it happened that Karmelina hated us and did these
things.'
(pp. 125/6, my italics)

Just as Marcell has to use a mental zoom lens the second time he
looks at the photos to *see* what is actually on them, we the readers
have to pay particular attention to certain phrases in the dialogue,
the ones I have italicized, to let us know what has really happened.
When we read the novel in a hurry, we could skim over these lines
and draw the wrong conclusion, as Wilson does when he says,
'The wife, Lenarda, has, as an adolescent, committed violence
against photographic images of her father, and fears all men . . .'[37]
Ebejer explains in his interview with Massa:

Lenarda has been violated by her father and the family gardener –
the older generation – sins of the fathers – when she was young. And
now she's frigid to men.[38]

How could we possibly understand this *from the text*? The clues
are there. The way the gardener hovered in the background. The
way his servile manner disappears at the time of a key question.
The way he says, 'the beautiful Lenarda.' The way the darker
people are sexually attracted to the fair Lenarda: her father is
swarthy. The way the child slashed the photos. The way Marcell
keeps saying that sexually, Lenarda is like a child.

The violation of Lenarda is symbolically tied to that of the
village so Sarid's direction to Marcell regarding the village seems
to be a profound solution. But does Marcell understand that
Lenarda has been violated by her father and the gardener? The
text suggests that though he is close to understanding, there is
something in his mind that blocks out that understanding: and the
something is the very thing that caused the two males to violate
her, otherwise he (Marcell) would have been protective of, and
patient with, her instead of feeling his manhood hurt by his
inability to sexually arouse her. When he had thought of her
lovemaking earlier, after his brother had taunted him, 'it had
crossed his mind how helplessly, how unresponsively, she had lain
against him.' (p. 232)

Marcell returns to his task of bringing the people and the land back to life. And he gets involved with Dirjana:

> It was as if for the first time he was loving a woman. And this
> woman was loving him as a man, and he marvelled how peaceful it
> could be. No outside thoughts from beyond the hill.
> (p. 92)

But it was of Sarid that Marcell thought most of all:

> Sarid was there, straddling his mind, even in his wildest love, as real
> as if he could reach out and touch him.

Their love-making forms 'one incandescent offering to Sarid' (p.
93). And yet 'at the exquisite moment, he had thought only of
Lenarda.'

Marcell's method of bringing the land and the people back to
life is resolutely non-violent. Mansweta says to him that Sarid has
been saying

> How he's known you for a long time, how gentle and considerate
> you've been to him. That's very good. My master loves gentleness
> and gentle people.
> (p. 86)

But is Marcell actually gentle? What about the killing of the eagle?
What is the significance of 'the young stranger' he keeps seeing
(page 156, for example)? He seems suspiciously like an *agent
provocateur* for Sur Bert. Yet he is more than that to Marcell.
Violence does finally break out between the villagers and Sur
Bert's men, having been literally triggered off: Sa Tereza Kate,
who has the intention of protecting her son Georg from the wiles
of Lenarda, shoots at her with a rifle but injures a young man
instead; the villagers, who could not see Sa Tereza, blame
Lenarda and then believe it came from Sur Bert's forces. Later, a
fire breaks out, which leads to the fighting since the people are
tense. Marcell does not try to cool things down, despite the
pleading of the doctor, who finally screeches that he is a fraud:

> Still uppermost in his mind lay the desire and hope for the right
> word or action that would put a stop to all the savagery. But just as
> his breath was constantly knocked out of his body, so did the idea
> begin to recede from him, the intention to dissolve into an

indefinable sadness. In its place a new impulse was gathering strength, soon turning into a deeply felt desire to strike out like the rest. From his hands to his armpits to the back of his head, the tingling, bristling force rose and expanded him into an object of wrath.

Once or twice he heard himself call out: 'Stop, please, stop.' Yet he knew that he was not really shouting it but simply mouthing it inside his own head, opening and shutting the jaws of his skeleton self inside the cavern gloom of his brain. His hope for the miracle of a single peaceful action that might stop this awful battle and scotch his own fury – he looked for it within himself in the midst of the knocking, the swearing, the frenetic screaming. It was not there at all. Where it should have been, the flame of battle licked away, till at last it touched him. It leapt up, burning out once and for all, reducing to ashes, whatever there was of the message he had never uttered because he had felt strongly enough about it . . .

The face and body of Lenarda as he struck a man across his face. The hauntingly beautiful eyes of Lenarda as, screaming, he brought his stick down slashingly across a bearded man's eyes. He was now shouting at the top of his voice . . .

The mouth, all the sweet, enchanted caverns of Lenarda, as with another shrieking cry, oblivious to the fact that it was his own, *he plunged the end of the stick into another man's mouth.*

And into another's.

And another's.

The thighs and the breasts of Lenarda, he *struck*, infinitely beautiful and desirable and cold, he *struck*, Lenarda's groin, once his well of unearthly delight and of abjectness and self-denigration, he *struck*, he *struck* . . . Her rigidly closed eyes, her teeth biting her lip with cold, unuttered pain and repugnance, repugnance, he *struck*, screaming endlessly, he *struck* the man across his mouth. Then, much harder, *in his groin* . . .

The man's animal cries of pain shot through Marcell, setting off all the jangling chords of his own crushing and unutterable secret.

And they were, as he suddenly realized in that one flashed moment, Lenarda's own screams deep inside herself.

(pp. 226/7, my italics except for 'struck')

The scene is violent and sexual. Marcell is trying to destroy the Lenarda in him. We see from the next chapter that that is the very night when the 'stranger' and his allies rape Lenarda. She comes to Karmenu for help and pleads with him, child-like, not to be sexual. Later, her friends, Fonsu and Georg, take her off to the boat: and instead of protecting her, obsessed with her loss of purity, they drown her and spread the word that she committed suicide because of what had happened. Ebejer says in the Massa interview,

> Both the village and the woman are raped . . . The politics of the free
> port reflect/deflect from passions that appear unrelated. But
> everything is bound up. The psychological factors included.
> Marcell's trauma in the face of Lenarda's revulsion; Lenarda's
> violation as a child compared with the violation of the village's
> pristine beauty. If Lenarda's mother wishes to see her destroyed, she
> is not far apart from the free port entrepreneurs. Rape comes in
> various guises.[39]

However, one of the most important things about the scene is that Marcell had not recognized the stranger in himself, the violent self he had suppressed, and neither had his blind mentor, Sarid, who had praised his gentleness. Jung says,

> If we could see our shadow (the dark side of our nature), we should
> be immune to any moral and mental infection and insinuation. As
> matters now stand, we lay ourselves open to every infection, because
> we are really doing practically the same thing as *they*. Only we have
> the additional disadvantage that we neither see nor want to
> understand what we ourselves are doing, under the cover of good
> manners.[40]

Given the circumstances, though, the stranger in Marcell emerges, with terrible consequences.

Jung tells us that 'cultural symbols' can retain much of their original numinosity. 'Where they are repressed or neglected, their specific energy disappears into the unconscious with unaccountable consequences,' he says, continuing,

> The psychic energy that appears to have been lost is uppermost in
> the unconscious – tendencies, perhaps, that have hitherto had no
> chance to express themselves or at least have not been allowed an
> uninhibited existence in our consciousness.
>   Such tendencies form an ever-present and potentially destructive
> 'shadow' to our conscious mind. Even tendencies that might in some
> circumstances be able to exert a beneficial influence are transformed
> into demons when they are repressed.[41]

This is what has happened to Marcell: and he has given the name 'Lenarda' to his suppressed symbol. But so has everyone else in the novel. Karmenu says, 'Everytime I see her I get the fire in my blood like it scorches the whole desert and sends it up in flames,' both because of her whiteness and the fact that she is possessed by his lighter-skinned and more educated brother. (p. 131) Georg, the young student, mythifies Lenarda because he sees his mother in her and vice versa.

The mother, Sa Tereza Kate, sees Lenarda as a whore who might take her son away from her. This is tied in with her desire to have her son get an education and climb out of the village and also with her feeling that one day, Marcell's father was 'just about to whisper an assignation' when Marcell came in on his scooter and tore her new skirt 'and to this very day I don't know ... They must have been the most beautiful words I'd ever have heard in my life.' (p. 58/9) She blames Marcell and says he must do something for all the beauty he stole from her. This is why she is embittered about the village and Lenarda, seeing both as whores.

Georg had once tried to have sex with Lenarda but she just treated him like a child and pushed him off. Later, he converts his sexual obsession to love: which is worse since it leads to his killing her. Much of the time, he meets her on the boat of his mentor, Fonsu, an artist. The mother believes Fonsu too is attracted sexually to Lenarda: we know, as Sa Tereza does, that he was once the lover of Lenarda's mother and we further know, as she does not, or she might have kept her son away from him, that he is now a homosexual. Perhaps Lenarda senses that he is a homosexual and that Georg is a latent homosexual so she keeps their company, which ought to be safe but is not. They drown her because she is no longer the pure ideal they had thought of: then they take the body to her husband's flat, telling Karmenu that she had jumped overboard while they were asleep.

Lenarda is buried in her family's grave. Her mother burns the photos, saying, 'Now I can die.' The old gardener dies alone. Marcell goes to see Sarid, only to find that he is obsessed with his dog, which has died after being injured in a fall. 'Gentle, loving creatures deserve to be always remembered,' says Sarid. 'He'll lie there forever.' (p. 247) He tells Marcell that he must never forget the dog. We had credited Sarid with wisdom because he was old and concerned about the past. Michael G. Cooke says, 'If the hero is dead, the hero's hero is not. We may call to witness ... Sarid, in Francis Ebejer's *Leap of Malta Dolphins* . . .'[42] But Cooke is deceived. Sarid's obsession with the dog shows that he has given up on people. His call to Marcell to resist the free port was not a concern with people or with solving Marcell's problem but a concern with his own frustrated ideals. Marcell should have known from the beginning that Sarid was blind. For all his knowledge of the past, it seems as though Sarid has simplified it.[43]

Does that mean that Marcell was wrong to bring the village back to life? For up to a point, he had succeeded:

> As an island in itself, it began to live for itself, for its own people, for its own traditions, with its own ideas of happiness and progress, all welling up from its down deep, cultural founts. Within those people, most of them inhabitants of long-standing lineage, even to centuries back, a spirit moved.
> (p. 187)

But eventually Marcell fails. Does it mean that 'progress' was right? The novel has a sudden ending: a short Chapter 21 of less than five pages and a short Epilogue of less than two pages, comparable to the quick ending of *A Quality of Violence*. We whizz by without much thought: but when we turn back to think, we know something is lost.

> Then progress took up again where it had laid off. From valley to village and its bay, the sounds of men laboring dedicatedly for their livelihood and the achievement of their dreams and the fulfillment of their ambitions went on without stop or hindrance.
> (p. 248)

Sarid is old, the older fishermen and farmers ply their much-reduced trade 'under the indulgently sardonic gaze of their sons and daughters', the old priest who had come to life under Marcell's success is senile, the doctor is reduced to his old cynical self, Sur Bert goes about with bigger dreams of expansion, Sa Thereza Kate basks on her balcony watching 'that other whore, the village, putting on more paint over its gums and eye sockets,' Sarid hardly leaves his room and when he does it is only to go to his dog's grave. Dirjana, married to Marcell, has a daughter; when the child is four and Dirjana is expecting again, he takes the child to the center of the sacrificial chamber in the temple:

> He waited. It was a hot day. He listened hard. Then the child began to whimper. Marcell shushed her. But the child just could not stop

crying. Tearing her hand from her father's she ran off and out of the temple, stumbling over rock and dry thistle in her haste.

'Come back,' Marcell shouted after her. 'Come back, Karmelina.'

But the girl went on running. His daughter was always running to her mother . . .

He let the fury pass over him until he felt relaxed enough to listen again to the breeze. Perhaps its message was just for him alone, he thought hopefully.

When the breeze came on, a little heavily, as if it had aged, there was nothing he could make of it. Except the old name of Lenarda.

L-e-n-a-r-d-a.

Lenarda was a name.

He kept his eyes shut while he continued to listen to the breeze as it wrapped itself around him.

Again, confusion. None of the clarity of Sarid's time. There had been no ambiguity then, he mused.

But the name remained. Up here, too, on Sarid's hill.

And the same caterwauling breeze wrapped itself around it, and he knew that there could not have been Sarid and the village without Lenarda. Or Lenarda without Sarid.

And he would grow old on the hill wondering about that.

(pp. 251/2)

Is Marcell doomed to repeat history, naming his daughter Karmelina, a daughter who always runs to her mother? No: Marcell has accepted ambiguity, contradictions. He has embraced the totality of the history of the village. He knows the Lenarda and the Sarid in himself. Lenarda is not a myth or an obsession: she is a name.

The Epilogue is entitled 'The Last Leap of All'. Time moves on, the old gardener who used to place flowers each month on Lenarda's grave is dead, and a new tarmac road is built linking the free port to the airport, built over the cemetery so that there is a deconsecration ceremony by a priest. The ending is ambiguous: 'The tarmac is wide and gleaming and it has set hard. Some think, *forever.*' So the end is not necessarily an end. It may be a new beginning. What Marcell has learned is more complex than what Sarid could teach him. Next time around, perhaps there will not be failure because of the inability to recognize what has been suppressed.

'One of the most perplexing things about the trickster is that he is both remarkably destructive and remarkably creative,' says Lewis Hyde in 'Tricks of Creation[44].' He continues, a trickster's lies and deceptions are not so much immoral as they are a-moral. He does not operate by the sure polarities of the ethical life but works, rather, in the shadows where it is easy to confuse north and south, left and right, right and wrong. Tricksters are 'edgemen' – they live on the road and in the twilight; they pitch their tents in the space between wilderness and town, sunlight and dreams, fact and fiction . . . Trickster figures personify ambiguity.

Compare this to Ebejer's statement about Marcell that he is

'very, very ambiguous. That symbolizes the ambiguity of Malta's state now that we're independent. Most are not yet clear as to what Independence signifies.'[45]

Asked what his feelings are towards Lenarda, Ebejer says, 'Ambivalent. Ambivalent as I am with most of my characters – ambivalent.'[46]

The appropriately named Hyde says, 'Tricksters are invariably associated with fire.' Note that the beginning of the violence in *Leap of Malta Dolphins*, the one that triggers off Marcell's suppressed violence, is fire. Hyde says further that confidence men are modern cousins of the tricksters.

The confidence man conjures up our unlived life. He tells us the story we wish to hear (but don't know we wish to hear). To come back to 'ambivalence,' wherever we display a conscious virtue, the con man will call to its unconscious opposite. He wakes greed in the generous, generosity in the greedy, and fleeces them both.

But of course the con man is trying to fleece people for his own ends while the trickster is opening the doors of perception. So read the following statement by Hyde as applying to the trickster:

The con man knows that true believers never create new worlds. *The believers who live in the heartland have a repetition compulsion: they tell the same story over and over again the same style, unaware that it isn't the only story.* It takes someone from the border towns to see the artifice. The trickster can both fleece the locals and create new culture because *only he is aware that culture is a created thing in the first place.*
(My italics)

In *Leap of Malta Dolphins*, it is not that there is a trickster within the text but that the text itself functions as a trickster.

Chapter III

Heading Them Off at the Pass:
The Fiction of Ishmael Reed

The western stagecoach is being pursued by a posse. Cowboys. No, the pursuers are wolves. The driver's assistant and some of the passengers throw out bones of various sizes and shapes. The real loot is hidden. The leading wolves see these bones and stop to eat them, giving up the chase. Several wolves trip over these leaders. The dog in them leads others to fight for the bones. Not one Wolf, however; he side-steps the bones and the mess. He decides to run off in an oblique direction and head the stagecoach off at the pass.

Just watch the Loop Garoo Kid in *Yellow Back Radio Broke-Down*, Ishmael Reed's second novel, a western.[1] Loop Garoo is a black cowboy, like the famous Lash La Rue of the movies, wearing black and using whips. First appearing as Loup Garou in Reed's quintessential poem, 'I'm a Cowboy in the boat of Ra,' he means wolf. Chapter 20 of Reed's *Flight to Canada* is prefaced by a poem by Raven Quickskill which ends,

> 'Just like a coyote casetting amorous /Howls/in Sugar Blues/I airmail them to you/In packages of Hopi Dolls/*Ah ouoooooo! Ah ouoooooo!*'[2]

The coyote is a small prairie wolf, the poem ends as a blues, and the howl comes from Howlin' Wolf, the famous bluesman. We were prepared for this wolf howl because we have heard the low moan of a solitary wolf at critical points in the novel. The son of Ed Yellings who is taking care of business in *The Last Days of Louisana Red* is named Wolf.[3] When the President gets to the

Presidents' hell in *The Terrible Twos*, 'an animal in a white smock dashes by which appears to be a wolf or coyote'.[4]

Reed knows the heterogenity of experiences of modern people so he provides them with different entry points into the chase. The novel which gives me the best path is *Flight to Canada*. In this novel, three slaves have escaped Arthur Swille, the slave owner, who is simultaneously a multinational, and are trying to get to Canada. The chief character is Raven Quickskill, who wants to get to Canada literally. Although Raven entered Reed's fiction through the Southwest coyote stories, the movement to Canada is taken from black history: slaves did escape to Canada.[5] But when Raven finally gets into Canada, at Niagara, he meets a beaten-up Carpenter, a free black who had left of his free will for Canada, returning from Toronto, who tells him that Canada belongs to the Americans: they just let the Canadians run it. Raven is deeply disillusioned and decides to return to the United States.

I understand Raven. When I was in East Africa, Goans, my ethnic group, were always planning to fly to Canada. In 1975, my wife and I bumped into a Goan couple in Montréal who had left Uganda in 1970. The man said that he was thinking of moving to Toronto: he hadn't found his Canada in Montréal and was thinking of looking for it in Toronto. The following year, we met a Goan friend at a dance in Toronto. A travel agent, he had been trying to get to Canada since the late sixties and had only succeeded because of Amin's expulsion of Asians in 1972. He told us that we looked good, thanks, he said, to living in the United States. He wished he could move to the United States too. I met a Goan journalist in Toronto who had emigrated from India: he had been without a job since his arrival eight months earlier and was considering returning to India. When I chaired the first panel on Goan literature at the annual Conference on South Asia at Madison, Wisconsin on November 7, 1982, Professor John Hobgood presented a paper on the writings of Francisco Luis Gomes, a multi-talented Goan intellectual of the nineteenth century, from which I learned, to my astonishment, that Goans had been looking to Canada as the Promised Land a hundred years ago. Time for me was collapsed: past and present became the same. Yet I had not understood the Goan obsession with Canada until I read *Flight to Canada*: it is the flight from a long colonial oppression, the ravenous hunger for freedom, which is in the blood. If Goans could have read *Flight to Canada*, moving the desire for escape to the mind, their options could have been greater. Reed says in his Foreword to *Conjure*,

> If America had listened to me then, her son, her prophet, much of the agony of the following years could have been avoided.

Goans, too, could have avoided some of the pain.[6]

Getting to Canada is not simple. To make us see multi-faceted reality, Reed operates on multiple artistic levels. *Flight to Canada*, the novel, begins with a poem entitled 'Flight to Canada', written by Raven Quickskill to his erstwhile master, Arthur Swille. Within the poem, the poet says, 'That was rat poison I left/In your Old Crow.' The crow is a sort of raven, which brings to mind 'The Raven' by Edgar Allan Poe, which brings to mind his most famous work, *The Fall of the House of Usher*, which brings to mind an implied incestuous relationship in a Southern mansion, which is the underpinning of the novel that follows Raven's poem. The poem makes us laugh, and through laughter Raven both ridicules the enemy and makes us think. Escaped slaves frequently sent taunting letters to the master. This fulfilled a psychic hunger for justice. Turn the page and we realize that the poem is just that: a work of art. It is not reality. We should not be surprised for the blurb to the first edition of *The Free-Lance Pallbearers* says:

> This electrifying first novel zooms American readers off to a land they have never heard of, though it may strike them as vaguely, and disturbingly, familiar. It's a crazy, ominous kingdom called HARRY SAM, a never-never place so weirdly out-of-whack that only reality could be stranger.[7]

Reed frequently gives us reading clues in his blurbs, indicating to us that his fiction is *stylized*. Art has a complex relation to reality for it is not only mirror but also dynamo. The poem 'Flight to Canada' has set forces into motion, creating a new reality for Raven. Chapter 1 begins, in italics,

> Little did I know when I wrote the poem 'Flight to Canada' that there were so many secrets locked inside its world. It was more of a reading than a writing.
> (p. 7)

Raven the artist creates a work of art which then changes his life,

getting him an invitation to the White House and getting him to
Canada. Note the parallel with Reed: Reed the artist created a
novel, *Flight to Canada*, which got him invited to Alaska by the
Raven's Bones Foundation of the Tlingits. He says,

> 'I cannot express the uncanny feeling that came over me as I read
> Raven Quickskill's monologue, interior monologue, stream of
> consciousness, and narrative in *Flight to Canada*'s first chapter while
> a movie screen Raven . . . stared down at me.'[8]

Art is not a photograph of reality. When the two Nebraska
tracers, earning their way through college by tracking down
runaway slaves, catch up with Raven, one of them asks whether
the poem is autobiographical. 'I'm afraid it isn't,' replies Raven.
'See, I told you,' the questioner tells the other. 'They have poetic
abilities, just like us. They're not literal-minded, as Mr. Jefferson
said.' (p. 63) This is the racism that grows out of thinking
of black people as property, as things, lacking creative imagination. The two tracers say they have read his poetry in *The
Anthology of Ten Slaves*, which is in the anthropology section of
the library. Reed is being sarcastic about the widespread idea that
art is only created by white people, that black people cannot
create works of the imagination. *The Reader's Companion to
World Literature* says under the heading '*black literature*' in
America.

> The psychological and moral dehumanization of slavery, its brutality
> and corruption, have found a counterpart in and infected a black
> revolutionary literature where the 'black aesthetic' becomes a violent
> rage against all things Western and white . . . Much black literature
> is flawed by polemics, specious ideological arguments, and
> stereotyped situations and characters. But black writers have
> produced work of great passion and considerable art.[9]

Except for the ambiguous last line, this entry states that black
writing is only reaction, not creation. Before *they* can get away
with it, since *they* are part of the problem, *they* are put into a work
of art by Reed and undermined. Anthropology section? Turn the
tables. In the novel, the anthropologist is sent by his multinational father to the Congo to find out about natural resources,
which he will then grab: missionaries have become too obvious so

there must be a new cover. But the new Congolese are hip. They grab the anthropologist and feed him to the crocodiles. He comes back to haunt his parents.

This is an old function of art, art as magic. The good artist becomes a medium. Chapter 1 of the novel is a prologue whose action was sparked off by the poem which prefaces the prologue. Raven is speculating on art. 'Who is to say what is fact and what is fiction?' An important question for a colonized person, whose history has been stolen, denied or distorted. It is the artistic imagination that has to recover 'his story'. Raven speculates on Harriet Beecher Stowe. She took the story of *Uncle Tom's Cabin* from Josiah Henson, who made no money, his settlement named Dawn going broke while agents and a promoter producing a musical version of the novel get fabulously rich. 'Is there no sympathy in Nature?' Raven wonders. (p. 9) Perhaps there is, since Byron came out of the grave to get Harriet Beecher Stowe for spreading stories that he committed incest with his half-sister Augusta. Raven thinks that she was herself attracted to Byron, as revealed by her words. This prepares us not only for the necrophiliac incest of Swille with his sister but also for his sister's ghost, phantom or double coming to get revenge against him. *The Life of Josiah Henson, Formerly a Slave*, was short,

> but it was his. It was all he had. His story. A man's story in his gris-gris, you know. Taking his story is like taking his gris-gris. The thing that is himself. It's like robbing a man of his Etheric Double. People pine away.
> (p. 8)

Harriet Beecher Stowe stole the story of Henson, so if there is no sympathy in nature, there must be sympathy in art: Reed seeks artistic redress on behalf of Henson by putting her into an updated story of Uncle Tom, exposing her, and preventing her from doing it all over again. Reed demythifies history: she wrote the story of Uncle Tom not because she wanted to undermine slavery or the aristocracy but because she wanted to buy a dress. Uncle Robin is careful with *his story*: he commissions Raven to tell the story.

> Quickskill would write Uncle Robin's story in such a way that, using a process the old curers used, to lay hands on the story would be

> lethal to the thief. That way his Uncle Robin would have the
> protection that Uncle Tom (Josiah Henson) didn't. (Or did he
> merely use another technique to avenge his story? Breathing life into
> Byron.)
> (p. 11)

St. Augustine states that since all time is eternally present, it is
possible to change the past. He thought this could be done
through prayer. Reed does it through art. Max Kasavubu is an
expert on Wright's *Native Son* in *The Last Days of Louisiana Red*.
He begins dreaming that he is Mary about to be raped by Bigger.
Then he dreams he is Bigger about to kill Mary – and he does kill
'Mary', his fellow-conspirator, Nanny Lisa. Mess around with the
work and the work will get you.

But art is a two-edged sword. When Edward Said visited the
University of Iowa in early 1982, he said he was very angry with a
review of his book *Orientalism* by a friend, published in an Arab
paper. This friend said that in writing the book, Said was serving
the purposes of the C.I.A.: whereas before the book, the C.I.A.
exploited the Arabs inefficiently, after it, they had the means to
exploit them efficiently. Said said that he had stopped talking to
his friend. First, there was the likelihood that careless readers
would conclude that he was a C.I.A. agent; and second, he was
really troubled that what the friend said was right. I told him his
dilemma had already been presented by Reed in Raven's story.
' "Flight to Canada" was the problem,' Raven thinks.

> It made him famous but had also tracked him down. It had pointed
> to where he, 40s and Stray Leechfield were hiding. It was their
> bloodhound, this poem 'Flight to Canada'. It had tracked him down
> just as his name had.
> (p. 13)

In a dream/vision while ill in the White House – the whole scene
could be a dream – Raven becomes an 'it', property, and hears
Swille closing in:

> The poem had pointed to where *it*, 40s, Stray Leechfield were hiding.
> Did that make the poem a squealer? A tattler? What else did this
> poem have in mind for *it*. *Its* creation, but in a sense, Swille's
> bloodhound.
> (p. 85)

The chapter ends,

> But it was his writing that got him to Canada. 'Flight to Canada'
> was responsible for getting him to Canada. And so for him, freedom
> was his writing. His writing was his HooDoo. Others had their way
> of HooDoo, but his was his writing. It fascinated him, it possessed
> him; his typewriter was his drum he danced to.
> (pp. 88/9)

Raven would not be able to achieve his freedom without taking the risk of being tracked down.

Raven's speculation before the story gets going becomes an important guide to the novel as art. It gives us the questions by which the artist is to fly, just as a jazz musician starts with a theme and then soars (the title of one of Grover Washington Jr.'s LPs is *Reed Seed*[10]). When we get to what we might consider pre-posterous, we must remember this is stylized, not naturalism. It is absurd to read Reed naturalistically, as Sondra A. O'Neale has done in a review of *Flight to Canada*. She says,

> And after all the painful realism of the effective time collage, the
> reader is left with an ending that is inappropos for Reed's sardonic
> humor. Master Swilles cannot be programmed into leaving all their
> money to faithful Uncle Toms. All will not end happily ever-after –
> not in 1868 or 1978. The black man's dilemma is insanely funny –
> enough to make one die laughing.[11]

But *within* the work of art, it is entirely plausible that the 'faithful' Uncle Robin ends up owning Swille's estate. Swille gets to depend on Robin after Raven escapes because he suffers from dyslexia. The significance of the dependency relationship is recognized by Bessie Head's chief-to-be Maru when he sees a painting by Margaret Cadmore Jr. of the Masarwa slaves of the society:

> You see, it is I and my tribe who possess the true vitality of this
> country. You lost it when you sat down and let us clean your floors
> and rear your children and cattle.[12]

Uncle Robin is a player: he is playing at faithfulness, waiting for the right time. Trusting his faithfulness, Swille gets him to write out his (Swille's) will. Robin consulted his own gods, who told him that he did not have to obey the gods and the laws of people who did not respect him as a human being. He doctored the will, and when the will is read, he is named as the heir. The judge has doubts and says,

> according to science, Robin, the Negro doesn't . . . well, your brain – it's about the size of a mouse's. This is a vast undertaking. Are you sure you can handle it? Juggling figures. Filling out forms.
> (p. 167)

Robin, who has actually being doing all this for Swille, and knowing what the white man's 'science' is regarding the black man (think of *The Shape of Skulls to Come* from Salkey's *The Adventures of Catullus Kelly*), goes through an act:

> 'I've watched Massa Swille all these many years, your Honor. Watching such a great genius – a one-in-a-million genius like Massa Swille – is like going to Harvard and Yale at the same time and Princeton on weekends. My brains has grown, Judge. My brains has grown watching Massa Swille all these years.'
> Then turning to Swille's relatives, Robin stood, tearfully, 'I'm going to run it just like my Massa run it,' he said, clasping his hands and gazing around toward the ceiling. 'If the Good Lord would let me live without my Massa – Oh, what I going to do without him? But if the Lord 'low me to continue –'
> (pp. 167/8)

This is burlesque; but the Ph.D.'d Cato mutters, 'Allow, allow', putting his hand to his forehead 'and slowly bringing it down in embarrassment.' Cato may or may not be Swille's bastard son biologically but he certainly is psychologically; in a few lines, Reed is exposing the brainwashing of western education accepted uncritically.[13] Uncle Robin's behavior is the diametric opposite. 'Uncle Tom' became a term of abuse in the radical sixties but Reed is showing that Uncle Tom techniques played an essential role in the survival of black Americans, techniques that are still required for survival. By remaining in the shadows and tomming when necessary, Robin lives up to his name and flies to freedom.[14] Robin could have fled for he often flew on business for Swille. But he knows what Raven discovers: that the Master owns it all, he owns Canada. And Raven too has to tom when he is in a jam. When the two Nebraska tracers come to his door to repossess him, he greets them calmly, even obsequiously, putting them off their guard. Noting that one of them has a cold, he says he is going to get some Vitamin C tablets from the bathroom and then he leaps out the bathroom window and makes his escape. Robin is not actually a faithful slave: he is a player, and so he recognizes that Lincoln is a player too for the President is less powerful than the multi-national capitalist.

Robin has never given the game away so that he could be bugged, like Moe, the white house slave. As the will scene continues, Robin says, 'If I can just go on, I'm going to try to make Massa Swille up in hebbin proud of me.' Ms. Anne Swille rises.

> Oh, Judge, don't be mean to Robin. Let him have it. My brother would have wanted it this way. It's in the will.

Donald Swille backs his sister: 'My brother often said he didn't know what he'd do without Robin. That Robin treated him as though he were a god.' While Robin, 'his head in his hands, was being comforted by Aunt Judy,' the Judge says, 'So be it.' In his deliberate exaggeration, a burlesque as in vaudeville, *we know* Robin is tomming. Reed the artist is playing too. Nathaniel Mackey explains this aesthetic technique as displaying

> the most indispensable ingredient of street-corner repartee, the ability to make one's opponent look silly through the creation of absurd scenarios and the use of outrageous images.[15]

One has to *read* the work, as Raven tells us, not impose on it. It is simply not true that, as Ms. O'Neale says,

> we get the distinct impression that Uncle Robin and his wife, Aunt Judy, have no intention of 'freeing the people.' Instead they simply fill the master's shoes. Life will continue as usual with the high-yellow nouveau riche in charge. It appears that the 'plantation niggers' are no nearer to owning themselves than they were when Swille was alive.[16]

In fact, Uncle Robin changes things. He frees Stray Leechfield, who is captured by the Nebraska tracers and brought back: he pays the tracers and lets Leechfield go. Leechfield thought he could buy his freedom with the money he made from his pornographic photos taken by Mel Leer and other schemes; Robin tells him, as Raven had done, that Swille did not want money, he wanted his property: and he considered his slaves to be his property. It was the slave in people he wanted; he wanted a world of slaves, and he could not afford to let them know through the example of Leechfield that there was another way. But Leechfield, blinded by his anger against house slaves, does not see that he owes his freedom to Robin. Robin also frees Raven, offering him the freedom to create his work of art without fear of pursuit: in other words, once his dream of Canada has been shattered, Raven is given the opportunity to create it through his writing. As for the estate, Robin wants to figure out what to do with it because it is too large for him. Aunt Judy feels the same way. Robin needs time to think. He has not given up his role in the shadows: after all, there are other forces around. He says,

> The rich get off with anything. I don't want to be rich. Aunt Judy is right. I'm going to take his fifty rooms of junk and make something useful out of it.
> (p. 179)

And in Chapter 1, we know that Robin has accepted Raven's proposal that the castle be used as an artists' and craftsmen's colony while he and Aunt Judy go to visit the Ashanti Holy Land.

Under colonial rule, the colonized were denied any knowledge of their history. 'A sense of history was totally absent in me,' says Bessie Head,

> and it was as if, far back in history, thieves had stolen the land and were so anxious to cover all traces of the theft that correspondingly, all traces of the true history had been obliterated.[17]

Insofar as there is history, it is imposed. For example, the Horatio Alger myth that you can make it within the system by hard work. Reed checks this idea out in *The Free-Lance Pallbearers*. Bukka Doopeyduk has the ambition of becoming the first black bacteriological warfare expert, works hard, goes backward, moves to the bottom in more ways than one, is to receive a golden bedpan for his faithfulness in his hospital work, but even that is denied him as he receives a boot on the bottom. One man's myth is another man's nightmare.

So you want your own history, huh? Here it is. This is all you can have: gnaw on it. 'Get back to your language,' they say,' says Adil Jussawalla in *Missing Person*.[18] Reed ridicules this dangerous kind of obsession with one's own history in a comic-book exchange between Raven and Mel Leer, an immigrant Russian Jew who is Leechfield's partner:

> 'Nobody has suffered as much as my people,' says Quickskill calmly.
>   The Immigrant, Mel Leer, rises. 'Don't tell me that lie.'
>   The whole café turns to the scene.
>   'Our people have suffered the most.'
>   'My people.'
>   'My people.'
>   'My people.'
>   'My people.'
>   'We suffered under the hateful Czar Nicholas!'
>   'We suffered under Swille and Legree, the most notorious Masters in the annals of slavery!'
>   (p. 68)

Blowing up the balloons, Reed lets them burst. He shows that the oppression of people, which has actually happened, can be turned into what Derek Walcott calls a career.[19] This is the accusation by the actress playing Desdemona to the actor playing Othello in Murray Carlin's play, *Not Now, Sweet Desdemona*. 'We have suffered,' she jeers.

> We know what suffering is. We are all refugees, so will you pay my hotel bill . . . Othello the Moor – and what is he? Another bloody self-pitying, posturing, speechifying Chairman of the Afro-Asian Delegation![20]

This is the danger of exploiting your people's exploitation. Princess Quaw Quaw Tralaralara enjoys the fame that comes from performing ethnic dances on college campuses.

Quaw Quaw is therefore hypocritical when she accuses Raven of being too obsessed by race. Race is his reality. When Carpenter tells Raven at Niagara that Canadian vigilantes beat up the Chinese and Pakistani and shoot the West Indians, she says, 'I'm a Native American.' (p. 160) When she is mistaken for Japanese by a racist United States immigration official, she gets mad. But real racism can make the recipient so touchy that he reacts to racism where it does not exist. Pirate Jack, a sophisticated exploiting middle-man, who controls the market and mass-taste behind the scenes, is helping Raven get to Canada on his private boat to elude Swille's men, even though Raven has something going with his (Jack's) wife, Quaw Quaw. There is the following exchange:

> 'You think that's manly. Huh? You think that's manly. One day I outwitted thirteen bloodhounds.'
>   'Preposterous.'
>   'I did. Thirteen bloodhounds. They had me up a tree.'
>   'That can't be. I've studied the history of bloodhounds since the age of William the Conqueror, and that's just a niggardly lie.'
>   'What did you say?'
>   'I said it's just a niggardly lie.'
>   'Why, you –' Quickskill rushes around the desk and nabs the pirate, lifting him up.'
> (p. 151)

The reader knows what Raven thinks of the word 'niggardly' – he thinks it is a racial insult. But Webster's *New World Dictionary* shows that the word comes from 'niggard', which probably comes from the Middle English 'negarde', which means 'stingy' or 'miserly'. Treating the subject on a comic level, Reed is showing that colonialism has programmed the colonized person to destroy himself if he is not cunning and self-knowledgeable. Pirate Jack was helping Quickskill elude Swille's men and get to Canada – his touchiness is jeopardizing this plan. Quaw Quaw jumps overboard to blot out the fighting and Raven nearly loses her.

The bitterness people feel over their exploitation can seldom attach itself to the force that is actually responsible for the exploitation, as we have seen from Salkey's *Come Home, Malcolm Heartland*. It is difficult for people in the belly of the whale to realize what is going on in the whale and where the whale is going. 'Day after day I'm more confused,' sings Dobie Gray in 'Drift Away.'[21] People keep fighting among themselves, destroying one another while the real exploiters remain out of reach, out of sight. Reed, drawing on Afro-American tradition, gives these invisible forces names, concretizing them. First, Louisiana Red, which is both a corporation and a hot sauce manufactured by the company:

> Louisiana Red was the way they related to one another, oppressed one another, maimed and murdered one another, carving one another while above their heads, fifty thousand feet, billionaires flew in custom-made jet planes equipped with saunas tennis courts swimming pools discotheques and meeting rooms decorated like a Merv Griffin Show set.
> (p. 7)

By refusing to use commas, Reed makes us read this description in an out-of-breath way, thus making us feel the gross accumulation of luxury. The reference to the Merv Griffin Show set both undermines the whole description through bathos and makes us understand the thing described in an instant because we all watch television. Reed goes on to identify a category of people who are manipulated by Louisiana Red, finding a clue in Cab Calloway's hit song of the thirties, 'Minnie the Moocher':

> Moochers are people who, when they are to blame, say it's the other fellow's fault for bringing it up. Moochers don't return stuff they borrow. Moochers ask you to share when they have nothing to share. Moochers kill their enemies like the South American insect which kills its foe by squirting it with its own blood. God, do they suffer. 'Look at all of the suffering I'm going through because of you.' Moochers talk and don't do. You should hear them just the same. Moochers tell other people what to do. Men Moochers blame everything on women. Women Moochers blame everything on men. Old Moochers say it's the young's fault; young Moochers say the old messed up the world they have to live in. Moochers play sick a lot. Moochers think it's real hip not to be able to read and write. Like Joan of Arc the arch-witch, they boast of not knowing A from B.
> Moochers stay in the bathtub a long time. Though Moochers wrap themselves in the full T-shirt of ideology, their only ideology is Mooching . . .
> The highest order of this species of Moochers is the President, who uses the taxpayers' money to build homes all over the world where he can be alone to contemplate his place in history when history don't even want him. Moochers are a special order of parasite, not even a beneficial parasite but one that takes – takes energy, takes supplies.
> (p. 17)[22]

The portrait of Minnie the Moocher is a hard one, particularly if we see her in terms of Angela Davis.[23] Reed is frequently accused of misogny. Sondra A. O'Neale says, 'for the black woman Reed intends no sympathy,' continuing,

> If Reed purposes to free the black man with his writing, let us hope that he will magnanimously enlarge his vision to free all the race – even his likewise-enslaved-to-unfair-stereotypes black sister.

Reed could be better understood if one looks at other black male novelists he is connected with. Al Young's *Sitting Pretty* and William Demby's *Love Story Black* are novels narrated by black males.[24] Reed once said that the runaway black man should be given equal time to present his side of the story instead of just being blamed for deserting the family and leaving the burdens entirely on the woman. This is precisely what Young does: grant his protagonist equal time. Not that Sitting Pretty is without fault: in his late fifties, he can recognize some of the areas in which he has been deficient, particularly towards his wife and children, but when younger, he had wanted freedom. The point is that he is a man, he has a voice and a point of view, he has a philosophy such that a black philosophy professor needs him to maintain his sense of identity, and he is a great hit on radio and T.V.

In Demby's novel, the protagonist is a black professor. He does not realize that he has been psysically castrated by the system, just as the black male was physically castrated in the past by certain forces. He goes to interview Mona Pariss, an old entertainer, to earn enough money from a black success magazine to pay off his credit cards. But she turns the tables. It turns out that the deeper level of her entertainment is that of high priestess. She has been waiting to restore the manhood of the black man. Mona Pariss is like Okot p'Bitek's Lawino in wanting to cure her man whose testicles have been smashed by large books. The popular T.V. sitcom, *Different Strokes*, had as its underpinning the idea that two young black boys cannot have a black father, they must be brought up by a great white father. The denial of black manhood can take many forms.

Why is Minnie always talking of shedding blood, PaPa LaBas asks her. Enough black people have been destroyed by colonial forces without them destroying one another in the name of some mythic freedom. Minnie is bringing disaster down on her family without realizing what she is doing. She springs Andy and Kingfish from jail and hijacks a plane for them on the assumption that every black man in jail is a political prisoner. In fact, both men were jailed for bulgarizing Amos's house, and they proceed to rob the passengers on the plane. Chorus is on the plane and shoots Minnie, whom he sees as Antigone. Minnie's case reminds me of what happened to a friend of mine in Kenya, a game-warden. He told me that the huge lump I saw on his head was the result of going on patrol with his dog. The dog disappeared into the forest, upset a herd of elephants, and then ran back to my friend – with the herd of elephants in pursuit. My friend turned to flee and tripped on his gun, which struck his forehead. He barely got away. Imagine the elephants programming the dog to lead them to the man . . . PaPa LaBas discovers, from Minnie's unconvincing language, which he realizes is second-hand, that she is being manipulated by her feminist nanny, who is teaching her man-hating stories, and her Marxist teacher, both of whom are agents of Louisiana Red. The nanny is not actually a black woman but a white woman acting as a black woman. This is the black-imitating-white-imitating-black tradition of the U.S. but it is also out of the cartoon tradition, where a person can change form.

Before condemning Reed for misogny, we have to look closely at the specific character and see how that character functions within the work. I was startled when seeing *Gone With the Wind* on T.V. to notice that the Mammy was exactly like Mammy Barracuda in *Flight to Canada* (as well as being a female Idi Amin). Like Professor in Wole Soyinka's *The Road*,[25] Reed finds clues to make his psychic arrests all over the place: literature, comics, newspapers, movies, T.V., radio, music . . . Nance Saturday, the maverick criminologist in *The Terrible Twos*,

> approached a problem as a romantic would. *He would read material.* He would study all the trivia connected with the case and all the facts he could sew together and usually the solution would come. (pp. 119/20 my italics.)

This shows the power of the subconscious and that of the word. Why was the Mammy figure so outspoken and so powerful in this popular precursor to the T.V. soap opera? There must be a meaning there, and Reed finds it in the hidden relationship between Mammy and the owner of the estate. We should not make the mistake of thinking that she is in charge of the plantation/multinational corporation: she is not. But she has power within the household because of her relationship to Swille, whom she brought up, and she is as dangerous as the factors Ayi Kwei Armah identifies in his novels, the Africans who were the middlemen in the slave-trade, who handed the slaves over to the white men. She believes the myth that the Africans have been saved from darkness by being Christianized and enslaved: no wonder she gives a great whoop of joy when she inherits Swille's whips. She is not a player out to win freedom, unlike Pompey and Bangalang, who react 'stupidly' and slowly when Robin tells them Swille is on fire and let him burn. Notice the looping relationship to the movie: Reed finds a clue in the Mammy of the movie, reinterprets her in *his* novel of southern aristocracy caught up in the Civil War, and then makes us see Mammy differently when we see the movie again. We know that Reed was conscious of this movie because the white woman acting as Minnie's nanny says, 'I have to shuffle about like Hattie McDaniel', who played Mammy in the movie, and Arthur Swille's dead sister is named Vivian, while Vivian Leigh played the Southern belle in the movie.

Reed creates what he wants out of what he sees. Underneath Minnie the Moocher, we find an Angela Davis figure from the seventies, Minnie the Moocher from a pop song of the thirties, Joan of Arc from the fifteenth century and Antigone from over four centuries B.C. Reed has unearthed another version of the Antigone myth, hinted at by Creon in Sophocles's play, in which Antigone is actually a man-hater in love with death. In Reed's value system, as Marian Musgrave points out, those to be admired are people who take care of business.[26] Creon got on with the job of keeping the state going. If Antigone wanted to do things for her brothers, why did she not stop the two from fighting? This is what Chorus asks; and the answer is that Antigone was in love with death and also she was a man-hater. Chorus is out to get revenge against her for making his role redundant: at the same time, one of his functions in the novel is to present that alternative version of Antigone as archetype, as a pattern that has continued through time. He also draws our attention to Reed's use of the particular myth underlying the novel so that we will not make the mistake of thinking that Reed's improvisation is without structure.[27] The simultaneous myths and histories in Reed, like the market studies by corporations which superimpose many polythene patterns onto one basic design, have the effect of retrieving *relevant* history and myth all at once. No pedestrian chasing after historical facts in a scholarly way, one element at a time: that way, we will never catch up with the coach.[28] Reed deals with simultaneous myths because he expects us to have the quick skill to connect things up on the run.

Since men are deliberately prevented by colonialism from achieving their manhood, the women have frequently to take on more than one role. Colonialism puts a heavy burden on women by making it possible for them to do things in areas where it blocks the men. When Canada took in Asians expelled from Uganda by Idi Amin in 1972, the women found it easy to get jobs while most of the men had to go through several humiliating rejections, frequently being told they lacked Canadian experience. The effect was to totally demoralize several of the men, particularly those qualified for high jobs: they were as unprepared as Carpenter and Raven for the existence of racism in Canada against 'West Indians' (all people originating from the Caribbean and Africa) and 'Pakistanis' (all people originating from the Indian sub-continent.) Very few of the Goan women in Canada, if any, realized while they were keeping the family together that the men were unemployed because of colonial forces rather than their innate uselessness. There was no alternate way of judging themselves for the system exerted hegemony: 'Slaves judged other slaves like the auctioneer and his clients judged them,' thinks Raven (p. 144). 'It hurt to see us folding in on ourselves,' says Angela Davis, 'using ourselves as whipping posts because we did not yet know how to struggle against the real cause of our misery.'[29]

Raven continues his pondering in Emancipation City:

> Was there no end to slavery? Was a slave condemned to serve another Master as soon as he got rid of one? Were overseers to be replaced by new overseers? Was this some game, some fickle punishment for sins committed in former lives? Slavery on top of slavery?
> (p. 144)

PaPa LaBas, really Legba, the god of communications and medium between the material and spiritual worlds, explains to Wolf why there are divisions in his family:

> The experience of slavery. I'm afraid it's going to be a long time before we get over that nightmare which left such scars in our souls – scars that no amount of bandaids, of sutures, no amount of stitches will heal. It will take an extraordinary healer to patch up this wound.
> (p. 100)

But there are healers at work in Reed's fiction. Aunt Judy is one of them. She is aware of the slave-master's hegemony. Although she had disagreed with Robin's providing Swille with slave-mothers' milk daily, she did not quarrel with him but asked him about it afterwards: and he explained that it was Coffee Mate with which he was poisoning the master. Mark Shadle points out that what Robin has been doing is feeding the multinational his own swill. 'Guede is here,' says Raven in Chapter 1. 'Guede got people to write parodies and minstrel shows about Harriet.' (p. 9) Guede is a Haitian loa that has the power to destroy people by showing them their own image. Thus Robin has been feeding Swille Coffee Mate, which is produced by the multi-national.

The attempt to end colonialism must incorporate, if not begin with, the restoration of manhood to the male. All the women who do not recognize this are acting, in Reed's fiction, as agents of Louisiana Red. These include Fannie Mae, Mammy Barracuda, Ruby and Minnie. All the women who understand the de-manning of colonialism and work against it and/or work with the men are admirable figures, women like Zozo Labrique, Joan, Sister, Aunt Judy, Bangalang, Esther, and Erline in *Mumbo Jumbo*.[30] Women who work against the men without realizing it but can be rescued are not damned: Quaw Quaw, Vixen and even Minnie, for whose life PaPa LaBas goes to the underworld to plead. The question of why Reed does not make a woman the protagonist of his novel is an aesthetic one, not a moral one: it is as absurd as asking Paule Marshall why she makes a woman the protagonist of *Brown Girl, Brownstones* and *Praisesong for the Widow*.[31]

So you want black manhood? Here is a man! See him on T.V. and in the papers! But Reed is already there. See, Reed says, Louisiana Red at work. Street Yellings: a selfish, greedy, vicious, mean thug, a murderer sprung from jail to be used against black people. This is the revolutionary leader?? There was a famous Street-type black leader of the sixties who killed a woman for the same reason as Street roughed up Ms. Better Weather: 'Do you know who I am? Don't you recognize my picture? Haven't you seen my picture all over? (p. 95) Also notice what happened to another Street, hiding out in Algeria and waiting to make the revolutionary against Amerika: it turned out that 'Amerika' was a brand of men's clothing he was going to market. Read is against sloppily attaching a heroic label to individuals who do not deserve it. Real manhood does not need to 'bully the blacks, to bully the women,' Vixen thinks in *The Terrible Twos*. (p. 105) It may work quietly behind the scenes, in the shadows, like Ed Yellings, PaPa LaBas and Uncle Robin. Not knowing her history and culture, Minnie wants to go public, thus exposing her people to further destruction. Mammy Barracuda never questioned the rightness of Swille's absolute ownership of human beings, having no knowledge of her culture but only that of suffering western Christianity, as indicated by the diamond crucifix she wears round her bosom:

> It's so heavy she walks with a stoop. Once she went into the fields and the sun reflected on her cross so, two slaves were blinded.
> (p. 20)

Uncle Robin knows his culture and his gods and knows, like Raven, that the slaves were kidnapped, not saved: so he is a player until the right time. Note the way he speaks: 'slave English' when speaking to the white people and 'good' English when speaking to those closer to him. Pompey and Bangalang knew he was playing a game, as they were, and they did not squeal on him.

No, Freedom is not easy to achieve. Stray Leechfield thinks he can buy his freedom by making money from posing for pornographic photos and other schemes with Mel Leer. 40s thinks he can protect himself with guns. Raven begins to recognize what Robin has known for some time: that Swille's ruling philosophy is the love of property, and he considers the slaves to be property. Swille does not need money: he controls the source and supply of money. But his love of property may be too abstract an idea to grasp, for slavery also attempts to put chains on the mind and the imagination. In *Yellow Back Radio Broke-Down*, Reed concretizes the western capitalist's love of property:

> Three horsemen – the Banker, the Marshal and the Doctor – decided
> to pay a little visit to Drag Gibson's ranch. They had to wait because
> Drag was at his usual hobby, embracing his property.
>
> A green mustang had been led out of its stall. It served as a
> symbol for his streams of fish, his herds, his fruit so large they
> weighed down the mountains, black gold and diamonds which lay in
> untapped fields, and his barnyard overflowing with robust and erotic
> fowl.
>
> Holding their Stetsons in their hands the delegation looked on as
> Drag prepared to kiss his holdings. The ranch hands dragged the
> animal from his compartment towards the front of the Big Black
> house where Drag bent over and french kissed the animal between
> his teeth, licking the slaver from around the horse's gums.
> (p. 19)

The difficulty for a critter – excuse me, critic is that Reed always
has a hundred things going on at the same time while the critic
goes in a straight line, pursuing one lead. Reed cautions us against
this kind of linear reading: on page 161 of *Mumbo Jumbo*, one has
to turn the book in circles to read what is being said at the bottom
of the page. We see the love of property concretized in terms of a
wild west pattern imprinted on our cowboy-loving minds: the
cowboy loves his horse more than anything else. But this is a horse
that has turned green from its nightmares. Nightmare – horse: the
connection is that of the stand-up comic who, in this hetero-
geneous America, finds all words funny, like Groucho Marx's
'Why a Duck?' The horse is green, as in 'greenhorn', again from
the cowboy yellowbacks. Then the horse is led away, covering its
eye with a hoof: this is out of movie cartoons. Raven mentions
Guede in *Flight to Canada*: we notice that the capitalist licks 'the
slaver'. Lest we dismiss the whole thing as 'unreal', we know from
the very beginning that the story is a tall tale, a tradition as old as
America:

> Folks, This here is the story of the Loop Garoo Kid. A cowboy so
> bad he made a working posse of spells phone in sick. A bullwhacker
> so unfeeling he left the print of winged mice on hides of crawling
> women. A desperado so ornery he made the Pope cry and the most
> powerful of cattlemen shed his head to the Executioner's swine.
> (p. 9)

Straight from the tall tale, from yellowback novels, and also from the storylines in black music.[32] The horse has turned green from nightmares: in its recurrent nightmare, it is about to be killed by Germans. The big American problem, says Reed, is that Drag, Swille and other American capitalists live in America but have their hearts in Europe. Arthur Swille is named after the Arthur of the mythic Camelot but he is actually no better than food for pigs, which is precisely the fate of Drag. The German chieftain hates green and wants his men to chop off the horse's head: the horse always wakes up just before they are to do so. In the horse's nightmare, 'The Germans burned down Yellow Back Radio in a matter of seconds – about the amount of time it takes for a station break.' (p. 66)

Yellow Back Radio Broke-Down is a title that tells several stories. The 'yellow back' is a wild west novel. It refers to the young people who have taken over the town because they do not have 'yellow fever': the fever for gold like many adventurers had when they were searching for El Dorado, and perhaps the paranoia against the Chinese and the Japanese. They are not afraid: they are not 'yellow'. The word 'radio' tells us that we are reading a radio script, that we are to hear the words that follow as we would on radio. The word 'radio' also brings to mind Reed's quintessential poem, 'I am a cowboy in the boat of Ra.'[33] The poem connects up 'Ra', the Egyptian sun god, with 'Radio', suggesting that there is a world beyond one's perceptions from which, if one is tuned in, one can receive messages; conversely, one can tune out bad messages. 'Broke-Down' suggests both that the whole system has broken down and that the radio has been 'exploded' so that we can understand it. The radio connection is extended to T.V. by the neighbouring town being named Video Junction. 'Yellow Back' has yet another meaning, mentioned in *Mumbo Jumbo*. Benoit Battraville from Haiti, which is fighting an invasion by white American soldiers, says to the black Americans,

> I know this is a strange request but if you will just 1 by 1 approach the Dictaphone, tell just how Hinckle Von Vampton propositioned you, the circumstances and the proposals he made to you, we will record this and then feed it our loa. This particular loa has a Yellow Back to symbolize its electric circuitry. We are always careful not to

come too close to it. It is a very mean high-powered loa.
(p. 151)

The word 'electric' is a clue that 'to loop' is to join so as to complete circuitry. Thus although it would make no difference on radio, the difference in the spelling of 'Loop Garoo' in the novel and 'Loup Garou' in the poem is significant. A loop is a sharp bend in a mountain road which almost comes back on itself like a snake. (So Loop fights Drag with a white python, Damballah.) In physics, a loop is an antinode, the node being the point, line or surface of a vibrating object free from vibration. To knock for a loop is to throw into confusion. And a loop antenna is used in direction-finding equipment and in radio receivers. Once you get to the multiple meanings, you, the reader, begin to loop. 'Garoo', according to Toma Longinović, a Yugoslav writer who was in the International Writing Program, means, 'essence'.[34] Reed's novel gets to the essence, doing more in 200-odd pages than a 600-page work, and Loop practises HooDoo, which is the essence of VooDoo. Reed wants us to short-circuit the whole mess, to break it down.

Reed's syncretism opens up 'the possibilities of exquisite and delicious combinations,' which is a Gumbo way of writing, as Reed's epigraph to *The Last Days of Louisiana Red* suggests, as does the poem 'The Neo-HooDoo Aesthetic', which is about gumbo.[35] Reed does not want black Americans to short-change themselves by denying what they are told is not in their tradition – 'Get back to your language.' The contributions of black Americans have penetrated everything that is American, even the wild west.[36] One of the epigraphs to *Yellow Back Radio Broke-Down*, from Henry Allen, says,

> America . . . is just like a turkey. It's got white meat and it's got dark meat. They is different, but they is both important to the turkey. I figure the turkey has more white meat than dark meat, but that don't make any difference. Both have nerves running through 'em. I guess Hoo-Doo is a sort of nerve that runs mostly in the dark meat, but sometimes gets into the white meat too.

As Americans, black Americans have to be open to possibilities of connecting up with other Americans. When Uncle Robin is taking care of business, he hears footsteps approaching. 'Uncle Robin takes a sip of coffee, looks innocent and begins to hum a spiritual.' (p. 41) He is actually as innocent as the Pope of the same name who comes to confront Loop Garoo. Moe is suspicious but cannot prove anything. Robin says,

> Sometimes it seems to me that we are all Uncle Toms. Take yourself, for example. You are a white man but still you a slave. You may not look like a slave, and you dress better than slaves do, but all day you have to run around saying Yessuh, Mr Swille, and Nossuh, Mr Swille, and when Mitchell was a child, Maybe so, l'il Swille. Why, he can fire you anytime he wants for no reason.
> (p. 41)

Moe's refuge is race: 'What! What did you say? How dare you talk to a white man like that!' Robin replies, 'Well, sometimes I just be reflectin, suh.' The word 'reflectin' shows Robin 'mirroring' – that is bouncing back, like Guede – and also thinking. The next moment, the red light begins to blink, which means that Swille wants Moe to come to his office. 'Moe wipes his mouth with a napkin, gulps the coffee down so quickly it stains his junior executive's shirt.' Robin cleans it quickly. The detail of the shirt shows that even an executive is a slave. The timing of the incident to prove a point is that of the T.V. sketch.

Moe is the 'white house slave'. If we heard this, which we would on radio and T.V., it would sound like 'White House Slave'. This takes us to *The Terrible Twos* in which the President, Dean Clift, a former model, is a slave to forces he never bothered to understand until he began to speak out against their interests. It is his black butler, trying to protect him, who tells him,

> Mr. President, everybody in the White house knows that you don't run the government, and that the Colorado gang is in charge . . . Mr. President, will you get it through your thick head that all they wanted to use was your model's face. They know that America gets butterflies in the belly over a pretty face. It was just your face, Mr. President.
> (pp. 158/9)

Shades of Benson!

But the President is locked up in an asylum after he blows the lid off the vicious anti-human schemes on T.V. This is not all a disaster, for a black American saying is, 'Suffering is seasoning.' (p. 173) It is a sort of purgatory for Dean Clift's days of selfishness. Justice demands a correction to, not a gloss over, historical crimes. In *Mumbo Jumbo*, there is a multi-cultural group going round reclaiming its stolen art from Western museums. Not all the members of the group agree with Berbelang's decision to include a white man, Thor Wintergreen, in the group on the grounds that he is different from the others because, the repentant son of a rich white man, he wants to end exploitation. Yellow Jack, a Chinese, does not trust the white man because of his history. In spite of the bitter exploitation of black Americans, Berbelang is willing to take a risk, a great risk. He sees the white man's history in terms of the myth of Faust. He is not the first thinker to see the West in terms of the Faust myth, which is usually interpreted as the willingness to sell one's soul for knowledge and power, or rather, for power through knowledge.

Berbelang approaches the myth from outside the Western perspective. He says that the real point is that Faust is a charlatan, a bokor, a thief magician, who one day finds to his surprise that something seems to be working. He then draws from various non-white peoples. He is thereafter haunted by his fear of being revealed. Thus Berbelang's interpretation of the myth is that perhaps deep down, Western man *knows* that he has been stealing the art and creativeness of non-Western man and *knows* that he is a fake, not a magician or a god. If so, the fear of exposure will make him continue to keep non-Western people down. Is this the case? 'I'm just 1 man,' says Thor Wintergreen. 'Not Faust nor the Kaiser nor the Ku Klux Klan. I am an individual, not a whole tribe or nation.' (p. 92) 'That's what I'm counting on,' replies Berbelang. 'But if there is such a thing as a racial soul, a piece of Faust the mountebank residing in a corner of the White man's mind, then we are doomed.' In the event, Thor is weakened by an appeal to his race, class and tribe by a descendant of the lower class of Europe, still serving the upper class that oppressed it and keeping European values going, preparing to take over and protect white civilization. 'Son,' says the tied Biff Musclewhite, 'this is a nigger closing in on our mysteries and soon he will be asking our civilization to 'come quietly' (p. 114). Thor tearfully unties Musclewhite, who proceeds to kill Berbelang, PaPa LaBas's French helper Charlotte, and finally Thor himself. The media call it suicide in two cases and justifiable homicide in the third.[37]

Must there always be Christian monotheistic domination? Zumwalt in *The Terrible Twos* is working for the North Pole Development Corporation, which has acquired monopoly rights to Santa Claus. He used to be a radical member of the S.D.S. in the sixties but got tired of the demands of black Americans. Western culture reasserted itself: it had never abandoned his mind. But he is not abandoned by the novel. He is ultimately saved by the Santa Claus and Black Peter exposure of the terrible crime he had carried secretly within him, that he had accidentally killed the President's son in his radical days and had had plastic surgery to change his identity. Deep down, Reed suggests, there is hope for ending the alienation of at least some powerful white people, including the President. Black Peter and Saint Nick reveal to these people the alienation from their own humanity.

So it is worth taking the risk of linking up with other people, selectively, because you can then go places you would be denied, see things you would miss, remember things your people have forgotten, and get a different perspective on yourself. In *Yellow Back Radio Broke-Down*, Chief Showcase, the lone survivor of a massacre by Drag, rescues Loop from Bo Shmo by helicopter. Showcase says,

> You see the tribe was so busy trying to organize they forgot that they were clandestine by nature, camouflage, now you see now you don't, what some blockheads call esoteric bullshit. But now I'm trying the same thing on him he put us through . . . Foment mischief among his tribes and they will destroy each other. Not only that. I have my secret weapon . . . If I can't get their scalps I'll get their lungs . . . this time it'll be done by an idea.
> (pp. 40/1)

The value of the shadows again. Drag permits his Chinese servant to say rude things about him. Drag enjoys it, and perhaps, with his Judeo-Christian consciousness, he wants to be whipped for his sins, just like Swille. Not too much, just enough to permit him to continue doing what he likes best, exploiting other people, owning them, killing off those who stand in his way, grabbing property. And why not permit his servant to let off steam? He is likely to feel better too, and nothing will change. Just shouting the truth will not make the walls of Jericho collapse. Was this what happened in the sixties, with radicalism going public? Reed's novels note that the real struggles are taking place between secret societies behind the scenes. In *Mumbo Jumbo*, the Atonists deliberately begin the Great Depression to put black artists out of work and stop Jes Grew. One of their agents is the 1909 version of Albert Goldman (p. 45): Albert Goldman, who did a hatchet job on Elvis Presley.[38] Another novelist who sees history in terms of plots between secret societies, Thomas Pynchon, says in his massive novel, *Gravity's Rainbow*,

> Well, and keep in mind where those Masonic Mysteries came from in the first place. (Check out Ishmael Reed. He knows more about it than you'll ever find here.)[39]

Real fighters do not underestimate the power of their antagonists. In fact, they do not underestimate power. There is a tendency for Third World intellectuals, not having tasted power and dealing with its structures and modes of operation, and also imitating powerless western intellectuals, to underrate power and profess to despise all powerful men. A deadly misjudgement since, as Wole Soyinka shows in *Kongi's Harvest*, a dictator knows how to exploit the weakness of intellectuals, giving them a taste of power in return for which they manufacture the words of legitimacy for him.[40] No: with Reed, power is given due respect, even when the adversary is hated. Aunt Judy sees as hypocrisy the fact that Lincoln (initially) only frees the slaves in the territories he has no control over. Not so Uncle Robin: he applauds the player in Lincoln. And as a true player, Lincoln wonders whether Uncle Robin is one too. Although Robin is secretly working to undermine his boss, when Swille is dead, he says, 'Well, you had to hand it to Swille. He was a feisty old crust. Lots of energy. What energy? Rocket fuel.' (p. 179) The stand-up comic again. In American culture, you can get away with murder through jokes.

Cunning people like Robin and Chief Showcase, learning from their history, are working indirectly. PaPa LaBas, knowing his culture, believes in wearing masks. Not that they know everything: PaPa LaBas seeks help to solve the murder of Ed Yellings by consulting Hamadryas, an older baboon god in the zoo (who may also be the Egyptian god Thoth). When Aunt Judy asks Robin whether it was not un-Christian of him to doctor Swille's will and end up owning the estate, he replies,

> I've about had it with this Christian. I mean, it can stay, but it's
> going to have to stop being so bossy. I'd like to bring the old cults
> back.
> (p. 171)

Loop Garoo fights Drag not with Drag's weapons, for then Drag
would win, but with HooDoo, spells, thought control, psychic
force, the mind. When Loop is winning, the problem gets serious
enough for the Pope to appear in the west. He knows how to fight
Loop since they are ancient enemies. The Pope wins a round but
not the fight. The Pope wants Loop to rejoin Christianity and
bring his strengths in. It is an old fight, the novel says. Christianity
designated all the African gods as the devil. Yet the West needs
the energy and creativeness of the black world. The fight is not for
total destruction but for Western hegemony. This is the same
fight in *Mumbo Jumbo* and *The Last Days of Louisiana Red* as in
the James Bond movie of the same time, *Live and Let Die*. In the
Bond movie, the action alternates between New Orleans and a
Caribbean island. There is even a white woman possessed by a
loa, who loses her power after being seduced by Bond and then
becomes a white virgin to be sacrificed by black voodooists. At
the end, there is a diversion: the conflict is presented as one
between the forces of good (the west) versus evil (black drug
dealers). Bond wins but Baron Samedi survives with his Geoffrey
Holder laugh. We can see why Reed takes movies seriously but
uses them in his own way. He has his own detectives, opposed to
the Bonds, detectives like PaPa LaBas and Nance Saturday, out
to make psychic arrests.

People's idea of history is created by the media: by fiction. The
kids at Yellow Back Radio have taken over and chased the
grown-ups out because they are tired of being taught miserable,
hateful lies. 'We decided to create our own fiction,' they say (p.
16). 'Who pushed Swille into the fire?' Robin speculates. 'Some
Etheric Double? The inexorable forces of history? A ghost?
Thought? Or all of these? Who could have pushed him? Who?'
While indications are that it was Pompey, who is a ventriloquist,
we must say *the logic of the fiction* pushes Swille in. J.R. McGuire
says of my novel, *The General is Up*, that from the Epilogue, it
appears that the novel we have read was written by the character
Ronald D'Cruz and

It seems, in light of the fact that Ronald worked for Damibia radio and television, that this is *his* language, his version of what happened in Damibia. But it also seems that he has recreated the reality of what happened such that *he* is the one who triggers the chain reaction in the last chapter. *He* is punishing those deserving within his own work of art. *Thus the text and its author are literally out to get and punish the General and his entourage for their monstrosities.*[41]

In the same way, Raven is writing the story, and as we know from his thoughts before he writes, he is out to get justice. Art is to seek justice through the working of its story, through Guede. Swille made every slave call him 'Massa Swille': saying it often, Robin must have got the idea of doctoring 'Massa's will'. Swille was committing necrophiliac incest with Vivian: so the story made Vivian's ghost come for him. (People think that Mrs. Swille pushed her husband into the fire, but she is found innocent: and ironically, she gets to Canada, getting a job at a museum in Toronto.) The anthropologist son of Swille sent to the Congo to find energy sources is thrown to the crocodiles and his ghost comes to haunt his father's mansion.

Everybody is haunted by past crimes. There are ghosts in the White House. President Dean Clift in *The Terrible Twos* is taken by Saint Nick to the President's hell, where he sees past presidents and would-be-presidents chained to their crimes against nature for not having had the courage to oppose dehumanizing actions: Eisenhower (Lumumba), Truman (Hiroshima) and Rockefeller (Attica). Reed's fiction haunts, too, changes things in our mind. Is Chief Showcase really seeking to defeat the white man by introducing him to smoking tobacco so that he will die of lung cancer? Well . . . we know that smoking causes cancer, and we know that Raleigh picked up smoking from the Indians . . . Uncle Robin has been poisoning Swille with Coffee Mate while Swille thought he was drinking slave-mothers' milk which would keep him young: will the F.D.A. suddenly announce that Coffee Mate causes cancer? Just look at those nasty ingredients listed on page 174. Reed the black American artist plants things in the mind and thereby changes the past. 'No one says a novel has to be one thing,' says Loop to Bo Shmo. 'It can be anything it wants to be, a vaudeville show, the six o'clock news, the mumblings of wild men saddled by demons.' (p. 36) We have seen the news and the demons. Vaudeville?

Reed the necromancer presented a vaudeville show in 1970 of

forthcoming attractions in his novels entitled, 'D Hexorcism of Noxon D Awful', which introduces almost the whole cast of Reed's characters in order to put a 'Nix on Noxon.'[42] Reed's writing is like an electronic series. This is suggested by the name 'Loop' since Reed himself appears in Loop's story: the shotgun messenger from the Black Swan Stagecoach says, 'Three black cowboys were seated on tree stumps drinking from some wooden bowl and grinning. One of 'em was playing the slide trombone.' (p. 55) Reed used to play the trombone. The staple unit of vaudeville on T.V. is the anachronistic historical sketch, where past and present are hilariously simultaneous. This is how Reed writes his fiction. When Professor Hobgood spoke on my panel at Madison on Goan literature, he produced a volume of Gomes's selected writings with the stamp of the Entebbe Goan Institute, of which I had been President three times and my father five times before me – and yet I had never noticed the volume! Suddenly all the layers of time were before me: summoned up by the introduction of a material medium of communication. This is what Reed does when he introduces the T.V. or radio into what we might think is the past. For example, Lincoln is assassinated with the T.V. cameras on him, there is instant replay, and an immediate interview with his wife – which Raven sees while making love to Quaw Quaw in a reproduction of a Ghanaian slave castle in Emancipation City. What presidential assassination is this? What time? What plot? Is the multinational involved? Reed would not call it anachronism. In *Shrovetide in Old New Orleans*, he says, 'The "time sense" is akin to the "time" one finds in the psychic world, where past, present and future exist simultaneously.' (p. 134) Through the constant T.V., radio, video and electronic references, Reed is also asking his people to acquire literacy as well as to leap to video and electronics or else they will be left far behind, as when they were denied literacy. Swille spells it out to Lincoln:

> We gave him Literacy, the most powerful thing in the pre-
> technological pre-post-rational age – and what does he do with it?
> Use it like that old voodoo. (pp. 35/6)

Raven Quickskill acquires *reading* and this makes him flee the condition of slavery outwards. Robin, who is put in charge because of the flight of Raven, also acquires *reading* and uses it to move inwards. The two need each other's skills: hence Robin gets Raven to write his story, which is also Raven's story. Watch the name: 'Raven' comes from a curing story, he is a healer through words. And, as Barry Lopez tells us, the raven is a friend of the wolf.[43]

The original spelling of Loop Garoo's name in 'I am a cowboy in the boat of Ra' is 'Loup Garou,' a wolf, actually a werewolf. The man who changes into a wolf does so to try to rescue the earth from the mess men of power have made in their blindness, greed and alienation from nature. The wolf also seeks to rescue those men of power who would be rescued. Thus in *The Terrible Twos*, Black Peter, Santa Claus and Saint Nick save Zumwalt, the aging soap-opera star who would be Santa, and the President. Even the President who was elected in 1980, setting off a Scrooge-like meanness in the spirit and a cold wave in nature, is not doomed because he did once take part in a movie in which he represented the plight of the oppressed. But some cannot be saved. The Christmas tree that an old Indian chief had tried to protect from the white man's bulldozers on the grounds that it was alive gets its revenge: when the President's wife turns the Christmas tree lights on, she is electrocuted and burned to a crisp. The switch let the current pass. The Yellow Back loa is mean. There is sympathy in Nature, LOUP GAROU, but it needs help from Art, LOOP GAROO, to close in on the western stage.

* * *

Tricksters run through Reed's first six novels. The baboon in the zoo in *The Last Days of Louisiana Red* is Hamadryas, who is also Thoth, the Egyptian god. Thoth became the Roman Hermes. Joseph L. Henderson says,

> Hermes is Trickster in a different role as messenger, a god of the cross-roads, and finally the leader of souls to and from the underworld. His phallus therefore penetrates from the known into the unknown world seeking a spiritual message of deliverance and healing.[44]

Lewis Hyde tells us that in the Pacific Northwest, Coyote is a trickster.[45] We saw the importance of Raven in *Flight to Canada*.

The other blackbird in the novel, Robin, is a player, that is, a trickster, as we see in the following scene after Raven has escaped:

> 'Robin, what have you heard about this place up North, I think they call it Canada?' Swille says, eyeing Robin slyly.
>
> 'Canada. I do admit I have heard about the place from time to time, Mr. Swille, but I loves it here so much that . . . that I would never think of leaving here. These rolling hills. Mammy singing spirituals in the morning before them good old biscuits. Watching 'Sleepy Time Down South' on the Late Show. That's my idea of Canada. Most assuredly, Mr. Swille, this is my Canada. You'd better believe it.'
>
> (p. 19)

We know that Robin is putting on Massa and we chuckle at his way of using the clichés of happy southern blacks. We think we are in on the act, that Robin is deliberately lying to Swille. We only realize at the end that we have been had. Robin was telling the truth. He did make Swille's castle his Canada – and Raven's as well.

Janet Giltrow reviews three books on Raven in *Canadian Literature* under the title, 'Raven's Lands.' She says:

> In *Raven the Trickster*, Gail Robinson collects and retells nine stories from North Coast folk narrative. The events described by these stories occurred 'when things were not ordered as they are now' – at a time, that is, when the ordinary laws of cause and effect had not been established, and almost anything could happen. The world was a work-in-progress, and this premise opens the door to fantasy: as modern narrators of science-fiction use the future as a setting and rationale for marvellous happenings, so native folk narrators referred to a distant past, out of reach of common sense reckonings.
>
> Managing this inchoate cosmos is Raven, the creator. He is very busy making the world, stocking it and adjusting it. Unlike more aloof creatures, who get the job done promptly, once-and-for-all, Raven seems to have no master plan. He makes mountains or creatures, or puts light in the sky, and then sits back to contemplate his project. Noticing areas that need refinement or development, he goes ahead with renovations and improvements.
>
> What moves Raven to creativity? Sometimes he is touched by petitionings from the Humans he has made, for he seems to have their interest at heart. When they get cold, they complain to Raven, who undertakes to get fire for them. But fire is owned by Qok, a vain and selfish owl. So, posing as a famous dancing deer, Raven tricks Qok, and steals a few flames for the chilly villagers. Although the

trick in a sense backfires – Raven's beautiful tale is burnt to a stump
– mankind benefits. Yet the boon is not the point of the story.
Rather, it is the trick that is most pertinent: Raven's insight into
Qok's vanity, and his ingenuity in outwitting this unworthy bird.[46]

As a writer, Reed's Raven is a creator. He tricks Swille by
pretending to be a faithful house-slave. As we saw in the chapter
on Ebejer, Lewis Hyde says that tricksters are invariably
associated with fire. Raven creates the text that pushes Swille into
the fire. The fire that Raven steals is a text: he brings a text back.
Reed twists the tale, though: instead of Raven's tale being burnt to
a crisp, he is given a chance by another blackbird, another
trickster, to create a longer story, his story. Reed looks on
tricksters favorably. In 'The Fourth Ali', he says, 'I posed for a
gag picture with Larry Holmes, WBC Heavyweight Champion
and one of the brightest students of the Ali style and a trickster
like Ali.'[47]

Henry Louis Gates, Jr. says of PaPa LaBas,

> He is the chief detective in hard-and-fast pursuit of both Jes Grew
> and its Text. PaPa LaBas' name is a conflation of two of the several
> name of Esù, the Pan-African trickster. Called 'Papa Lebga' as his
> Haitian honorific and invoked through the phrase 'eh là-bas' in New
> Orleans jazz recordings of the 1920s and 1930s, PaPa LaBas is the
> Afro-American Trickster from a black sacred tradition. His
> surname, of course, is French for 'over there,' and his presence
> united 'over there' (Africa) with 'right here.' He is indeed the
> messenger of the gods, the divine Pan-African interpreter, pursuing,
> in the language of the text, 'The Work,' which is not only *Vaudou*
> but also the very work (and play) of art itself. PaPa LaBas is the
> figure of the critic, in search of the text, decoding its telltale signs in
> the process.[48]

Keeping what Gates has said in mind, let us return to Giltrow,
who goes on to throw light on Reed's seventh novel, *Reckless
Eyeballing*:

> In most of the stories, Raven is protagonist. But two present plots
> that resemble those of European folk tales in which young human
> heroes have problems and adventures. In 'Cannibal' three brothers
> go forth to overcome a female monster who devours hunters. She is
> horrible: 'old and dried blood, sweet-smelling with decay, covered
> her wrists and elbows. Flies clung to her arms like burrs.' Readers

familiar with European tales about brothers might expect the youngest of the three to take this opportunity to show that he is brave and clever beyond his years, and defeat the bloodthirsty adversary single-handed, saving his siblings in the process. But all three brothers are equally irresolute and confused, and Raven must intervene at the end of the tale. In 'Sila' Raven does not actively intervene in the fate of the young heroine but appears intermittently as a sage and sensitive councillor. When Sila's doting brothers complain that she will not submit to her proper feminine role in the tribe, and goes swimming instead, Raven advises them: 'Let her swim the tides, for it is her nature to do so.'

* * *

In the first section, on Reed's first six novels, I created a critical form that reflected Reed's as a novelist, a form that loops through Reed's texts, demonstrates what he did, flying through his texts just as his texts fly through others. The essay does not move 'logically', i.e. from A to B to C, but leaps and loops from idea to idea, image to image, expecting the reader to keep something in mind until it comes back again. Reed implies that his work is 'gumbo' in which are found various ingredients according to the recipe of the cook: I created a critical gumbo into which I put every ingredient I wanted, that belonged to me. These include my Goan background, which my colonial education tried to remove from me for we were educated to be the middle-men between our people and the West. I included the rock 'n' roll I love and the blues from which it grows. Reed let me have his gumbo: and I prepared mine for him.

* * *

'You ain't nothin' but a gangster and a con artist . . . Tricking these people. You ain't nothin' but a trickologist with your fuzzy quick lines. You mischievous malicious bastard.'

So says Jake Brashford to Ian Ball in *Reckless Eyeballing*.[49]

Reckless Eyeballing is Ishmael Reed's seventh novel and his most famous. It led to Reed being invited to appear on T.V. shows such as *The Today Show* and *Tony Brown's Journal*. Why all the attention? Because on the face of it, his novel is an answer to Alice Walker's best-selling novel, *The Color Purple*[50] and the movie based on the novel directed by Steven Spielberg. 'Tremonisha

Smarts . . . is a famous black writer . . . whose hit play 'Wrong-Headed Man' . . . comes across as a sort of send-up of Alice Walker's *Color Purple*' says Michiko Kakutani in a review of *Reckless Eyeballing* under the title 'Gallery of the Repellent'.[51] It would appear that Reed's novel is a *roman à clef* with Tremonisha Smarts as Alice Walker (just as Minnie the Moocher was Angela Davis in *The Last Days of Louisiana Red*), Ian Ball as Ishmael Reed himself, and Jake Brashford as Ralph Ellison. The lone play written decades ago by Brashford is entitled *The Man Who Was an Enigma*; compare this to Ellison's *Invisible Man*. Raven Quickskill says in his poem 'Flight to Canada' that he caught a jumbo jet to Canada but he arrives there physically on a boat; similarly, Reed has moved the action in *Reckless Eyeballing* from novels to plays, the clue being that Ball has written a play of the same title, which triggers off the action, just as Raven had written a poem. The play that got Ball into trouble with the feminists is entitled 'Suzanna': think of the song which includes the line about going to Louisiana. '[The feminists have] been on my case since my 1974 novel *The Last Days of Louisiana Red*, because it includes a feminist radical whose speeches they disapprove of,' says Reed in 'Stephen Spielberg Plays Howard Beach by Ishmael Reed' [sic].[52]

Ishmael Reed has frequently been accused of being a misogynist. He says that after his exchanges with Barbara Smith on *Tony Brown's Journal*,

> Some of Ms. Smith's 'sisters' were not so friendly as Ms. Smith . . . Others dismissed me with feminist rhetoric in which *misogynist* was the frequent buzzword.[53]

Even Greil Marcus, a critic famous for his work on rock 'n' roll and sympathetic to Reed, says in a review of *Flight to Canada*, 'Reed's misogyny is as rampant as ever.'[54] 'Misogynist? Who, me?' says Johnnie Sobert in *Escape to an Autumn Pavement* (p. 80). In his seventh novel, Reed appears to take the accusation seriously and make a joke of it. Or to put it in the words of the engineer-in-chief in Conrad's *Nostromo*, perhaps Reed is 'putting the face of a joke upon the body of a truth.'[55] Reed said in his Self Interview in the seventies,

> I get my strongest criticism from some of the 'Sisters.' I guess this is

because they want me to improve and do better, God bless them.[56]

Note the following exchange between Tremonisha Smarts and Ian Ball:

> 'You got a thing about black women. They're either vamps or being
> subservient to some man. She stressed *man*. 'And then you give the
> old whorish white bitches in your play all the good lines, and don't
> leave no good lines for the sisters. I know all about your problem.'
>   'What do you want me to do, Tre?' he said, eager to mend his
> ways.
>   'I want you to do better.' She blew some smoke from the cigarette
> she held.
>   'I'll certainly work on it.'
> (p. 73)

There is an earlier exchange between the two:

> 'Man do you get a kick of running down black men?' This time his
> mother appeared in his mind's eye. She was wearing that bandanna
> on her head tied up in that certain way. 'But on the other hand,' he
> said before her frown appeared, 'A lot of them deserve it.'
> (p. 52)

This is the humor of the T.V. sketch or of the stand-up comic
(people were always saying Brashford could have made millions
as a stand-up comic, Ian thinks on page 29). So it would seem that
Reed is having his joke on the feminists, particularly the way two
feminists come to see him to apologize and to weep after his play
('The two feminists who had wrongly attempted to censor his
work cried even harder,' p. 108.) Reed even has descriptions of
himself attached to Ball and the Flower Phantom. Tremonisha
says of the Flower Phantom to O'Reedy, 'He was a large man . . .
He had the cheekbones of a well-fed cat.' (p. 10) Martha Ball
thinks of Ian, 'He had his father's Olmec face, his adobe-colored
skin, and his gray eyes.' (p. 144)
     But is Ian Ball Ishmael Reed? And are we to take Ball's views as
Reed's, views we must identify as those of the novel?
     Ms. Kakutani's review begins as follows:

> The way 'Reckless Eyeballing' starts off reminds you of a seedy
> 1940's detective novel gussied up with some contemporary bigotry

and anger: a large man, wearing sunglasses and a raincoat, has been
assaulting prominent feminists. He ties them up, shaves off their
hair, chastises them for giving black men a bad name, and leaves a
chrysanthemum behind as a calling card. His explanation is that this
is what the Resistance did to whores who collaborated with the Nazis
and that women today who help perpetuate ugly stereotypes about
black men deserve a similar punishment for their sins.

Ms. Kakutani does not know how to read because this is not the
way the novel begins. The opening paragraphs are as follows:

> At first the faces were a blur, but then he was able to identify the
> people who owned them. It was a painting he'd seen in a book about
> Salem, of the Puritan fathers solemnly condemning the witches, but
> in place of these patriarchs' faces were those of Tremonisha Smarts
> and Becky French. He couldn't hear what they were saying. They
> were moving their lips. They were mad. He was sitting in the dock
> where they kept the witches. Becky said something to a guard and
> the guard started toward him. The guard was about to take him
> away to the gallows, he'd gathered from the logic you get in dreams,
> but when the guard looked up from underneath the black Puritan's
> hat she wore, she wasn't a guard at all but his mother.
>   Becky and Tremonisha said cut it, cut it, and then the dream cut
> to a scene in the desert. He was cowering behind a huge cactus plant
> as a snakeskinned hand was about to cut off a rattler's head with a
> large gleaming blade. He shot up in bed.

Why does the novel begin with a dream? And why this particular
dream? A clue is provided as the paragraph continues:

> He was sweating. He looked next to him. The cover had been pulled
> aside and the woman he'd brought home from the evening of
> nonreferential poetry had left. Her subtle perfume still hung in the
> air. While he'd been making love to her he kept thinking of that ad
> for Jamaica that contained the line: 'Come daydream in a private
> cove.' At one point, they were fucking so heavy that they began to
> warble involuntarily like birds. He'd had about three gin and tonics.
> This drink always brought out his romance. He got up and put on a
> robe.

Romance? Sounds surprisingly like sexism. Get that name: I. Ball,
Iron Ball, eyeball, etc. In his play which has the same title as the
novel, the skeleton of Ham Hill (suggesting Emmet Till) is to be
exhumed to be tried by a court for recklessly eyeballing a woman,
an action she claims was as bad as rape and led to his lynching:

twenty years later, she is a lesbian feminist and wants a trial to remove any shadow of doubt that she was to blame for leading the young man on. Ball is trying to be nice to the feminists to get his play produced and his name removed from the sex list.

So why does the novel begin with that particular dream? The novel itself provides us with a clue: on page 100, Ball has gone up from the production of his play at the Queen Mother to watch a feminist play about Eva Braun at the Lord Mountbatten in which she claims she was an innocent victim. Near the end of the play (and the end of Chapter 19), after Eva has shot and killed Hitler, she turns to the priest who had come to marry them:

> 'Please don't shoot me,' the priest says. 'It was his fault. He made me do it. He made all of us follow him. He swayed us with his brilliant oratory and mesmerized us with pageants and fireworks, he somehow managed to tap into our collective un –' (Eva kills the priest with one shot.)
> (p. 100)

The statement Eva interrupts with her shot is the phrase made famous by Jung, 'the collective unconscious.' *Reed is telling us to look at Jung.* In an interview with John O'Brien, Reed quotes Jung favorably, saying the end of *Yellow Back Radio* was based on an introduction Jung wrote to Milton's *Paradise Lost*.[57] He quotes Jung several times in *Mumbo Jumbo* (pp. 62, 161, 208, 209) and lists Jung's *Psychology and Religion: West and East* in the Partial Bibliography at the end. Earlier, I said that the long list of books discovered by the narrator in Tayeb Salih's *Season of Migration to the North* was an indication to the reader that books had to be found to juxtapose with this text to help it acquire its true meaning: Reed is giving us the same type of clue by his Partial Bibliography. Jung provides us with the meaning to the opening paragraph of *Reckless Eyeballing* and therefore will help us understand the novel as a whole. I quote extensively from *Man and His Symbols* edited by Jung and in particular from his opening chapter, 'Approaching the Unconscious' and the chapter by M-L. von Franz. Jung says:

> The general function of dreams is to try to restore our psychological balance by producing dream material that re-establishes, in a subtle way, the total psychic equilibrium. This is what I call the

complementary (or compensatory) role of dreams in our psychic make-up. It explains why people who have unrealistic ideas or too high an opinion of themselves, or who make grandoise plans out of proportion to their real capacities, have dreams of flying or falling. The dream compensates for the deficiencies of their personalities, and at the same time it warns them of the dangers of their present course. If the warnings of the dream are disregarded, real accidents may take their place. The victim may fall downstairs or may have a motor accident.[58]

What does the dream reveal about Ball's imbalance? Turn to von Franz:

If the dreamer is a man, he will discover a female personification of his unconscious and it will be a male figure in the case of a woman . . . Jung called its male and female forms 'animus' and 'anima'.

The anima is a personification of all feminine psychological tendencies in a man's psyche, such as vague feelings and moods, prophetic hunches, receptiveness to the irrational, capacity for personal love, feeling for nature, and last but not least – his relation to the unconscious. It is no mere chance that in olden times priestness (like the Greek Sibyl) were used to fathom the divine will and to make connection with the gods . . .

In its individual manifestation the character of a man's anima is as a rule shaped by his mother. If he feels that his mother had a negative influence on him, his anima will often express itself in irritable, depressed moods, uncertainty, insecurity, and touchiness. (If, however, he is able to overcome the negative assaults on himself, they can serve to reinforce his masculinity.)

(pp. 186/7)

Another way in which the negative anima in a man's personality can be revealed is in waspish, poisonous, effeminate remarks by which he devalues everything. Remarks of this sort always contain a cheap twisting of the truth and are in a subtle way destructive. There are legends throughout the world in which 'a poison damsel' (as they call her in the Orient) appears. She is a beautiful creature who has weapons hidden in her body or a secret poison with which she kills her lovers during their first night together. In this guise the anima is as cold and reckless as certain uncanny aspects of nature itself, and in Europe is often expressed to this day by the belief in witches.

(p. 190)

Ball clearly does not understand himself. He says to Jim about the Flower Phantom, 'Sounds like a real screwball. My mom always taught me to respect women.' (p. 17) But we know that Ball is sexist towards women. Look at how the chapter opens:

> Good grief, look at the tits on that one,' Jim said.
> 'Jesus. Would you look at that. I'd like to take that one for a horseback ride all night long. Yeeeooooww.'
> (p. 13)

This is obviously sexist. Whereas, then, some readers have jumped on Reed's novel and taken it to be an attack on Alice Walker, *The Color Purple* and on feminists generally – 'Feminists object to the central character of Reed's novel, the playwright Ian Ball, a sexist womanizer,' says Maya Harris[59] – in fact Reed is beginning his novel by showing us the lack of balance in his protagonist, Ian Ball, who needs to recognize his anima.

Ball's friend, Jim Minsk, is a famous and powerful director who is going to direct his play. However, he is killed in a horrifying way in a southern university named the Mary Phegan college. The novel notes that this type of anti-semitism is very old in Christianity: it is an old paranoia, of a white Christian blonde woman being raped by Jewish men and later by black men. This is the connection between Jim and Ian; but Jim had not believed his father, a Russian immigrant, who said that anti-semitism was increasing in the United States. Jim was invited South ostensibly to watch the annual play of the Mary Phegan college but in fact as a sacrificial victim to born-again Christian paranoia. The person responsible for leading Jim into the trap is an old black radical, a 'Mau Mau' who looks more white than black; so much for Ms. Kakutani's implication that black males are not seriously criticized in the novel:

> Mr. Reed does not appear to taken an entirely even-handed stance. Some kinds of prejudice seem to concern him more than others . . . the sexist banter of men tends to come off as sort of 'boys will be boys' silliness.

After Jim's death, Becky French, the feminist who controls what will be put on in the theater, gives Ian a new director: Tremonisha Smarts.

Wha? Ishmael Reed is to be guided by Alice Walker? Isn't Ishmael Reed criticizing Alice Walker? Didn't Ms. Kakutani say,

> Mr Reed tends to stack the cards against certain characters by
> having them all too neatly recant at the end of the book: Tremonisha
> Smarts makes a lengthy confession, admitting that she's been used as
> a tool by white feminists, that she now intends to tend house, take
> care of her man and get pregnant?

But let us pay attention to the name: Tremonisha Smarts. Her
name sounds very much like the title of an opera by Scott Joplin
that was not produced in his lifetime because ragtime was not
quite accepted as serious music on the same plane as classical
music: *Treemonisha*. Reed says in *Mumbo Jumbo*.

> Scott Joplin has healed many with his ability to summon this X
> factor, the Thing that Freud saw, the indefinable quality that James
> Weldon Johnson called 'Jes Grew.'
> (p. 211)

In *Treemonisha*, the protagonist is found near a tree by a white
woman named 'Monisha', who gives her her name. She gets
formally educated, thanks to her mother, and she gets very smart.
But why does Reed drop one 'e' from the name? By dropping the
'e', 'tree' becomes 'tre', which, in sound, suggests *French* for
'very': added to 'monisha', her name suggests 'very mother',
which brings in once again the question of mother=anima.
Towards the end of the opera, Treemonisha saves the community
from the root workers, the evildoers who were deceiving it by its
(the community's) superstitious beliefs.[60] Ian Ball actually begins
learning from Tremonisha:

> She knew her business. He had a tendency to tell rather than show,
> and she was teaching him the art of description. The art of
> movement. The art of character differentiation.
> (p. 72)

For the first time in a novel, Reed actually describes the contents
of rooms before he gets to the characters. Tremonisha also has a
good effect on Ball on a personal level: 'Tre had taught him to
communicate to a woman without having to devise strategies for
getting them into bed.' (p. 120) And Ian does not get, or try to get,
Tremonisha into bed, although he recklessly eyeballed her early
in the novel.

Ian almost beats up a critic, Paul Shoboater. (Watch that name:

naming is very important to black Americans, who were denied the power to even name themselves.) Shoboater made a negative reference to his mother, and Ball almost lost control. From the Dozens, we know that Ball is not strong because he could not control himself after the reference to his mother. He does not know his father. He has found a father-substitute in Jake Brashford, the Ellison figure. He is always quoting Brashford, e.g. about the Flower Phantom, he says to Tremonisha,

> Brashford said that throughout history when the brothers feel that they're being pushed against the wall, they strike back and when they do strike back it's like a tornado, uprooting, flinging about, and dashing to pieces everything in its path. A tornado has no conscience. He says the fellas feel that they are catching it from all sides.
> (p. 51)

The reference to 'the fellas' shows that there is a community, a male community, out there watching what is going on in the world; it also shows Ball's lack of balance with the feminine in himself. He is in two minds about the Flower Phantom, who has been striking at feminists, shaving their heads because he said this is what the Resistance did to the French women who collaborated with the Nazis during the occupation, and then leaving a chrysanthemum as a calling card. Tremonisha was his first victim. When Ball is waiting to meet Tremonisha:

> Tremonisha was about forty-five minutes late, which gave him an opportunity to read *The New York Pillar*. The Flower Phantom, as the man who assaulted Tremonisha Smarts was called, had struck again, this time tying up at gunpoint and shaving the head of a feminist writer who had suggested in a book that the typical rapist was a black man. The newspaper was calling the culprit a hair fetishist because of his practice of collecting the victim's hair and placing it in a black plastic bag. A sketch of the Flower Phantom appeared in all of the newspapers. Panels of experts discussed him on television. Some black men began to appear in public wearing a chrysanthemum pinned to their clothes. Ian's head told him that this man was a lunatic who should be put away for a long time, but his gut was cheering the man on. His head was Dr. Jekyll, but his gut was Mr. Hyde.
> (pp. 50/1)

The problem of the lack of balance because of lack of recognition of the anima can be seen in the portraits and fates of other characters, chief among them Detective O'Reedy. This is how Ms. Katutani introduces and describes him:

> To make his points with full shock value, Mr. Reed himself employs stereotypes, creating a gallery of repellent characters, all painted in the flat, bright primary colors of farce. Detective Lawrence O'Reedy ('Loathsome Larry'), the cop who's pursuing 'the Flower Phantom,' is an Irish bully who combines the worst traits of Archie Bunker and Dirty Harry and is forever romanticizing 'the old days' when 'white men were in charge' and police brutality was never a community issue.

The description is accurate as far as it goes, but it does not go far enough. True, O'Reedy is based on Dirty Harry. Just as Dirty Harry made a statement before he blasted criminals to hell, so too does O'Reedy: and just as Reagan quoted the saying, so too we are told O'Reedy's line 'became immortal, even quoted by politicians' (p. 10). What is O'Reedy's line? 'Give me something to write home to Mother about.' (p. 7) Is this just a *Mad Magazine* rewriting of Dirty Harry's line, 'Make my day'? Is O'Reedy Dirty Harry/Clint Eastwood? (On page 73 we are told Clint Eastwood was his idol.) Look again: it has 'Mother' in it. So O'Reedy has the same problem as Ian Ball: he is a sexist because he has not come to terms with his anima. And this lack of balance means he blasts 'criminals' without any qualms of conscience. But who are these 'criminals' he blasts with the gun he names 'Nancy', a woman's name, also coming from 'Aunt Nancy', i.e. 'Anansi', in the south? Those who society, because of its stereotyped beliefs reinforced by commercialized art, believes are criminals. He had just loved *Wrong-Headed Man*; he too loves seeing black men as sexual beasts (King Kong, Mighty Joe Young): the play has reinforced his idea of the black man as criminal.

Did I say without qualms of conscience? Note the following extract:

> Recently he had been having bad dreams in which he'd seen the faces of the dead he'd dispatched to the land of ghosts, blown-up before him. And then, this morning, was it a man, with a part of his skull missing and blood on his shirt, in his house, sitting in his chair, reading his newspaper? It looked up from the newspaper and grinned

at O'Reedy, a mass of putrefying flesh hanging from its skull. He screamed and ran back into the bedroom to grab Nancy. Betsy said that she was sure that he was just having a nightmare, but when he went back to get the newspaper, the man had gone, yet the newspaper was scattered about the floor and not outside, on the doormat, folded neatly. Must have been the spaghetti and meatballs he ate the night before. The way he looked at it, those men deserved to die. I mean, they were running away, weren't they, so they must have been guilty. Well, maybe that black jogger was innocent, but it was dark the morning he shot him. He couldn't see so well, and besides there had been a number of rapes in that park. Everybody knew that all black men did was rape white women, so too bad for the jogger, but, well, the way O'Reedy looked at it, this was war, and in war a lot of innocent people get killed. But then, the other day he had opened the shower curtain and those three P.R.s he'd shot one night after a rooftop chase were standing there in the shower, nude, and singing some song in Spanish, and the bullet holes were still visible on their chests, and he didn't understand the Spanish. What really haunted him was the jogger's name: O'Reedy, same as his. (pp. 8/9)

O'Reedy's conscience forces its way up through dreams and hallucinations. The black jogger he has killed has the same name as he: from Jung, as we saw in the chapter on Ebejer, we can tell that the black jogger is O'Reedy's shadow. On one level, this is a classic American song and act, Me and my Shadow, the white man and his black partner in a vaudeville sketch. On another level, the *shadow* is explained by Ahmad Harb as

> an archetypal figure which represents the qualities which the ego considers negative, or does not need and so they are pushed aside or repressed. The shadow symbolizes our 'other side', our 'dark brother' who is an invisible but inseparable part of our psychic totality.[61]

The black jogger, then, is the shadow of O'Reedy: and both are manifestations of Ishmael Reed, who discovered a few years ago that he has some Irish ancestry.[62] Detective O'Reedy has therefore also not come to terms with his shadow. Since he has not come to terms with his anima, he continually asserts his manhood, putting down women, fondling his gun Nancy, killing non-white men, condemning men who are effeminate.

His son suddenly tells him that he wants to teach Irish studies:

'I think he's doing the right thing, dear,' Mrs. O'Reedy said.

'Who's asking you. Get back into the kitchen.'

'Yes, dear,' she said, returning to the kitchen.

'What can you learn about Irishmen in a university that you can't down at the local gin mill?'

'Look, I have to go, Dad. My date.'

'Probably some fucking hippie like the last one. Kept interrupting all of the male guests with her crazy ideas, embarrassing me in front of my buddies and their wives. She wouldn't even offer to help with the dishes. Yet you got all high and mighty when I tried to introduce you to those hookers that time when I was trying to help you learn things.'

'You hate yourself, Pop, you're Irish, yet you don't think that the Irish have produced anything worthwhile. You and your father, just carrying out the orders of people who hate you, who treat you no differently than they would a stage Irishman, a clown –'

'Now, you wait –' O'Reedy said, rising.

'A great Irish-American writer like James T. Farrell had to borrow money from friends because the Irish were so busy trying to assimilate that they didn't support their artistic geniuses, ignored them because they were considered too ethnic by people on the make. Reminded them of a world they wanted to leave behind, and so they use your pop –'

'How would you like to get a good belt –'

'That's right. Be their Dirty Harry Callahan. If you can't get your way, use violence. You're like the middle men all over the world, the muscle, the fists for people who spit on your kind, you're protecting their property by beating up people. You and your father, both mercenaries. At the turn of the century they used your father against the Jews on the Lower East Side and against other Irish. Why do you think they call those vehicles that transport prisoners paddy wagons? Did you ever think of that? And now they use you against the blacks and the Puerto Ricans.'

'That's enough outta you.'

'Don't you think I don't know about those three Spanish guys and that jogger –' O'Reedy knocked his son over the sofa he was standing in front of.

'Get up! Get up! I'll teach you.' His wife ran from the kitchen screaming.

'You keep out of this,' he said. One Spanish guy was standing behind Sean. He was thumb-nosing O'Reedy, mocking him. The other two Spanish guys sat on the edge of the couch behind which Sean was beginning to rise. One had a radio next to his head and the other was popping his fingers. They were wearing party shirts and dark glasses. O'Reedy stepped back, a look of horror on his face.

'Dad, what's wrong?' Sean said. As he said that, the black jogger ran through the room, entering through one wall and exiting through

another. O'Reedy went for his gun, but before he could fire Sean
knocked it out of his hand.

'I . . .' his father was in a daze. Sean and Mrs. O'Reedy escorted
him to the couch.

'I'll be all right. I just need a drink. Son, I'm sorry I just
haven't . . .'

'It's all right,' Sean said, going to the kitchen to remove a bottle of
whiskey from the cabinet. O'Reedy's wife remained in the room. She
sat next to him on the couch. He put his head in her lap and began
to sob.

'Don't worry, dear,' she said. 'You'll be retiring soon.'
(pp. 91/2)

O'Reedy does retire, from his job and from his one-sidedness. He
makes his speech in which he apologizes for all the wrong he has
done. The crowd keeps yelling, 'Give me something to write home
to Mother about,' but significantly *he* does not say it. Instead, he
praises his wife and his son, thanks Lieutenant Brown for saving
him from the alleged Flower Phantom, and says:

I was against Brown, the other blacks, the Hispanics, and the women
coming on the force. You know how hard it is for an old guy like me
to change, but you know, now that they're here I'm wondering, hey,
how did we get along without them all these years . . .
(pp. 122/3)

He looks at the dome ceiling, sees an ascension mural – and sees
the black jogger and other people floating towards heaven,
including 'the Amazon who had laid down her sword and
removed her helmet,' his relatives, 'his Mom and Dad,' the three
Spanish guys. 'Wait for me, wait for me,' he calls out and
collapses. He says to his wife, 'You've been so great to me, and
I've been like a – a – I stink – I had my whores.' (p. 124) To his son,
he admits he was right, he was 'their errand boy.' With this
confession seeking wholeness – note that he sees his Mom *and* his
Dad – it is no surprise that O'Reedy's shadow comes to take him
up and that the Amazon laid down her sword and removed her
helmet, thus indicating that he was no longer at war with his
negative anima. In contrast, note Ian Ball's dream about the
Amazons:

all of those giant Amazon women that Shoboater had said were on
the walls of museums on the domed ceilings of churches, and on

public buildings in Europe had escaped and were chasing him and
the fellas through the streets. These giant women didn't seem to have
much difficulty in catching them, despite the heavy clothing they
were wearing. None of them tripped over her skirt. They were
'monstropolous,' as Zora Neale Hurston would say.
(p. 88)

Ian Ball and Detective O'Reedy are two possibilities of the same person: namely, Ishmael Reed.

The problems caused for black men by *Wrong-Headed Man* cannot be dealt with merely with a scathing attack on the play and the author, although this is what some critics assume Reed has done. 'To think oneself free simply because one can claim – can utter – the negation of an assertion is not to think deeply enough,' says Henry Louis Gates, Jr.[63] Reed's criticism is deeper than the negation of an assertion: it is that Tremonisha's play is un-balanced and both reflects and reinforces the lack of balance in the society. Since Ian Ball listens to rock 'n' roll, we can provide the other side to *Wrong-Headed Man* from a hit by Elvis Presley from the 1958 movie *King Creole*, 'Hard Headed Woman', which begins,

Well a hard headed woman, soft hearted man
Been the cause o' trouble ever since the world began
Oh yeh, ever since the world began – uh-huh-huh-huh
A hard headed woman been a thorn in the side of man.[64]

Trumpets mock and trombones wail while the singer gives examples from Biblical history where hard-headed woman has caused soft-hearted man problems, coming down to present times. This blues-based song would be as one-sided as *Wrong-Headed Man* if it were not for the fact that at the end, the singer recognizes how much he would miss his woman if she left. Only the last verse is actually sung in the movie.

Art has power, art has an effect. Becky French has been influenced in her thought and behavior by a Nazi propaganda film, *Jud Süss* (p. 60). Reed says,

Film and television, besides being sources of entertainment, are the
most powerful instruments of propaganda ever created by man, and
the Nazi period has proved that, in sinister hands, they can be used
to harm unpopular groups and scapegoats.[65]

We are told by Jake Brashford what art should be:

> Hell, if I'm writing articles about freedom all the time, and they
> bored with that, then let them be bored, because *in the old African
> tales we came here with* – the ones we knew before they took our
> brains to the cleaners – *the god of drama demands that you tell the
> truth*, so lying is violating some sacred oath in a manner of speaking.
> (p. 26, my italics)

Given the rock 'n' roll connection – Ian has 'rock and roll records'
on page 121 – we realize that the line when Brashford calls Ball a
gangster and a con artist can be related to Jerry Leiber and Mike
Stoller's 'Hound Dog', turned into hits by Big Mama Thornton
and Elvis Presley, particularly in the live version on *Elvis as
Recorded at Madison Square Garden*.[66] Alice Walker has a story
based on the Elvis/Big Mama Thornton/'Hound Dog' connection, narrated by the Big Mama figure, entitled 'Nineteen
Fifty-Five' in the collection, *You Can't Keep a Good Woman
Down*.[67]

It is the lack of balance, of coming to terms with the anima, that
leads to a desire to aggressively assert manhood and nationhood.
This is what lies behind racism and anti-Semitism as well.
Thinking of Becky French's decision to produce a play about Eva
Braun in which Eva is presented as an innocent victim, Trem-
onisha says to Ian that she discovered that on the night of his
Austrian triumph, Hitler slept in a bed with a picture of Josephine
Baker hanging above the head. He hated jazz and was always
scolding Eva about her collection of jazz records, Tremonisha
says, so why didn't he order Josephine Baker's picture to be
removed? 'He was getting even with his mother,' she says (p. 64).
She goes on to explain:

> He had her [his mother's] picture on the wall of his bedroom, but the
> night that he's away from his room, sort of a shrine to his mother, he
> fantasizes about sleeping with the demon princess, the wild temptress
> Lilith, Erzulie, the flapper who brought jazz dance to the Folies.

She says that Jesus had the same problem: 'Jesus, Hitler, both had
weak fathers and strong, manipulative mothers.' (p. 65) She goes
on to say that Hitler was part Jewish. Ian is startled. 'Tremonisha,
are you saying that World War Two happened because Hitler was

trying to pass for white?' 'Overzealous assimilation,' she replies, 'it happens all the time.'

Before we conclude that this is too simplistic, we have Ian telling Shoboater that

> Tremonisha says that Hitler was Jewish and that the reason he hated Jews was because he actually hated himself, or wanted the approval of white people.
> (p. 85)

'She got it all wrong,' Shoboater replies.

> It was the German nation that tried to become white . . . The Germans have too much Tartar blood to be Nordic. The Khans left onion-shaped domes all over Germany, and that is not all they left. Hitler probably had more Mongol blood than anything else; most of those people come out of central Asia. There's still no hard evidence that Hitler was Jewish, regardless of what Tremonisha says. It was the German nation that went crazy trying to be white; they tried everything, they tried to claim the Greeks, they tried to claim the Egyptians. Nothing worked, and so Hitler came along and said *you're white* so often that they believed it, and so for as long as Hitler was in power, every German person stood in front of his mirror and didn't see himself, but saw a blond, blue-eyed Aryan. Talking about schizophrenia. He had them mesmerized.
> (p. 86)

As Paul and Ian continue talking, this is what happens:

> 'I got to hand it you, Ball. You're the original malevolent rabbit. You couldn't care less about what happened to Brashford. As soon as you stop using him, you'll use somebody else. Your mother was like that. Wasn't she arrested?' Ball leaned over and grabbed the sucker by the collar. The diners looked at the pair, but Ball didn't care. He let him go. Shoboater was trembling . . .
>   'I'm sorry, Paul. But when somebody puts my mother down, I just go crazy.' Besides, he wanted Shoboater to write a good review of *Reckless Eyeballing*.
> (p. 87)

Ball is being connected to Hitler through the reference to the mother, a reference that is stressed when Ball attends the play about – and, as we discover, *by* – Eva Braun a few pages later. The Eva character says,

> Look at that bitch . . . God, that woman has been dead these many years, but she still controls him. Sometimes when he's making love to me, if you want to call it that, he calls out her name. Klara. Oh, Klara. It's disgusting. And if you knew what I know about him in bed, then you'd understand why he's trying to conquer all of these countries and be such a big man.
> (pp. 97/8)

I am not saying that Ball is as bad as the genocidal Hitler or that their mothers are equally bad: just that they have a similar problem, according to the novel, expressed through an unbalanced relationship with the mother and a lack of a true relationship with the father.

Various characters accuse others being tools of racism or of acting against black men. The chief accusation is against Tremonisha Smarts. She is the first victim of the Flower Phantom. When O'Reedy comes to investigate, she tells him, 'He said all sorts of political things. Said that I was giving the black man a bad name.' (pp. 10/11) 'Probably some psycho with wounded masculine pride,' O'Reedy says, not realizing that this applies to himself. Her play is the thing: and it is causing problems for her too. As she says over the phone to the person producing the film, 'It's fiction, I told you – you keep asking me did it really happen? No, I never had incest with my father.' (p. 11)

As a Jew, Jim is very familiar with scapegoatism. He tells Ball, 'The Europeans were massacring Jews before they went into Africa after the blacks. Ancient Christians hated the Jews.' (p. 15)

> I just hate misinformation, Ian. The Jews own the media, the Jews own the garment district, the Jews own this, the Jews own that. They just libel Jews with that shit so's to take their minds off those who really own it. That's the same shit they used against you blacks.
> (p. 16)

It is Brashford who has the most political explanation about the black-male-bashing:

> It's these white women who are carrying on the attack against black men today, because they struck a deal with white men who run the country. *You give us women the jobs, the opportunities, and we'll take the heat off of you and put it on Mose* [the black American male], is the deal they struck. They have maneuvered these white boys who

run the country, but they have to keep the persecution thing up in order to win new followers, and so they jump on po' Mose. They get Tremonisha and Johnnie Kranshaw to be their proxies in this attack. Sort of like the rich used to hire poor people to fight their wars. As for these Jewish women who are putting a hurtin' on black dudes in print – they know they can't change Abraham, Isaac, and Jacob, so they're rehearsing on us, and backing these literary sleep-in maids who are coming down on the brothers in a foul and horrendous manner. Now I don't approve of violence, but I can't help secretly applauding what – that crazy dude did to Tremonisha.
(pp. 26/7)

We tend to believe that Brashford is speaking for Reed since he is like a father to Ian. In this particular case, his view seems to be borne out by the rest of the novel. It is foolish to dismiss conspiracy theories by definition, as Ms. Katutani does. Larry Abraham says in *Call it Conspiracy*:

Those who believe that major world events result from planning are laughed at for believing in the 'conspiracy theory of history.' Of course, no one in this modern day and age really believes in the conspiracy theory of history – except those who have taken the time to study the subject. When you think about it, there are really only two theories of history. Either things happen by accident neither planned nor caused by anybody, or they happen because they *are* planned and somebody causes them to happen. In reality, it is the 'accidental theory of history' preached in the unhallowed Halls of Ivy which should be ridiculed.[68]

We note from the above that it explains one of the meanings of the title of Reed's sixth novel, *The Terrible Twos*, where conspiracies are seething under the surface and only a few people find out. When the President goes on T.V. to expose a big one, he is locked up in an insane asylum. Abraham continues,

the most effective weapons used against the conspiratorial theory of history are ridicule and satire. These extremely potent weapons can be cleverly used to avoid any honest attempt at refuting the facts. After all, nobody likes to be made fun of. Rather than be ridiculed most people will keep quiet; and this subject certainly does lend itself to ridicule and satire. One technique is to expand the conspiracy to the extent it becomes absurd . . .
'Intellectuals' are fond of mouthing clichés like, 'The conspiracy theory is often tempting. However, it is overly simplistic.' To ascribe

absolutely everything that happens to the machinations of a small group of power hungry conspirators *is* overly simplistic. On the other hand nothing is more simplistic than doggedly holding onto the accidental view of major world events.
(pp. 10/11)

Abraham notes that history books are full of the schemes of small groups of men which have conspired to bring the reins of power into their hands. He says,

> there *have* been Hitlers and Lenins and Stalins and Caesars and Alexander the Greats throughout history. Why should we assume there are no such men today with the same ambition?
> (p. 20)

So we should tread carefully before dismissing the conspiracies in Reed's fiction without doing any reading ourselves. The colonizers did not succeed by telegraphing their objectives. The colonial 'scouts' went out on behalf of forces at home.

Tremonisha is smart and discovers that she has been used. Ian overhears an argument she is having with Becky about his play:

> 'I'm not going to produce that play as it is. We have . . . standards to uphold.' In his mind's eye, he could see Becky shake her head like a filly when she said *standards*.
> 'It's not standards. You're worried about that monologue. It's political, isn't it? You don't like the monologue, you bitch, admit it. You white feminists sound more like the white man with each passing day. In fact, the only thing your dipshit movement has produced is more white men. Standards. All the mediocre shit that you produce by these junior womanists. You've got your nerve talking about standards. Why do you always feel the need to castrate the black man?'
> (p. 75)

Becky blames Tremonisha, saying she is the one the black men picketed. But Tremonisha says that it is Becky's fault because she listed her as a spokesperson for all black women in the press release and insisted she write in the scene about the man throwing his wife downstairs. Becky gets mad and says,

> Look, Ms., I made you and I can destroy you. I filled that theater with women and got you those interviews in the magazines. You

were nothing. Reading your diatribes in quaint little coffee shops on
the Lower East Side. I created you. I gave you prominence. But
don't get smart. There's always somebody else who'll take your
place.
(p. 76)

But thanks to her work on Ian's play, Tremonisha gets wise while
Ian is the person who takes her place. Later, the black feminist
writer who had preceded Tremonisha says, 'Now that Tre has left, I
I wonder who Becky's whore is now.' Ball drops his cup of coffee.
(p. 143) He had changed the ending of his play so that it would get
produced and he would be taken off the sex-list, altered it so that
Ham Hill is found guilty of reckless eyeballing. Brashford had
seen the ending of Ball's play while Ball was watching the play
about Eva Braun in the same building. Brashford called him 'a
gangster and a con artist', 'a trickologist', a 'mischievous
malicious bastard', saying, 'I'm your literary father, you shit. And
look at what you've done to me.' (pp. 106/7) Ball does not care
because two feminists 'who had wrongly attempted to censor his
work' had been crying in repentance in his arms. One said,

> Mr. Ball. I have an apology to make . . . I was chairperson of
> women's studies at a small obscure university in Cincinnati and . . .
> One of my students wanted to write a dissertation on your plays and
> I – I – . . . I turned her down. I said you were a notorious sexist even
> though I hadn't seen any of your work.
> (p. 105)

The 'person' found guilty of 'reckless eyeballing' is a skeleton
with no eyes – and strictly, no sex – while others are guilty of the
deed: Ian Ball, Jim Minsk, and even O'Reedy.

As for Tremonisha, she leaves for Yuba City and writes Ian a
long and wise letter after she has felt some pain, that is, after she
smarts:

> I was writing about some brutal black guys who I knew in my life
> who beat women, abandoned their children, cynical, ignorant, and
> arrogant, you know these types, but my critics and the people who
> praised me took some of these characters and made them out to be
> *all* black men. That hurt me. The black ones who hated me and the
> white ones who loved me were both unfair to me. Nobody takes the
> crude and hateful white men like Hoss and Crow in Sam Shepard's
> plays and says that these men represent all white men. Has anybody

> ever said that Richard III represented all white men? That all white
> men craved to lock children in a tower somewhere for perverse
> reasons? [Her producer is named Towers.] Nobody ever said Lady
> MacBeth or Medea represented all white women. That all white
> women manipulated their husbands into committing acts of murder
> or desired to murder their children. I thought they were my fans,
> those feminists, but some of them would have drinks and ask me
> about the 'raw sex' and how black men were, you know. Others used
> my black male characters as an excuse to hate all black men,
> especially some of these white women. Then they wouldn't feel so
> guilty for taking their jobs.
> (p. 130)

She has also discovered that Ian was right: that it wasn't so much
black men killing women as women killing the men and getting
off. Her new play is about a woman who leaves her husband for
another woman only to discover she was a batterer for 'this is a
problem that the male-loathing feminists don't want to discuss:
women beating up on women.' (p. 131) She is with her man, Dred
Creme, whom she is bringing back to health and good music. In
Alice Walker's *Meridian*, the protagonist, a black woman, helps
the black man, Truman Held, find himself at the end.[69]

Ms. Kakutani says that Reed 'tends to stack the cards against
certain characters by having them all too neatly recant at the end
of the book.' Haven't we heard the phrase 'too neatly' before,
when Griffiths dealt with *The Late Emancipation of Jerry Stover*?
Ms. Kakutani has missed the real ending. She says of the end,

> Tremonisha Smarts makes a lengthy confession, admitting that she's
> been used as a tool by white feminists, that she now intends to tend
> house, take care of her man and get pregnant; another black female
> writer makes a similar admission.

But aren't we suspicious of the too neat killing off of 'the Flower
Phantom', who turns out to be Randy Shanks, who had had a
good thing going as a black writer living in Europe until
Tremonisha's writing got the women there to turn against him
and who was the doorman to Tremonisha's apartment building?
Structurally, does his death not come too soon: thirty-eight pages,
i.e. a quarter of the way from the end? No: the end is different
from what Ms. Kakutani says.

Ball goes home from New York City. Whereas we had assumed

that 'south' meant the American south, it is even more south than
that, 'south' as the Third World is 'south', a Caribbean island like
Haiti named New Oyo. (This is also the country Paul Shoboater
comes from: Ian can see the Shoboater estate when he arrives.)
When he gets to his mother's spacious house, he embraces his
mother and gives her the Tina Turner albums she asked for.

> His mother and her friends were crazy about Tina Turner, way down
> here, and come to think of it his mother did resemble Tina Turner,
> full in the thighs her hair worn down the sides of her face, and the
> kind of lips that you get when you cross an Arawak and a
> Congolese.'
> (p. 133)

He thinks,

> The fellas had said that Ms. Turner's song, 'Private Dancers'
> symbolized the bond between white men and Third World women all
> over the Americas. It was their love anthem.
> (pp. 133/4)

Ian meets Johnnie Kranshaw, who is now staying with his mother
and who explains to him how she broke from Becky French. A
friend of hers had written a book about natural childbirth and the
black community and she (Johnnie) asked Becky to see if she
could get it published:

> 'Boy, did that bitch get hot. She turned red as a beet, and started
> talking so loud some of the other people in the restaurant started
> looking our way. She said that neither she nor her friends in
> publishing would have anything to do with a book whose subject
> matter was even remotely connected to the penis.
>   She said that the penis had been used as a weapon against all
> women for thousands of years and that there would be no peace in
> the world as long as men were not disarmed of their penises.' The
> fellas were right about Becky, Ian thought.
>   'What did you say?' Martha asked. Johnnie Kranshaw closed her
> eyes and transmitted her answer to Becky. 'I turned to the bitch, cool
> as you can be, and I said, "Heifer, you wouldn't even be here if it
> wasn't for some man's thing."
> (p. 139)

The result was that whereas Johnnie's photo, supposed to appear
on the cover of the feminist magazine, *Mama* (note the mother

connection again – Tremonisha was called 'Ms.' earlier) was replaced by that of Tremonisha,' just as surely as Eddie Murphy had replaced Richard Pryor.' All the praise they had heaped on her play, *No Good Man*, was taken back and nobody in New York was doing her work.

Becky had turned against men because of some bad experiences she had had with them. She had not, therefore, come to terms with her animus. Tremonisha had also had bad experiences with men. Her man, Dred Creme, a musician, had been beating her when Ian had come in and saved her. He asked her, 'why do middle class women like you go out with guys who want to beat you up and take your money?' Later, as we have seen, she writes that she is in Yuba City and is helping Dred Creme recover. So unlike Becky, she is not running away from man but is going to help save him. *She is coming to terms with her animus.* On a broader level, the novel asks the question of whether the white blonde virgin such as we see in the play to which Jim is invited represents to Christians the anima they will not recognize. Ian's mother sees the problem in literal terms, saying cynically to Johnnie that maybe the American male

> can't find no sexual satisfaction at home so he uses these military exercises as a cover for finding exotic women, women that will give him the pleasure he don't get at home. They have been leaving those Anglo women since the Crusades, going over into the Arabian countries, raping women. Trying to find women who won't give them none of that 'Dear, I have a headache tonight.' Look at all the different kinds of babies that the Caucasian man has left all over the world.
> (p. 140)

Martha Ball has never told her son that his father was Koffee Martin, the revolutionary leader who had been executed and who was the national hero. Koffee's first wife wouldn't let him go. She and Martha were the only people in New Oyo with 'the Indian gift,' the gift of second sight. She told on Koffee to the police. He went to the United States, where he became a famous leader. But he was framed and deported and was beaten to death in jail in his country. The night before, Martha had bribed guards to let her into the cell and 'when she left Koffee she was one going on two.' (p. 146) When Abiahu, the first wife, found out that Martha was pregnant with Ian,

> she told everybody that she's put a hex on the child and that he
> would be born a two-head, of two minds, the one not knowing what
> the other was up to.
> (p. 146)

Martha opens the bags and finds videotapes, whose titles are
listed, the most significant one in terms of my interpretation in the
first section of the chapter being *The Werewolf of London*. She
thinks,

> Had the green fingers. Could he bring up a flower, and that favorite
> flower of his, the chrysanthemum, that smelly flower, people said
> couldn't grow down here, but he grew it. That greenhouse that she
> built for him out back. He used to go all over the island, giving away
> chrysanthemums. Chrysanthemums became his calling card. I bet he
> doesn't remember any of that . . .
> (p. 147)

Within a few lines, our suspicions are confirmed:

> She went over to the last bag, a green army bag, that he sometimes
> used to carry his belongings. She opened it. It smelled sour. Inside
> was a dirty, crumpled leather coat. A beret. A dirty white air force
> scarf, and a black mask. Underneath this she found human hair.
> Many textures and colors. Fuzzy, frizzy, straight, silky, stringy,
> brittle. 'Johnnie come up here. I need your help,' she screamed.
> (pp. 147/8)

So Ian Ball is the Flower phantom and did not know it. He is a
split personality, or 'schizophrenic', to use the incorrect but
popular term mentioned by Paul Shoboater. There was a clue
earlier, when we were told Ball thought of himself as Jekyll and
Hyde, but we did not pay attention, taking it to be just a turn of
expression. Why the chrysanthemum? One meaning is contained
in the joke told by Brashford:

> A Jew, a Pole, and a black man arrive at the pearly gates and are
> told by Saint Peter that they can only enter the Kingdom if they spell
> a word. The Jew and the Pole are asked to spell God. They do and
> are admitted. The black man is asked to spell chrysanthemum.
> (p. 28)

But there are other explanations. Chrysanthemums are commonly known in the United States as 'mums', which is the British spelling of 'moms'. It would not be stretching the imagination too far to see the flower as the mandala. Von Franz says, 'The contemplation of a mandala is meant to bring an inner peace, a feeling that life has again found its meaning and order.'[70] Everyone needs to find wholeness, not only the women or only the men. It is because Ball has no wholeness that he cannot make love to a woman. For example, notice the way he makes love to Cora Mae's lawyer from his play, the ex-wife of Towers Bradshaw the movie director: 'He took her home and fucked her until she was sore.' (p. 109) In contrast is his father as remembered by his mother: 'Making love to that man was what making love to chocolate or rum would be like if they could assume a human form.' (p. 145) This is a positive linguistic use of the enslaving products of colonial monoculture. As for Ian, his hair fetish comes from his yearning for woman and for wholeness: Tina Turner has a mane of hair, which is even more of her trademark than her thighs, and 'his mother did resemble Tina Turner, full in the thighs, her hair worn down the sides of her face.' (p. 133) Tremonisha and O'Reedy find wholeness while Ian Ball is his mother's problem at the end. This is the first novel which Reed does not end on an optimistic, upbeat or humorous note. Instead, it ends with a challenge comparable to that in Salkey's first novel. Ball's mother seeks the help of a wiser black feminist: 'Johnnie, come up here. I need your help.'

While several of the characters lack balance, *the novel* is not unbalanced. For example the anti-semitism of Brashford and Randy Shanks is balanced by the pro-Jewishness of Paul Shoboater, who says to Ian,

The Jews are the only ones standing between black people and these barbarians from Europe that are over here. What do you think that the Posse Comitatus, the Order, and the other right-wing outpatient clinic is talking about when they say 'bleeding heart liberals.' They're talking about the Jews. Plain and simple. And every year I send one-tenth of my salary to the Anti-Defamation League because they're keeping an eye on these people who not only hate the Jews but hate blacks too. You can't depend upon this black middle-class to do that, or the black intellectuals . . . If it wasn't for Jewish morality these people would be burning niggers left and right.
(pp. 83/4)

Shoboater could be echoing Fanon:

> It was my philosophy professor, a native of the Antilles, who
> recalled the fact to me one day, 'Whenever you hear anyone abuse
> the Jews, pay attention, because he is talking about you.'[71]

It should be no surprise, then, that Shoboater is the only critic
with the integrity and insight to write the truth about Ball's
play:

> *Reckless Eyeballing* is marred by flat characters, but that's not the
> worst offense that Ian Ball has committed in this piece of rubbish.
> Mr. Ball has a way of talking out of both sides of his mouth, as
> though he were of two heads or of two minds. When misogyny was
> in, he wrote *Suzanna* . . . If Ian Ball was as good a playwright as he
> is a cunning opportunist, and a flexible equivocating and ambitious
> knave, maybe he would deserve the overpraise that this play is
> bound to receive.
> (p. 127)

Reed has already placed a judgement of Ian Ball within the novel
yet hostile critics did not notice. They did not read. As for Ian, he
does not care about the truth of Shoboater's review since it is
buried on page 68: what matters to him is the favorable review by
the feminist critic on the front page.

Michele Wallace got fooled by *Reckless Eyeballing*. Viciously
attacking Reed in *The Village Voice*, in 'Female Troubles: Ishmael
Reed's Tunnel Vision,' she says:

> Ian Ball, *clearly a stand-in for Reed*, doesn't know his ass from his
> elbow when it comes to American feminism – which, I suppose,
> makes him yet another Afro-American trickster figure, like PaPa
> LaBas in *Mumbo Jumbo* and *The Last Days of Louisiana Red*, like
> Raven Quickskill in *Flight to Canada*, like Black Peter in *Terrible
> Twos*. In Afro-American folklore, tricksters are characters steeped in
> motherwit who turn the shortcomings of powerlessness to advantage.
> Reed has grafted on this agenda the conflicting demands of an edenic
> triangle that owes most of its inspiration to patriarchy.
> Consequently, his tricksters have been undergoing a fierce process of
> degeneration and an identity crisis that won't wait.[72]

Ms. Wallace has picked out the trickster figures in Reed and still
has been tricked. She does not seem to know enough about the

uses of the trickster in Afro-American culture. After narrating a trickster tale, Jay Edwards says in 'Structural Analysis of the Afro American Trickster Tale' that 'The important thing is that in this (and other Anansi-type tales) Trickster also assumes the role of the Dupe.'[73] Ms. Wallace got so carried away with 'Balling' Reed that she did not realize that the Irish lieutenant and the jogger were also Reed. Saying without any proof that Reed was 'next up for inclusion in the canon in the 70s, but his career seems to be in decline – precipitated, in no small part, by his perversely misogynistic views,' Ms. Wallace discusses the opening of *Reckless Eyeballing* in Freudian terms, overlooking the clues about Jung in the novel and the negative remarks about Freud in *Mumbo Jumbo* (pp. 237/8) and concludes,

> The presence of the mother as executioner evokes 'the suffocation of the mother' – a popular name in the 17th century for the choking sensation considered a common sympton of 'feminine' hysteria, a symptom used to confirm the diagnosis of witchcraft.

Not only does Ms. Wallace misunderstand the beginning of the novel, as seen earlier from my analysis, but she also overlooks all the positive references to women in the novel, Toni Cade Bambara (p. 119), Toni Morrison (p. 119), Zora Neale Hurston (p. 120), Paule Marshall (p. 128), and Tina Turner (p. 133), among others. She also misses a clue provided in the text that we are not to take Ball to Reed: just when we have concluded that Brashford is Ellison, Brashford says, 'Ralph Ellison was right' (p. 30), thus setting up a distance between himself and the real author.

Reed says of Ms. Wallace's article,

> I think that the article was designed to make me feel bad, because it contained a number of unfriendly remarks, many of them erroneous, about my writings, my career, and about me. I found it odd that Ms. Wallace, who has expressed her disdain for 'patriarchy' in article after article, used the critical tools based upon the ideas of one of the most notorious and misogynistic of patriarchs, Sigmund Freud, to discuss my 'perverse misogyny.' Here was a man who concealed the fact that his friends were seducing their daughters (certainly a film project for Stephen Spielberg). [sic] Also, for someone attempting to explain my ideas about 'NeoHoodooism' to the *Voice*'s readership, Ms. Wallace spends a lot of time 'psychoanalysing' the image of the serpent in my novel *Reckless Eyeballing* without so much as a

reference to the fact that the serpent is at the heart of Vodun, neo-African religion, upon which 'NeoHooDooism' is based.[74]

Despite Reed's understandably hurt feelings at being misread, he has succeeded – in drawing out of Ms. Wallace what lies buried within, namely, the patriarch Freud. The text is instrumental in revealing that within this black feminist lies a patriarchal white man. Fanon says, 'Like it or not, the Oedipus complex is far from coming into being among Negroes.'[75]

Does it follow that every feminist, or every black feminist, must hate Reed's novel? It depends on how one reads the text. 'Some women call Reed an incredible misogynist, but I think he's been misread,' says Carolivia O. Herron, continuing, 'I don't think he's against Black women. *Reckless Eyeballing*'s conclusion contradicts any anti-feminist reading.'[76] Patricia Holt is very favourable to the novel in her review, 'A Hideous and Hilarious Novel from Ishmael Reed', in *The San Francisco Chronicle*:

> Reed dazzles and infuriates us with his splatter effect, blistering our sensibilities with portrayals of black-hating whites, man-hating women, power-hungry feminists, duped blackwomen, gut-exploding bullets, a sexual hit list, Nazi chic, 'sand niggers' and killer Christians until we find it impossible to know where he stands.
>
> This is Reed's intention, of course: He doesn't want us to know where he stands, at least not at first; he wants us to know there is a *perception*, true or not (he think it's true) that white feminist editors are today censoring works by black men and that black women writers are making black men look like monster rapists and killers . . .
>
> But Reed is more complicated than sideline polemics, and 'Reckless Eyeballing' as a result is hilarious, hideous, infuriating and brilliant.[77]

This is a good critique, although the conclusion overshoots the mark. 'Reed's characters are one-dimensional and self-serving, his ideology is sometimes screwy, his history always distorted,' Ms. Holt says, continuing,

> . . . but his message – that hypocrisy runs so deep in all of us that we don't know the lies we tell or the double lives we lead – is absolutely invaluable.

As we have noted, certain characters are deliberately one-dimensional, and it is a matter of perception whether Reed's history is distorted and his ideology screwy. It is not hypocrisy but history that runs through us. Ms. Holt is tending to read the characters rather than the text.

Just as not every feminist will necessarily hate Reed, not every black man will necessarily understand him. Richard Wesley, a black American, says in *Ms.*,

> If black women writers such as Gayl Jones, Audre Lorde, Ntozake Shange, or Alice Walker are to be hounded from one end of the century to the other for decrying the insensitivity of black men to black women, then should not those black male writers such as Ishmael Reed be brought before some of these 'image tribunals' to account for *their* literary transgressions? But more important, there should be *no* 'tribunals' at all.[78]

Despite the sub-title, Wesley is not 'reading between the lines.' Even though he says that there should be no 'image tribunals', there are two questions to be asked. First, who has proposed that there should be such tribunals? Second, if Wesley does not know how to read, although he is a script-writer in Hollywood, who is to judge that Reed is committing 'literary transgressions'? No wonder Reed took the statement seriously and issued a press release on November 1, 1986, challenging *The Village Voice* and *Ms.* to hire black women for executive positions, stating, 'black women occupy key positions in the two foundations and businesses I've established,' that his I. Reed Books and *Quilt* anthology have published more black women than the two magazines, and adding,

> I find it strange . . . that my novel, *Reckless Eyeballing*, which gives what I feel to be a fair, ironic, and comic assessment of the conflicts between Blacks and Jews, men and woman, has been greeted with such outrage by the same black and white feminists who praised Susan Brownmiller's *Against Our Will*, in which the author expressed sympathy for the murderers of Emmett Till.

Reed is reading between the lines and concluding that Wesley's statement about literary tribunals has the endorsement of *Ms.*, making Wesley a kind of Ball.

The relationship of the sexes must not be read at face value in the novel. The mother may not stand for the real mother but for the anima and the same goes for the father-as-animus. In an otherwise sensitive essay on Salkey's *Escape to an Autumn Pavement*, Anthony Boxill takes the relationship of the protagonist to the father and mother too literally. He says,

> this domination by women plays a great part in Johnnie's emasculation. The hostility he shows towards women in the novel . . . indicates his resentment of the domination of his mother and his grandmother . . . The reader can sense in his turning to Dick that this is the affection that he has always longed to give his father, and the choice which Johnnie must make between Fiona and Dick is rendered more difficult because it involves a choice between his mother and his father.[79]

But Fiona is not a stand-in for Johnnie's mother and Dick is not a stand-in for his father. When O'Reedy has made his speech of wholeness and is about to die, he sees both his father and his mother.

Ahmad Harb says,

> The anima/animus dynamics [sic] relate to the *persona* which Jung defines as 'the complicated system of relations between the individual consciousness and society, fittingly enough a kind of mask, designed on the one hand, to conceal the true nature of the individual.' If the individual identifies greatly with his/her persona, difficulties will arise. The persona, 'the ideal picture of a man as he should be,' is inwardly compensated by a feminine weakness, if the individual outwardly plays the strong man, and by masculinity if the individual (a woman) is possessed with her femininity'.[80]

Ms. Kakutani says that there is a lot of 'ugly talk' by the characters. This is true. If the men say crude things to one another and use four-letter words about the women, the women say even worse things to and about one another and about the men. For example, Tremonisha says to Becky, 'All of you white bitches are like that . . . You treacherous cunt.' (p. 74) Is this being unfair to the women, saying that they are as crude as the men? Not if we go by what a founding editor of *Ms.*, Letty Cottin Pogrebin, says in an article entitled '#@%&*@!'. She says that language taboos are a form of social control: when certain kinds of words are forbidden to one group, that group is excluded from full participation in the culture. Language is a way of encoding difference and dominance, she continues, explaining that the use of profanity has been men's prerogative but hiding it from women is no favor to them for what is really going on is assertion of turf and power. The refusal to let women use swear-words is a means of denying them power.[81] So through the crude language, Reed is actually helping liberate the women and agreeing with a feminist! What Reed appears to be doing and what his novel is actually doing are two different things.

The crudeness of what the characters say in the novel is the truth of what they think much of the time. Lies must be opposed with the truth. Tremonisha has been guilty of distorting the truth, as she recognizes. She writes to Ian, 'All of us who grew up in the middle class want to romanticize people who are worse off than we are.' (p. 131) We have seen the distortions of Ian, done because he wants to get off the sex list and become famous and wealthy. Yet he contains within himself the possibility of truth. His play could have told the truth, and indeed it appears that it did so in the version Brashford had read before he (Ian) changed it so that Becky would find it acceptable. Shoboater says, 'Why are you so hung up on eyes? I remember in that travesty of yours, *Suzanna*, there were a lot of eye monologues and dialogues.' Ian replies,

> Eyes reveal a person's true intentions. They are, as Rousseau said, the soul's mirror. I use the term 'reckless eyeballing' because on one level the play is about people intruding into spaces that don't concern them.
> (p. 81)

The references to plays and playwrights tell us that the novel, *Reckless Eyeballing*, is, like its namesake, like a play. It is full of dialogue. The descriptions of rooms are like set descriptions. This is done deliberately: Reed is *placing scenes before our eyes because he wants us to see*. How are we to read Reed? Not necessarily by attaching weight to every word, although, contrariwise, we must attach weight to every word. Reed finds everything to be significant. Thus Reagan's visit to the cemetery at Bitburg, and his placing of flowers on the grave of the Nazis, is not seen as an accident: it is a sign of the resurgence of anti-semitism and racism. The poet Alurista told me that he thought of Reed as being like a fisherman who threw out several hooks and what caught caught. But I read differently: the reader is inescapably involved in the task of interpreting the text or he/she will get misled, ending up reinforcing his/her own prejudices instead of responding to the text. Why did many feminist readers get misled when they read *Reckless Eyeballing*? Because many readers *assume* from some words that Ian Ball is Ishmael Reed and therefore represents the authorial point of view in the novel. Thanks to this assumption, such a reader does not notice that Ball has no opinions: he is always quoting first Brashford and later, when he gets to admire her, Tremonisha. *Reed has used himself* to play a trick on the reader who would be tricked, a trick by which she/he will misread because of her/his preconceptions.

We thought the play about and by Eva Braun would merely be an apology for the innocence of a guilty woman, something we could dismiss scornfully and righteously, but in fact we actually learned something of key importance (about Jung and about Hitler) from it. Since we assume that Ball is Reed, we assume that Ball represents Reed instead of being unbalanced. It is no improvement when Ball becomes nice to the feminists and switches from writing plays they do not like to plays they do: he is still unbalanced and his work is a lie. At the end, Ian's mother calls out to Johnnie Kranshaw for help. Why 'Johnnie'? Isn't it commonly a man's name? I relate the name to the classic song of female revenge against a wrong-headed man, 'Frankie and Johnny.' In the song – recorded, among others, by Sam Cooke, who had it at No. 14 on the *Billboard* Hot Hundred in 1963 and who was shot in cold blood by a black woman a year later – a woman kills her two-timing lover Johnny. Here, Frankie *is* Johnny, as implied by the spelling, thus suggesting Johnnie has come to terms with her animus. By the end of the novel, it is the two black feminists and the Irish lieutenant who have achieved wholeness, not Ian Ball.

'Man is in the last stage of his evolution. Women will be here.' – Raven Quickskill.[82]

Conclusion

'Do you ever write a straightforward novel?' I wrote to Andrew
Salkey in frustration several years ago. It is a valid question: why
not write straightforwardly? Several good writers such as Ngũgĩ
wa Thiong'o do so in the sense that although they may structure
their fiction in complex ways – Ngũgĩ's *A Grain of Wheat* and
Petals of Blood have a non-linear, spiral form – they do not use the
form of the text to let the reader run the risk of misleading
himself/herself. One possible explanation for why the fiction of
writers such as Salkey, Ebejer and Reed are tricksters in form
while that of Ngũgĩ is not is implied by Ngũgĩ in *Decolonising the
Mind: The Politics of Language in African Literature.*[1] He says that
the literature of post-independent Africa and the Third World
was directed at the nationalistic bourgeoisie and the petty
bourgeoisie. Ngũgĩ himself is from the peasantry and increasingly
speaks for and to them: he has explained in several of his volumes
of prose that he re-educated himself at the feet of the peasants.[2] It
could be argued that his primary duty is to tell them the truth,
which they already know to a large extent anyway since their
interests are diametrically opposed to those of the ruling class.
Furthermore, they are not steeped in literary texts such that
parody or literary word-play makes sense to them, although they
are familiar with trickster figures from their own stories and
although they appreciate the ability to tell stories and to re-tell
familiar tales with new flourishes. Therefore one does not need to
play tricks in form even if one does in content, that is, if one tells
the story of tricksters. In contrast, Salkey, Ebejer and Reed are
from the lower-middle class, a class that misperceives the world
because of its own vacillating class interests since, in Ngũgĩ's
words, 'Like a chameleon it takes on the colour of the main class

with which it is in the closest touch and sympathy.'³ Using this argument, Salkey, Ebejer and Reed would have to play tricks on the perception of their readers because it is their class that misperceives the world, not the class of workers and peasants. Salkey, Ebejer and Reed have to make the members of their class see what they do not want to see. Literature written by a member of the working class or peasantry about and to that class will naturally be straightforward.

Such an argument not only misrepresents the complex nature of literature but also overlooks the fact that, as Ayi Kwei Armah shows in his *The Beautyful Ones Are Not Yet Born* and *Fragments*, all classes among the colonized people were affected by colonialism and neocolonialism.⁴ Ngũgĩ shows in his most famous novel, *Petals of Blood*, that neocolonialism sucks the blood of the village of Ilmorog, taking away the young people, then the land, and finally everything.⁵ Only one of the novel's five main characters, two of whom are petty bourgeois, begins to see the world accurately, in working-class, trade union terms, after he nearly loses his mind through reading too many radical Third World texts. Reed would provide another answer. Replying to Amiri Baraka's accusation that he praises the bourgeoisie, Reed says that when he spoke of the middle class, he did not mean those who dominate the economic life of the United States but people whose income is above the poverty line. 'The middle class I was referring to is a working class,' he says.⁶

Colonialism created an imbalance by denying manhood to the colonized males (and having an equivalent effect on the colonizers since they had to be excessively male, male as god). Thus in the search for assertion, things can frequently go wrong because the colonized individuals do not come to terms with the hidden and the suppressed in the context of continuing political and economic repression and exploitation. One can get trapped into seeing the external world in a way that is dangerous because of what lies unrecognized within, thanks to the colonial experience and the lack of control and self-knowledge it entails. Merely rising up and asserting oneself, claiming innocence, does not throw off the chains since these chains are also inside. Salkey, Ebejer and Reed seek to make us open doors which swing two ways, into the outer world and into ourselves: thus getting us to come to terms with our complex selves so that we can deal with and master a complex and dangerous world. They know we may not see because we may not want to see or may not realize that we are not letting ourselves see: so they find literary ways of getting past our defences.

Reed's way is to use multiple techniques. You cannot pin him because his next text is genrically different from his previous one. His first novel is a gothic one, his second a western tall tale, his third a ragtime mystery, his fourth a modern version of a Greek classic, his fifth a vaudeville show, his sixth a parody of Dickens's *A Christmas Carol* (thus bringing the novel back home since Dickens conceived the idea for the novel while he was in America), and his seventh a what? Well, it signifies on *The Color Purple*. And this introduces us to the fact that coming out of black American history, in which, for example, black people were once forbidden literacy on pain of having their tongues removed, there is the imperative for the black American artist to say things without endangering himself and his people. He does this by 'signifying'. Critics such as Henry Louis Gates, Jr. and Michael G. Cooke have written about the Signifying Monkey in black American literature. Cooke says,

> The trickster figure that is the signifying monkey sees more than it is prudent to say, and more than it is wholesome to deny. Instead of making scenes, he creates scenarios that amply indicate his sense of the Lion's credulity, insecurity, pride, and proneness to painful error. He submits only to subvert.[7]

Gates quotes Roger D. Abrahams's definition of signifying:

> Signifying seems to be a Negro term, in use if not in origin. It can mean any of a number of things; in the case of the toast about the signifying monkey, it certainly refers to the trickster's ability to talk with great innuendo, to carp, cajole, needle, and lie. It can mean in other instances the propensity to talk around a subject, never quite coming to the point. It can mean making fun of a person or situation. Also it can denote speaking with the hands and eyes, and in this respect encompasses a whole complex of expressions and gestures. Thus it is signifying to stir up a fight between neighbors by telling stories; it is signifying to make fun of a policeman by parodying his motions behind his back; it is signifying to ask for a piece of cake by saying, 'My brother needs a piece of cake'.[8]

Abrahams concludes, Gates says, that essentially, signifying is a technique of indirect argument or persuasion, a language of implication, of goading, begging, boasting by indirect verbal or gestural means; the name itself

> shows the monkey to be a trickster, signifying being the language of trickery, that set of words or gestures achieving Hamlet's 'direction through indirection.'

But Gates goes further than Abrahams in that he says that the Monkey is not only a master of technique, 'he *is* technique, or style, or the *literariness* of literary language: he is the great Signifier.'[9]

Ishmael Reed has a whole range of trickster figures, chief among them an almost invisible one, the Signifying Monkey. In *Reckless Eyeballing*, Ian Ball's favourite cartoon character is Bugs Bunny, that is, the trickster rabbit. Andrew Salkey, as we have seen, has a major trickster figure that runs through a great deal of his work, the spider Anancy. What about Francis Ebejer?

At first, it would seem that the connection with Ebejer's fiction is not the trickster but Jung. Ebejer says in an unpublished interview with Adrian Stivala that his novels

> are mythological stories, in the Jungian sense; but when not taken as such – each book carries a straightforward story on the primary level – they are also individualistic. I mean by this that my characters are persons in their own right: they move and talk like most of us, always allowing, of course, for the heightened and larger than life concentration of fiction. But they are also archetypal, myth-making.

Ebejer tells Stivala further,

> It is the *anima* in a male writer, or the *animus* in a female one that triggers off the yearning for outward expression, however polarized the *anima/animus* and the Self are to begin with.

Explaining Jungian concepts, Ahmad Harb notes that the function of the unconscious to consciousness 'is *compensatory . . .* If consciousness denies "the unconscious counterweight", the unconscious forcibly imposes itself and the state of compensation is disturbed.'[10] In Ebejer's first three novels, it is hard to detect any elements of the trickster. Ebejer wrote to me on August 7, 1987,

myth of course comes in, as it does (again this has been pointed out
to me) in nearly all of my work. I have been described as an intuitive
writer. That's why I still find it difficult to note the 'trickster'
element, though I'm sure it's there.

And yet we note that as the reality gets more complex, Ebejer's
fiction increasingly takes on the qualities of the trickster until
Leap of Malta Dolphins deceives the wilfully blind critics just as
much as Salkey's *Come Home, Malcolm Heartland* and Reed's
Reckless Eyeballing. So I probed further in a phone conversation
with Ebejer; and I received a letter from him dated August 17,
1987 in which he said yes, there was a trickster figure in some of
his works: the national 'clever idiot' *Gahan*:

> *Gahan*, the prankster the clever idiot, the purveyor of truth even
> while he jested . . . starting nine centuries ago, reflecting the
> idiosyncrasies of the Mediterranean races. The first time I used a
> variation of him was with the artist-cum-rebel Blonk in my play
> *Boulevard*. Remember how he beguiled the others with his highest
> achievement, a blank canvas? Then, too, there's Kos in *Requiem*.
> And two years ago, in my three-Act Maltese play, *Il-Gahan
> ta'Bingemma* where he acted himself, the real Gahan, mouthpiece,
> scapegoat, whipping-boy, flagellator, truth-machine for the whole
> Maltese race.

Paul Xuereb said in a review of *Il-Gahan ta'Bingemma*:

> Ebejer has had the genial idea of setting most of the play on the
> heights of Bingemma into which are hewn graves from prehistoric,
> Punic, Roman and Arab times: a site that witnessed the forging of
> the Maltese nation. He has had the even more genial idea of making
> Gahan, the idiot boy of Maltese – and Mediterranean – folklore the
> Chorus. This Gahan, however, is no ordinary idiot, but the wise
> fool, the jester who can tell the deepest truths. Gahan's well-known
> exploit of dragging his house's front door behind him . . . is
> transformed brilliantly into a symbolical opening of the doors of
> ignorance, apathy and prejudice (akin to the breaking down of walls
> in Ebejer's own *Hitas*).[11]

'Why are sterility and spiritual decadence such important themes
in your novels?' asks an unnamed interviewer in an unpublished
interview. Ebejer replies, 'I have portrayed spiritual decadence
and sterility, but with the aim of pointing out paths out of them.'

Who can point out paths out? Emma Jung and Marie Von Franz say that *the trickster-figure* is 'the one who can bring the unconscious problem of opposites up into consciousness and in this way might act as "lightbringer" for man.'[12]

So Ebejer has used a trickster figure, like Salkey and Reed. This is an indication of their awareness that breaking through the reader's barriers is a complex matter. It is the novels that are to perform the task of trickster, but how do novels point to ways out? Mario Vargas Llosa says,

> in fact, novels do lie – they can't help doing so – but that's only one part of the story. The other is that, through lying, they express a curious truth, which can only be expressed in a veiled and concealed fashion, masquerading as what it is not.[13]

He continues,

> Every good novel tells the truth and every bad novel lies. For a novel 'to tell the truth' means to make the reader experience an illusion, and 'to lie' means to be unable to accomplish that trickery.

As we noted in the Introduction, Marlow lacks the courage to tell the truth to Kurtz's fiancée when he gets back from Africa so he lies to her about Kurtz's death, telling her that he died with her name on her lips whereas we know his famous death lines.[14] But this is a *straightforward* lie; Marlow, like Jim in *Lord Jim*, wants a second chance. His telling of the story is the second chance. But notice how he tells the truth: the story is hedged, hesitant, and qualified. The point of his story seems to be his tracking down of the best that Europe has produced, namely, Kurtz: he seems to see the brutalized Africans only incidentally along the way. And when he gets to Kurtz, the man dedicated to an idea has become a 'savage' in pursuit of ivory: he has become a brute by performing the real task European colonialism wants of him, not because of the supposed savagery of Africa.

Marlow is telling his story on the Thames, the waterway on which English imperialist agents set out, and he is speaking to the levers of imperialism, those who are benefitting from imperialism and yet who have a clear conscience because they do not see the cruelty and brutality of the enterprise since the Kurtzes are the ones doing the dirty job. Will they not resist a story showing them directly how they benefit from brutality? So Conrad tells them the story indirectly, the point of the story appearing to be what Europe has done to one of its finest, Kurtz: and in the process, the brutalizing of the Africans is sneaked in through the story, all the more cunningly because Marlow uses the standard racist terms towards them, comparing them to animals, whereas *the story* shows us that by the end it is Kurtz who is like an animal crawling on all-fours. 'And this also,' begins Marlow with his cunning story, 'has been one of the dark places of the earth.' He goes on to talk of how when the Romans arrived there 'nineteen hundred years ago – the other day,' they saw 'sandbanks, marshes, forests, savages.' In other words, they saw the ancestors of the civilized English as savages, just as the English – like Marlow himself – see the Africans they have conquered as 'savages.' Or as Reed's Pirate Jack puts it, 'The difference between a savage and a civilized man is determined by who has the power.' (p. 149) But there is more: in Part II, Marlow suddenly says, 'The mind of man is capable of anything – because everything is in it, all the past as well as all the future.'[15] What Marlow is really saying, when we connect these statements, separated by several pages, is that in the mind of the English is the memory of the time they were the slaves of the Romans – and their behaviour as the civilized beings lording it over the Africans they have colonized comes from their days of slavery, for nineteen hundred years ago is just yesterday. Marlow is able to note the brutalizing of the Africans because the English are willing to believe that the Belgians, *not they* are brutal: but all the generalizations he makes about imperialism apply to them too. *The story* thereby breaks past the defences of the listeners so successfully that the narrator – who is not Marlow but one of the comfortable listeners – no longer feels as confident of the Thames and London at the end as he did at the beginning. From a Third World point of view, there is more to say, and Reed says it by signifying on *Heart of Darkness*, among other works, in *Flight to Canada*.

The clue that Reed is conscious of the Conrad text is provided in *Reckless Eyeballing*: Reed refers to 'An expedition into the heart of darkness, as it were' (p. 79). Swille's son could be looked on as Son of Kurtz: he goes to the Congo to look for energy resources. The Snake Society in the Congo throws him to the crocodiles. 'All I wanted to do was bring home some shrunken heads for my museum collection,' his ghost tells his mother (p. 126), reminding us that Kurtz's house was surrounded by heads. Instead, the crocodile that swallows him regurgitates his head, which is sent to his father, who donates it to the National Archives and takes it off his taxes. Meanwhile, Uncle Robin has been poisoning Swille with what appears to be slave mothers' milk but is actually Coffee Mate, produced by the multinational. When we turn back to *Heart of Darkness*, we have to wonder if the Africans really treated Kurtz as a god: we recall that Swille's brother said at the reading of the will that Swille said 'Robin treated him as though he were a god' (p. 168). How do we know that the mysterious illness that was killing Kurtz was not slow poisoning by the Africans?

The novels of Salkey, Ebejer and Reed 'lie', that is, they tell the truth. In their last novels under consideration, all three novelists go as far as possible to let the readers' misread the text, themselves and the world.[16] They do this by *using themselves* in their fiction. As we have seen, Malcolm Heartland seems to be Andrew Salkey, Ian Ball seems to be Ishmael Reed, and, according to Keith Wilson, Sarid is Francis Ebejer. Wilson's reaction to Ebejer is instructive: by assuming that a particular character represents the author, he goes off on the wrong track and misunderstands the complex exploration of the group, the individual and history. Suddenly, like a slap in the face, the reader reaches a totally different conclusion from what he/she expected. Malcolm is killed, Ian Ball turns out to be the Flower phantom, and Sarid is only concerned with his dog while Lenarda is dead and Marcell has a daughter from Dirjana named Karmelina. Unless the reader decides that the novelist does not know how to write – as some critics in unexamined superiority do – he/she has no choice but to re-read the text to see where he/she went wrong. Actually, all three writers have made fleeting appearances in their texts at various times, Salkey in his Author's Note to his second novel and the fact that Sobert, like Salkey, was born in Panama, Reed as the trombonist in his second novel, and Ebejer as Lorenz (to some extent) in the fifth novel. In all cases, these appearances are red herrings as well as clues, making readers go off the track if they are so inclined. The appearance of the novelist in the novel is a clue that we should pay attention to *the novel*. Wilson Harris says, we may be closer than we think to the Hermetic arts of Bruno and the alchemical imagination where the filter of the mind was as much part of the process of experiment as the material itself under scrutiny.[17]

In tracking down the meaning of the novels by the three novelists, I have used Jung extensively. However, we have to return to the qualifier I made at the beginning of this book. The three novelists are Third World novelists, that is, they are dealing with people who have had the experience of colonialism and neocolonialism. Fanon points out that Jung has certain limitations when it comes to the colonial experience. Fanon says,

> European civilization is characterized by the presence at the heart of what Jung calls the collective unconscious, of an archetype: an expression of the bad instincts, of the darkness inherent in every ego, of the uncivilized savage, the Negro who slumbers in every white man. And Jung claims to have found in uncivilized people the same psychic structure that his diagram portrays. Personally I think Jung has deceived himself. Moreover, all the peoples that he has known – whether the Pueblo Indians of Arizona or the Negroes of Kenya in British East Africa – have had more or less traumatic contacts with the white man . . .
> On this level one would have only to demonstrate that Jung has confused instinct and habit. In his view, in fact, the collective unconscious is bound up with the cerebral structure, the myths and archetypes are permanent engrams of the race. I hope I have shown that nothing of the sort is the case and that in fact the collective unconscious is cultural, which means acquired.[18]

Fanon's point is that colonialism and racism affect the collective unconscious: for example, the *anima* of the colonized Antillean black man is almost always a white woman and the *animus* of the Antillean is a white man. This, according to Fanon, happens because of the imposition of European values through colonial racism on the Antilleans. In other words, the political plays a key role. Thus, using Fanon's insights, we may see that the protagonist of Ebejer's *Come Again in Spring* who is European and aspiring to be European in America is confronting his positive *anima* when he has to make love to a black American woman but sees God in her. Thus all three novelists are not writing Jungian novels in an unchanging context: they are writing in the context of colonial relationships, which their texts seek to end.

If so, how does this make them different from other Third World writers? At first glance, Julio Cortázar would appear to be a writer like the three. Gregory Rabassa says of *Hopscotch*:

> A form is of its own making, an object is defined by its use, as Ortega y Gasset has said, and the reader really creates his own novel as he goes forward. This is the starting point of *Hopscotch*, where Cortázar gives us a carefully ordered alternate version and also invites us to go to work and bring forth further variations. We have before us a rich lode of chiastic possibilities. When the novel was first published in the United States, a great many critics did not know that along with the interesting possibilities put forth to them they were also being had. *Cortázar shook his head in dismay at this straitlaced interpretation and agreed that it would be awful to have to read any novel through twice*, this one above all. What he did do, however, was to point out the possibilities of reality, and this can best be done and perhaps only be done by recourse to fiction, to the lie . . .
>
> As we put the pieces of *Hopscotch* together we find that the puzzle is the novel itself, that we are in a sense writing it as we read it . . .[19] (my italics)

We note that Rabassa talks of fiction as a 'lie' and of the problem of critics reading the text in a strait-laced way when the readership is part of the problem and even creation. But the chief difference between Cortázar on the one hand and Salkey, Ebejer and Reed on the other is that it is clear with Cortázar's novel that one is dealing with a puzzle from the beginning whereas with the other three the trick rather than the puzzle is found to have been so at or by the end. Therefore in the case of the three, *one must go back and re-read the text*. Reed is like Cortázar in one respect, though: both writers are concerned with the problem of reading in a linear way. Cortázar alternates lines so one must read two sets of sentences simultaneously in Chapter 24 of *Hopscotch*[20] while Reed makes us read page 161 of *Mumbo Jumbo* by turning it round and round like a record. One must *detect* what is going on. Hence one of Reed's trickster figures is PaPa LaBas, who, just called 'LaBas' in *The Last Days of Louisiana Red*, is a detective, a psychic detective. Nance Saturday in *The Terrible Twos* is also a detective, a maverick criminologist (who is ahead of *Man* Friday since 'nance' is an effeminate man as well as being a shortened version of 'Aunt Nancy', that is, 'Anansi').

Chinua Achebe's Ezeulu, the Chief Priest, says to his son when deciding to send him to the Christian school at the point at which colonialism is consolidating itself in West Africa, 'The world is like a Mask dancing. If you want to see it well, you do not stand in one place.'[21] And Ngũgĩ notes that the linear unfolding of a story is removed from the actual social practice of the people.[22]

'A text is a coded structure which must somehow be decoded,' says Henry Louis Gates, Jr. in 'Criticism in the jungle'.[23] The novels of Andrew Salkey, Francis Ebejer and Ishmael Reed are tricksters, light-bringers because they want to bring things up from the depths, because they want us to stop feeding history peanuts, because they want us to take hold of our history, control it and change it.

Every creation myth has a trickster in it.

The trick is to read.

Notes

Introduction

1 See the chapter 'The Individual Versus the State' in Peter Nazareth, *Literature and Society in Modern Africa*. Nairobi/Kampala/Dar es Salaam: East African Literature Bureau, 1972. Published as *An African View of Literature*, Evanston: Northwestern University Press, 1974.

2 Peter Nazareth, *The Third World Writer: His Social Responsibility*. Nairobi. Kenya Literature Bureau. 1978.

3 Ibid., p. 73.

4 Ibid., p. 74.

5 Ibid., p. 84.

6 *South*, London: South Publications Ltd.

7 Tayeb Salih. *Season of Migration to the North*, trans. Denys Johnson-Davies, London: Heinemann, 1969.

8 Jonah Raskin, *The Mythology of Imperialism*. New York: Dell, a Delta book, 1971, p. 161.

9 See Peter Nazareth, 'Out of Darkness: Conrad and Other Third World Writers,' *CONRADIANA*, ed. David Leon Higdon, Lubbock: Texas Tech Institute, Vol. XIV, No. 3, 1982, pp. 173/87. Mawuena Logan points out in 'Cultural Pluralism: Henty and the Ashantis' that the protagonist of G.A. Henty's *By Sheer Pluck: A Tale of the Ashanti*, a young Englishman named Frank Hargate, goes to Africa as 'a bearer of the torch of enlightenment to the heart of darkness.' (*The Children's Literature Association Quarterly*, Battlecreek, Michigan, vol. 16, No. 2, summer 1991.) Henty's novel was first published in 1884 while *heart of Darkness* was first published in 1899 – which suggests that Conrad was using the title ironically, particularly in *Lord Jim* Conrad shows the destructive effect on adolescent boys of adventure stories (such as Henty was writing).

10 Omolara Ogundipe-Leslie, 'To a "Jane Austen" Class at Ibadan University', *African Writing Today*, special issue of *Pacific Moana Quarterly*, Hamilton: Outrigger Publishers, Vol. 6, Nos. 3/4, July/October, 1981, p. 12.

11 See Mary Lou Emery, *Jean Rhys at 'World's End'*, sub-titled *Novels of*

Colonial and Sexual Exile, Austin: The University of Texas Press, 1990, pp. 14/15.

12. Alex La Guma, *A Walk in the Night*, Ibadan: Mbari, undated but probably 1962.

13 See Abdul R. JanMohamed, *Manichean Aesthetics*, Amherst: University of Massachuesetts Press, 1983.

14 Umberto Eco, *The Name of the Rose*. trans. William Weaver. Harcourt Brace Jovanovich, 1983.

15 Ayi Kwei Armah, *Fragments*, Boston: Houghton Mifflin, 1969.
Ayi Kwei Armah, *Why Are We So Blest?*, New York: Doubleday, 1972.

16 F.R. Leavis. *The Great Tradition*. London: Chatto and Windus, 1948.

17 Raskin, op. cit., pp. 5/6.

18 See Peter Nazareth, 'The Narrator as Artist and the Reader as Critic,' Mona Takieddine ed., *A Casebook on Tayeb Salih's 'Season to the North'*. Beirut: The American University of Beirut, 1985, pp. 123/34.

19 Ayi Kwei Armah, *The Beautyful Ones Are Not Yet Born*. Boston: Houghton Mifflin, 1968.

20 Peter Nazareth, 'Brave New Cosmos,' David Cook. ed. *Origin East Africa*, London: Heinemann, 1965.

21 Peter Nazareth, *Two Radio Plays*. Nairobi/Kampala/Dar es Salaam: EALB, 1976.

22 O.R. Dathorne, *African Literature in the Twentieth Century*. Minneapolis: University of Minnesota Press, 1975, p. 336.

23 Peter Nazareth, *In a Brown Mantle*. Nairobi/Kampala/Dar es Salaam, 1972.
Peter Nazareth, *The General is UP*, Toronto. TSAR Publications, 1991.

24 Philip Roth, *Reading Myself and Others*, New York: Bantam, 1977, p. 196.

25 Peter Nazareth, 'Practical Problems and Technical Solutions in Writing My First Two novels,' *CALLALOO*, ed. Charles H. Rowell, Lexington: University of Kentucky, Vol. 4, Nos. 1/3, Feb./Oct., pp. 56/62.

26 See Peter Nazareth, 'The Confessor,' *Short Story International*, ed. Sylvia Tankel, Great Neck, No. 28, 1981.

27 J.R. McGuire, 'The Writer as Historical Translator: Peter Nazareth's "The General is Up"', *Toronto South Asian Review*, ed. Moyez Vassanji, Vol. 6, No. 1, Summer, 1978, pp. 17/23.

28 Lambert Mascarenhas, *Goa Today*, ed. Lambert Mascarenhas, Panjim: Vol. XIV, No. 8, March, 1985, p. 42.

29 'Francis Ebejer – His Novels (Part Two),' *Civilization*, Hamrun, No. 21, 1985, p. 568.

30 Ibid, p. 570.

31 Albert Wendt, ed., *Lali: A Pacific Anthology*, Auckland: Longman Paul, 1980, p. xiv.

32 See my Afterword to Violet Dias Lannoy, *Pears From the Willow Tree*, Washington, D.C.: Three Continents Press, 1989.

33 Henry Louis Gates, Jr., 'Criticism in the jungle,' *Black Literature and Literary Theory*, ed. Henry Louis Gates, Jr., London/New York: Methuen, 1984, p. 9. My italics.

34 David Haworth, *New Statesman*, London, 14 February, 1969, p. 230.
Graham Hough, *The Listener*, London: BBC, October 22, 1959, p. 698.
The Times Literary Supplement, London, February 15, 1968, p. 149.
35 Wole Soyinka, *Collected Plays*, Vol. I, London: Oxford University Press, 1973.

Chapter One: Andrew Salkey

1 Andrew Salkey, *A Quality of Violence*, London: Hutchinson, 1959. The novel was reissued by London/Port of Spain: New Beacon, 1978. All page references are to the Hutchinson edition.
2 Ivan Van Sertima, *Caribbean Writers*, London/Port of Spain: New Beacon, 1968, p. 16.
3 Kenneth Ramchand, *The West Indian Novel and its Background*, second Edition, Port of Spain/London/Kingston: Heinemann, 1983, p. 129. My italics.
4 Gerald Moore. *The Chosen Tongue*. New York/Evanston: J.&J. Harper, 1969, p. 8.
5 Bill Carr, 'A Complex Fate', *The Islands In-Between*, ed. Louis James, Ibadan/Nairobi: Oxford University Press, 1968, pp. 102/3.
6 Andrew Salkey, *Anancy's Score*, London: Bogle-L'Ouverture, 1973, my italics.
7 See Michael Gilkes, *Wilson Harris and the Caribbean Novel*, London/Trinidad/Jamaica: Longman Caribbean, 1975, p. 41.
8 Mervyn Morris, 'Anancy and Andrew Salkey,' *Jamaica Journal*, ed. Olive Senior, Kingston: Institute of Jamaica Publications Ltd., Vol. 19, No. 4, November 1986/January 1987.
9 Andrew Salkey, ed., *Breaklight*, New York: Doubleday, 1973.
10 See Andrew Salkey, *Georgetown Journal*, London/Port of Spain: New Beacon, 1972.
11 Martin Luther King, 'Letter From a Birmingham Jail,' *The Random House Reader*, ed. Frederick Crews. New York: Random House, 1981, p. 294.
12 See my play 'X' in *Two Radio Plays*.
13 Ngũgĩ wa Thiong'o (James Ngugi), *The River Between*, London: Heineman, 1965.
14 Wilson Harris, *Tradition the Writer and Society*, London/Port of Spain: New Beacon, 1967, pp. 24/5.
15 Ishmael Reed, *Flight to Canada*, New York: Random House, 1976, p. 177.
16 Margaret Atwood, *Second Words*, Boston: Beacon Press, 1984, p. 149. My italics.
17 Andrew Salkey, *Escape to an Autumn Pavement*, London: Hutchinson, 1960. All page references are to this edition.
18 Frantz Fanon. *The Wretched of the Earth*, trans. Constance Farrington.

Preface by Jean-Paul Sartre, New York: Ballantine, 1973.

19 Gerald Moore, op. cit., p. 106.

20 Bill Carr, op. cit., 104.

21 Samuel Selvon, *The Lonely Londoners*, London: Allan Wingate, 1956.

22 William Riggan. *Pícaros, Madmen, Naïfs, and Clowns: The Unreliable First-Person Narrator*. Norman: University of Oklahoma Press, 1981, pp. 19/20. My italics.

23 *ASA Review of Books*, eds. Barbara Lewis & Allen Howard. Waltham: African Studies Association, Vol. 4, 1978, p. 63.

24 Anthony Boxill, 'The Emasculated Colonial,' *Présence Africaine*, Paris, No. 75, 3rd Quarterly, 1970, p. 146.

25 *Flight to Canada*, p. 42.

26 Fanon, op. cit., pp. 152/3.

27 Andrew Salkey, *The Late Emancipation of Jerry Stover*, London: Hutchinson, 1968. All page references are from this edition.

28 Bill Carr, op. cit., p. 108.
    Wole Soyinka, *The Interpreters*, New York: Collier, 1965.

29 Contrast this with Sam Selvon's celebration of pay day of the workers in *Turn Again Tiger*, London: Heinemann, 1979, pp. 53/4. It may be partly a matter of temperament and purpose that the description is enervating in Salkey and energizing in Selvon, but it is also a question of the class of the people concerned and the relationship to the land.

30 Violet Staub de Laszlo, ed., *The Basic Writings of C.G. Jung*, New York: Modern Library, 1959, p. 167.

31 Gareth Griffiths, *A Double Exile*, London: Marion Boyars, 1978, p. 130.

32 Ibid., p. 132.

33 Ibid., p. 134.

34 V.S. Naipaul, *Finding the Center: Two Narratives*, New York: Knopf, 1984.

35 Wayne Brown, *On the Coast*, London: André Deutsch, 1972, p. 17.

36 Ibid., p. 7.

37 Earl Lovelace, *The Dragon Can't Dance*, London: André Deutsch, 1978, pp. 188/9.

38 David Rubadiri, *No Bride Price*, Nairobi: East African Publishing House, 1968.

39 Ayi Kwei Armah. *The Healers*. Nairobi: East African Publishing House, 1975.

40 *Webster's New World Dictionary of the American Language*, Second College Edition, ed. David B. Guralnik, New York: Simon & Schuster, 1980.

41 Andrew Salkey, *The Adventures of Catullus Kelly*, London: Hutchinson, 1969. All page references are to this edition.

42 E.R. Braithwaite, *To Sir With Love*, Toronto/London: The Bodley Head, 1967. The book was first published in 1959. The movie, starring Sidney Poitier, was made in 1967.

43 Christopher Booker, *The Neophiliacs*, London: Fontana/Collins, 1969, p. 56.

44   David Black. 'Hot Secrets,' *Playboy*, Chicago, August, 1985, p. 74.
45   Frantz Fanon. *Black Skin, White Masks*. trans. Charles Lam Markmann, New York: Grove Press, 1967, pp. 63/82.
46   Fanon, op. cit., pp. 158/9.
47   Ishmael Reed, *Mumbo Jumbo*, Garden City: Doubleday, 1972, p. 47.
48   Albert Wendt, *Flying Fox in a Freedom Tree*, Auckland/Hawthorn: Longman Paul, 1974, p. 81.
49   Similarly, Modin in Ayi Kwei Armah's *Why Are We So Blest?* is warned by a white homosexual about the predatory Aimée, op. cit., pp. 168/74.
50   Andrew Salkey, *Come Home, Malcolm Heartland*, London: Hutchinson, p. 15.
51   Andrew Salkey, *Away*. New York/London: Allison & Busby, 1980, p. 39.
52   Ibid., p. 40.
53   See Peter Nazareth, 'Alienation, Nostalgia and Homecoming: Editing an Anthology of Goan Literature,' *World Literature Today*, ed. Ivar Ivask. Norman: University of Oklahoma. Vol. 59, No. 3, Summer, 1986, pp. 374/82. The essay shows the difference between nostalgia and homecoming: and how exiled colonials tend to mistake the former for the latter.
54   Raskin, op. cit., pp. 12/13.
55   *Black Skin, White Masks*, p. 63.
56   *Away*, p. 58.
57   Andrew Salkey, *The One*, London: Bogle-L'Ouverture, 1987.
58   Ibid., p. 33.
59   *The Mabinogi and Other Medieval Welsh Tales*, trans. and ed. Patrick K. Ford, Berkeley/Los Angeles/London: University of California Press, 1977, p. 35.
60   Ibid., pp. 36/7.
61   Philip Agee, *On the Run*, Secaucus: Lyle Stuart, 1987.
62   *The New York Times Book Review*, August 2, 1987, p. 7.
63   David Morrell, *Blood Oath*, London: Pan, 1982.
     David Morrell, *The Brotherhood of the Rose*, New York: St. Martin's/Marek, 1984.
64   Carl C. Jung, 'On the Psychology of the Trickster Figure,' in Paul Radin, *The Trickster*, New York: Schocken Books, 1972, pp. 206/7.
65   R.D.E. Burton, 'Derek Walcott and the Medusa of History,' *Caliban*, ed. Roberto Marquez, Amherst, Vol. III, No. 2, Fall-Winter, 1980, pp. 3/4.
66   *Away*, pp. 54/7.
67   Ishmael Reed, *Conjure*, Amherst: Amherst University Press, 1972, p. 50.
68   Andrew Salkey, *Jamaica*, London: Bogle-L'Ouverture Publications, 1983. The book was first published in 1973 by Hatchinson.
69   Andrew Salkey, 'Lecture Notes, Talking Points and an Outline towards a Definition of the Responsibility of the Intellectual in the Third World,' published in Conference Papers, *The Role of The Intellectual in the Third World*, Havana, 1968.
70   Peter Nazareth, *Two Radio Plays*, p. 26.

Chapter Two: Francis Ebejer

1 'Francis Ebejer – his novels,' *Civilization*, Hamrun, No. 21, 1985, p. 569.
2 John Paxton, ed., *The Statesman's Year-Book*, 118th edition. New York: St. Martin's Press, 1981, p. 841.
3 Ibid., p. 735.
4 In Daniel Massa, ed., *Individual and Community in Commonwealth Literature*, Valetta: University Press, 1979, p. 221.
5 Francis Ebejer, *A Wreath for the Innocents*, London: MacGibbon & Kee, 1958. Reissued as *A Wreath of Maltese Innocents*, Valletta: Bugelli Publications, 1981. All page references are to the Bugelli edition.
6 Albert Wendt, *Sons for the Return Home*. Harmondsworth/New York/Ringwood/Markham: Penguin, 1987. First published by Longman Paul in 1973.
7 Lucio Rodrigues, 'It Happens', *Goan Literature: A Modern Reader*, special issue of the *Journal of South Asian Literature*, East Lansing: Michigan State University, ed. Peter Nazareth with the assistance of Joseph K. Henry, Vol XVIII, No. 1, Winter/Spring, 1983, p. 239.
8 Francis Ebejer interviewed by Adrian Stivala, unpublished. Ebejer sent me a number of interviews which have not been published to date.
9 Daniel Massa, 'Interview with Francis Ebejer,' *World Literature Written in English*, ed. G.D. Killam, Guelph: University of Guelph, Vol. 23, No. 2, Spring 1984, p. 480.
10 Ebejer sent me a copy of his replies to questions by the Torinese student, written in 1984.
11 Francis Ebejer, *Evil of the King Cockroach*, London: MacGibbon and Kee, 1960, pp. 85/6. Reissued as *Wild Spell of Summer*. Malta: Union Press, 1968. The pagination is the same in the two editions.
12 Francis Ebejer, *In the Eye of the Sun*, London: MacDonald, 1969. All page references are to this edition. The novel was completed in 1959.
13 Chuck Berry's version, recorded in 1956, is available on *Chuck Berry – The Great Twenty-Eight*, New Jersey: Chess, 1982 while Elvis Presley's is on *Elvis Sings Flaming Star*, Hamburg: RCA Camden, 1969. The monkey in the title is also the trickster figure. Elvis emphasizes the notion of the blonde-haired woman by singing the verse twice.
14 D.H. Lawrence, *The Woman Who Rode Away and Other Stories*, London: Penguin, 1950.
15 Francis Ebejer, unpublished interview.
16 Okot p'Bitek, *'Song of Lawino' and 'Song of Ocol'*, Nairobi: East African Publishing House, 1972, p. 191.
17 Francis Ebejer, unpublished description.
18 Francis Ebejer, *Come Again in Spring*, New York/Washington/Atlanta/Los Angeles/Chicago: Vantage, 1979.
19 See Peter Nazareth, 'Waiting for Amin: Two Decades of Ugandan Literature,' G.D. Killam, ed., *The Writing of East and Central Africa*, Nairobi/London: Heinemann, 1984, pp. 7/35.
20 Francis Ebejer, unpublished interview, 1982.

21 Ishmael Reed, *Shrovetide in Old New Orleans*, New York: Doubleday, 1978, p. 286. Ebejer was in the U.S. in 1962 on a Fullbright Scholarship.

22 Mark Shadle makes the point about ragtime in his Ph.D. dissertation, *Mumbo Jumbo Gumbo Works: The Kaleidoscopic Fiction of Ishmael Reed*. University of Iowa: American Studies, May, 1984.

23 Francis Ebejer, *Requiem for a Malta Fascist, or The Interrogation*, Malta: A.C. Acquilian & Co., 1980. All page references are from this edition.

24 Ebejer asked these questions in 'The Bilingual Writer as Janus,' Commonwealth Literature Conference, University of Venice, September 23-26, 1987. He said:

> It may be interesting to note here that nature itself seems to have pointed out the way to political and cultural twinning from practically all sides; in fact, right down from the start of things, from even before the creation of the Mediterranean Basin as we know it: 'this tideless, dolorous, inland Sea' as Swinburne, somewhat pessimistically, described it, even if for Sophocles it was a 'frog-pond'.
>
> I am referring to the fact that our Islands lie squarely on the European continental plate: the water that flows deep underneath our surface comes from the European Appennines; from the South, from North Africa, whence had come, via Sicily, the bountiful semitic-Arab features of our language, sand sometimes blows over to add rich nutrients to our soil; fossilized remains of the bison and the dwarf elephant from the landmass which later became known as Europe lie side by side in our caverns with those of the ancestors of the elegant North African gazelle.
>
> From the East came our Christian faith and Judeo-Islamic-Christian culture; from the West, occidental influences, from the Normans, the Spaniards, the Knights, the French, the Italians, the British. Symbiosis, some say a happy one, has thus been achieved by means of a mixture of Latin, Mediterranean-semitic and Anglo-Saxon languages and cultures. The broad vernacular base, however, remained and still remains solidly Punico-Carthagenian, at least in so far as this relates to the Maghrebian: solidly, in spite of, or perhaps because of the weight it had to carry.

25 *Newsweek*, New York, August 24, 1987, p. 65.

26 Carl G. Jung, ed., *Man and His Symbols*, New York: Laurel, undated but probably 1964, pp. 5/6. Page references are from this edition.

27 Keith Wilson, 'Malta's Francis Ebejer: Defining a Context,' *World Literature Written in English*, ed. G.D. Killam, Vol. 23, No. 2, Spring, 1984, p. 475. My italics.

28 See 'Two Halves' in *An African View of Literature*. The section on *No Bride Price* was written shortly after Amin's coup.

29 *World Literature Written in English*, Vol. 23, No. 2, Spring, 1984, pp. 487/8.

30 Francis Ebejer, *Leap of Malta Dolphins*, New York/Washington/ Atlanta/Los Angeles/Chicago: Vantage, 1982.

31 Letter from the Cousteau Society, 930 West 21st Street, Norfolk, Virginia 23517.

32 Keith Wilson, op. cit., pp. 477/8.

33 See Francis Ebejer, 'The Bicultural Situation in Malta,' *Individual and Community in Commonwealth Literature*, ed. Daniel Massa.

34 *World Literature Written in English*, pp. 480/6.

35 Ibid., p. 482.

36 Helena Kosek, 'The Demolisher of False Myths,' *World Literature Today*, ed. Ivar Ivask, University of Oklahoma: Norman, Vol. 54, No. 4, Autumn, 1980, p. 567.

37 *World Literature Written in English*, pp. 476/7.

38 Ibid., p. 483. As for the question of seeing: Ebejer says in an answer to the Torinese student, 'I have rediscovered a first love, painting; people have remarked [that] what I portray is in eight out of ten cases happening on high ground, with a view of cliff!' Compare the cliffs with the mountain at the end of Salkey's *The Late Emancipation of Jerry Stover*.

39 *World Literature Written in English*, p. 483.

40 Carl C. Jung, op. cit., p. 73.

41 Ibid., p. 83.

42 Michael G. Cooke, *Afro-American Literature in the Twentieth-Century*, New Haven/London: Yale University Press, 1984, p. 49.

43 When I drew Ebejer's attention to Cooke's reference to his Sarid, he wrote to me on March 16, 1986: 'It was nice seeing "Sarid" mentioned in Professor Cooke's book. Not bad for a character I created and killed off in a 1952 radio-play, and brought back after all those years for *Dolphins*. The title of the radioplay was '*Is-Sejha Ta' Sarid*' ('Sarid's Call – or Summons").'

44 Lewis Hyde, 'Tricks of Creation,' *Boston Review*, Vol. XII, No. 1, February, 1987, p. 5.

45 *World Literature Written in English*, p. 485.

46 Ibid., p. 486.

Chapter III: Ishmael Reed

1 Ishmael Reed. *Yellow Back Radio Broke-Down*. Garden City: Doubleday, 1969. All page references are to this edition.

2 Ishmael Reed, *Flight to Canada*, New York: Random House, 1976, p. 124. All page references are to this edition.

3 Ishmael Reed, *The Last Days of Louisiana Red*, New York: Random House. All page references are from this edition.

4 Ishmael Reed, *The Terrible Twos*, New York: St. Martin's/Marek, 1982, p. 109. All page references are to this edition.

5   Ishmael Reed, *Shrovetide in Old New Orleans*, New York: Doubleday, 1978. All page references are to this edition. Ralph Ellison quotes 'an old slave verse' in his famous interview in *The Paris Review* which contains three characters, Aunt Dinah, Uncle Jack and Uncle Ned, who want to get to Canada, freedom. Ellison comments, 'It's crude, but in it you have three universal attitudes toward the problem of freedom. You can refine it and sketch in the psychological allusions, action and what not, but I don't think its basic definition can be exhausted. Perhaps some genius could do as much with it as Mann has done with the Joseph story.' Ralph Ellison, *Shadow and Act*, New York: Signet, 1966, pp. 173/4. Reed is that genius.

6   Ishmael Reed, *Conjure*, Amherst: University of Massachusetts Press, 1972, p.vii. Goa, in India, was conquered by the Portuguese in 1510.

7   Ishmael Reed, *The Free-Lance Pallbearers*, New York: Doubleday, 1967.

8   *Shrovetide in Old New Orleans*, p. 2.

9   Lillian Herlands Hornstein, C.D. Percy & Sterling A. Brown, eds. *The Reader's Companion to World Literature*, second edition, revised and updated by Lillian Herlands Hornstein, Leon Edel and Horst Frenz. New York/Scarborough: New American Library, 1973, p. 65.

10   Grover Washington, Jr., *Reed Seed*, Hollywood: Motown, M7-910R1, 1978.

11   Sondra A. O'Neale, 'Ishmael Reed's Fitful Flight to Canada: Liberation for Some, Good Reading for All,' *CALLALOO*, ed. Charles H. Rowell, Lexington: University of Kentucky, Vol. 1, No. 4, October, 1978, p. 176.

12   Bessie Head. *Maru*. London: Heinemann, 1971, p. 109.

13   *Flight to Canada*, p. 54. Also see Reed's poem, 'Badman of the guest professor,' *Conjure*. p. 77. 'They gibbed me a Ph.D.,' says Cato (p. 53). Cato's language moves in the opposite way to Robin's: in a pressured situation, it breaks down, as though he is of two minds.

14   Mark Shadle makes the point that in British usage, a man-servant is a 'batman'. So Robin *is* Batman. And we note that Batman grew out of The Shadow.

15   Nathaniel Mackey, 'Ishmael Reed and the Black Aesthetic,' *CLA Journal*, Baltimore, Vol. XXI, No. 3, March, 1978, p. 358.

16   Sondra A. O'Neale, op. cit., p. 175.

17   Bessie Head, 'Social and Political Pressures that Shape Literature in Southern Africa,' *World Literature Written in English*, ed. Robert E. McDowell, Arlington: The University of Texas, Vol. XVII, No. 1, April, 1979, p. 21. The paper is included in the Appendix to my study guide, *Literatures of the African Peoples*, University of Iowa: Center for Credit Programs, 1983.

18   Adil Jussawalla, *Missing Person*, Bombay: Clearing House, 1976, p. 15.

19   Derek Walcott, *Dream on Monkey Mountain and Other Plays*, New York: Farrar, Strauss & Giroux, 1970, p. 20.

20   Murray Carlin, *Not Now, Sweet Desdemona*, Nairobi: Oxford University Press, 1969, pp. 43/4.

21   Dobie Gray's 'Drift Away' was No. 5 on the *Billboard* Hot 100 in early

1973 (Decca 33057). Ray Charles's version is on *Ain't It So*, New York: Atlantic, SD 19251, 1979.

22 A new recording of 'Minnie the Moocher' by Cab Calloway is on the original soundtrack recording of *The Blues Brothers*, New York: Atlantic, SD 16017, 1980. Cab Calloway performed the song in the movie.

23 It is difficult on the first reading to avoid linking Minnie the Moocher with Angela Davis. I bought *The Last Days of Louisiana Red* and *Angela Davis/An Autobiography* at the same time: they were published simultaneously by Random House. Reed says in his Self-Interview, originally published in *Black World* in 1974, 'The abuse of the term [Political Prisoner] by people like Baldwin and Professor Angela Davis harms the cause of those who are truly political prisoners.' *Shrovetide in Old New Orleans*, p. 136. This point is also made against Minnie in the novel.

24 Al Young, *Sitting Pretty*, New York: Holt, Rinehart & Wilson, 1976. William Demby, *Love Story Black*, New York: Reed, Cannon & Johnston, 1978.

25 Wole Soyinka, *The Road*, London: Oxford University Press, 1965. The 'Professor' belongs to the oral tradition and believes in *the word*.

26 Marian E. Musgrave, 'Ishmael Reed's Black Oedipus Cycle,' *OBSIDIAN: Black Literature in Review*, ed. Alvin Aubert, Detroit: Wayne State University, Vol. 6, No. 3, 1980, p.64. Jerome Klinkowitz explains the way some people have misunderstood Reed's concern with taking care of business, taking the meaning of the word 'businessman' at face value. ('Reed's Syncretic Words,' *The American Book Review*, May-June, 1983, pp. 16/17.)

27 For example, see J.A. Avant's review of the novel in *Library Journal*, Whittinsville: R.R. Bowker, Co., Vol. 99, 1974, p. 3147.

28 Reed says 'the essay is the ditch-digging occupation of writing. I spend a lot of time running up and down the stairs for Facts!' *Shrovetide in Old New Orleans*, p. 6.

29 Angela Davis, op. cit., p. 95.

30 Ishmael Reed, *Mumbo Jumbo*, Garden City: Doubleday, 1972. All page references are to this edition.

31 Paule Marshall, *Brown Girl, Brownstones*, New York: Avon, 1972. The novel was first published in 1959.
Paule Marshall, *Praisesong for the Widow*, New York: G.P. Putnam's Sons, 1983. Paule Marshall shows how colonialism undermines manhood in her fiction. She has major male characters in all her work, particularly her *tour de force*, *The Chosen Place, The Timeless People*, but even here the protagonist is a woman. See my chapter, 'Colonial Relationships, Colonized People,' in *The Third World Writer: His Social Responsibility*.

32 'Now this here's the story 'bout the "Rock Island Line",' begins Lonnie Donegan's imitation of Leadbelly's 'Rock Island Line', which reached No. 8 on the British pop charts and No. 10 on *Billboard*'s Hot 100 in 1956, setting off the skiffle craze in England. A whole generation of

English boys were inspired by Donegan to start their own skiffle groups, including those who became the Beatles and the Rolling Stones, and to discover black blues. Supposedly, Bill Skiffle was the first man in New Orleans to hold a rent party, using instruments like a washboard and box-bass. *Lonnie Donegan*, Scarborough: Pye, FILD 011, 1977, is a collection of Donegan's 26 hits. *Putting on the Style*, Los Angeles: United Artists, UA-LA827-H, 1977 is an updated Donegan backed by his musical heirs. One of Leadbelly's versions can be found on *Leadbelly*, Hollywood: Capitol, SM-1821, undated.

33   *Conjure*, pp. 17/8.
34   Toma Longinović writes minimalist fiction. See his Reed-like novel, *Moment of Silence*, San Francisco: Burning Books, 1990.
35   *Conjure*, p. 26.
36   For example, see Philip Durham & Everett L. Jones. *The Adventures of the Negro Cowboys*, New York/Toronto/London: Bantam, 1969.
37   At the end of *Mumbo Jumbo*, Biff Musclewhite boards the Titanic. In 1987, Telly Savalas hosted a special on T.V. about the sinking of the Titanic. He gave many reasons for the sinking of the leviathan. The first of these was the mummy curse: many people who had dealt with the mummy removed from its tomb in Egypt had died mysteriously. As a result of yet another death, the mummy was being sent to New York from London on the Titanic, Savalas said. We recall that Raven speculates at the beginning of *Flight to Canada*, 'Do the lords still talk? Do the lords still walk? Are they writing this book? Will they go out to Long Island and touch these men who were musing in the restaurant about the money they were going to make on the musical comedy *Uncle Tom's Cabin*? Will they get the old mummy grip?' (p. 10)
38   Albert Goldman, *Elvis*, New York: Avon, 1981. I am aware of the notion that Elvis ripped-off black music. But the story is more complex. The singers he copied, learned from, mimicked, or brought in run into the dozens, chiefly but not exclusively black. He always added something to what he got, particularly when he seemed to do straight imitation as in his version of Chuck Willis's 'I Feel So Bad.' Elvis was a twin – his twin brother was born dead, and he 'twinned' himself to others all his life. Little Richard says in his *Rolling Stone* interview,

> Like, see, when Elvis came out, a lot of black groups would say, 'Elvis cannot do so and so and so, shoo shoo shoo [huffs and grumbles]. And I'd say, 'Shut up, shut up.' Let me tell you this – when I came out they wasn't playing no black artists on no Top 40 stations – but it took people like Elvis and Pat Boone, Gene Vincent, to open the door for this kind of music, and I thank God for Elvis Presley. I thank the Lord for sending Elvis to open that door so I could walk down the road, you understand?

The Rolling Stone Interviews: Talking with the Legends of Rock & Roll, New York: St. Martin's Press/Rolling Stone Press, 1981, p. 92. Goldman was deliberately chopping down a person who had opened the door, as he was to do later with John Lennon.

39 Thomas Pynchon, *Gravity's Rainbow*, New York: Bantam, 1974, p. 685.

40 Wole Soyinka, *Kongi's Harvest*, London: Oxford, 1965. Bob Krantz in *The Terrible Twos* refers to Uganda in 1990 and says, 'We wouldn't have expected that these nations would spend an eternity under military rule and unemployed intellectuals.' (p. 55)

41 J.R. McGuire, op. cit., p. 22.

42 Ishmael Reed, 'D Hexorcism of Noxon D Awful,' *Amistad 1*, ed. John A. Williams & Charles F. Harris, New York: Vintage, 1970, pp. 165/82.

43 Barry Wolstun Lopez, *Of Wolves and Men*, New York: Charles Scribner's Sons, 1978, pp. 67/8. For the raven in a 'curing story', see *The Greenfield Review*, issue on American Indian Writing, ed. Joseph Bruchac III, New York, Vol. 9, Nos. 3 & 4, Winter, 1981/82, pp. 136/8. When raven comes to the door, he has come to cure. The song about the red robin bobbing along seems to be a pop version of the curing song. See also 'Trickster: 1977' by Wendy Rose in *The Remembered Earth: An Anthology of Contemporary Native American Literature*, ed. Geary Hobson, Albuquerque: University of New Mexico Press, 1981, p. 384. The poem says, 'The Trickster's time/is not clicked off neatly/on round dials . . . when you have stretched/to your limit and can/no more bear to hear the frozen words/circle like ravens above you . . . We'll say he is the whistling coyote . . . Let the bones melt into the rain and/disappear; let me disappear/and let those soft bones go.'

44 Joseph L. Henderson, in *Man and His Symbols*, p. 155.

45 Lewis Hyde, *The Boston Review*, p. 7.

46 *Canadian Literature*, ed. W.H. New, Vancouver: University of British Columbia, No. 96, Spring, 1983, pp. 126/7.

47 Ishmael Reed, *God Made Alaska for the Indians*, New York/London: Garland, 1982, p. 50. Reed does not use the word 'trickster' favorably on one occasion. (*Shrovetide in Old New Orleans*, p. 142). By the time of *Reckless Eyeballing*, Reed uses the word 'trickologist' when he means it to be unfavourable.

48 Henry Louis Gates, Jr, 'The "Blackness of Blackness": A Critique of the Sign and the Signifying Monkey,' *Critical Inquiry*, University of Chicago, Vol. 9, No. 4, June, 1983. The chapter is included in Henry Louis Gates, Jr., *Black Literature and Literary Theory*, London/New York: Methuen, 1984. It is further included in Henry Louis Gates, Jr., *Figures in Black*, New York: Oxford University Press, 1987.

49 Ishmael Reed, *Reckless Eyeballing*, New York: St. Martin's, 1986, p. 106. All page references are to this section.

50 Alice Walker, *The Color Purple*, New York/London: Harcourt Brace Jovanovich, 1982.

51 *The New York Times*, Saturday, April 5, 1986.

52 *Black American Literary Forum*, ed. Joe Weixlmann, Terre Haute: Indiana University Press, Vol. 2, Nos. 2 & 2, 1986, p. 10.

53 Op. cit., p. 9.

54 Greil Marcus, 'Uncle Tom Redux,' *The Village Voice*, New York, November 15, 1986, p. 49.

55 Joseph Conrad, *Nostromo*, London/New York: J.M. Dent & Sons/ E.P. Dutton & Co. Inc., 1960, p. 316.

56 *Shrovetide in Old New Orleans*, p. 137.

57 John O'Brien, *Interview With Black Writers*, New York: Liveright, 1973, p. 178.

58 *Man and His Symbols*, p. 34.

59 Maya Harris, 'What is to Be Done?', *The Harvard Crimson*, February 26, 1957, p. 5.

60 I am indebted for my information about *Treemonisha* to Dr. Lee Cloud. He did one of the parts in the first reading of *Treemonisha* in Atlanta, 1972.

61 Ahmad Harb, *Half-way Between North and South: An Archetypal Analysis of the Fiction of Tayeb Salih*, Ph.D. dissertation, University of Iowa: Department of English. May, 1986, p. 13.

62 *God Made Alaska For the Indians*, pp. 97/100.

63 *Black Literature and Criticism*, p. 7.

64 'Hard Headed Woman' by Claude Demetrius, copyright © 1958 by Gladys Music, copyright renewed. All rights administered by CHAPELL & CO. Inc. International Copyright secured. All rights reserved. Used by permission. The track can be found on two Commemorative Elvis LPs issued in 1987, *The Number One Hits* and *The Top Ten Hits*, New York: RCA, Nos. 6381-1-R and 3683-1-R.

65 *Black American Literature Forum*, pp. 15/16.

66 *Elvis as Recorded at Madison Square Garden*, New York: RCA, LSP-4776, issued in 1972. 'Hound Dog' and its hit version by Elvis can be found on both LPs listed in n. 64. and in *Elvis Presley Sings Leiber & Stoller*, RCA International, NL 89099, issued in 1980. Big Mama Thornton's version can be found on *Rock & Roll: The Early Years*, New York: RCA AFM 1-5483, issued in 1985. In his version, Elvis fingers the hound dog, saying it cannot catch the rabbit, that is, the trickster. *The Terrible Twos* is partially dedicated to Jerry Leiber.

67 Alice Walker, *You Can't Keep a Good Woman Down*, New York/San Diego/London: Harcourt Brace Jovanovich, 1981, first published 1972. 'Nineteen Fifty-two' is also included in Margaret Busby, ed. *Daughters of Africa*, New York: Pantheon, pp. 642/52.

68 Larry Abraham, *Call it Conspiracy*, Seattle: Double A Publications, 1985, pp. 8/9.

69 Alice Walker, *Meridian*, New York: Pocket Books, 1976.

70 *Man and His Symbols*, p. 230.

71 *Black Skin, White Masks*, p. 122.

72 Michele Wallace, 'Female Troubles: Ishmael Reed's Tunnel Vision,' *The Village Voice Literary Supplement*, December, 1986, p. 11. My italics.

73 In *Black Literature and Literary Theory*, p. 91.

74 *Black American Literature Forum*, p. 13.

75 *Black Skin, White Masks*, pp. 151/2.

76 Quoted by Maya Harris, 'What is to Be Done?', *The Harvard Crimson*, p. 5.
77 *The San Francisco Chronicle*, Friday, March 28, 1986.
78 Richard Wesley, *'The Color Purple' Debate*, sub-titled 'Reading Between the Lines,' *Ms.*, New York: Ms. Foundation for Education and Communication, Vol. XV, No. 3, September, 1986, p. 91.
79 Anthony Boxill, op. cit., p. 149.
80 Ahmad Harb, op. cit., p. 320.
81 *Bottom Line/Personal*, New York: Boardroom Reports Inc., Vol. 8, No. 10, August, 1986, pp. 9/10.
82 *Flight to Canada*, p. 106.

> Lee Bartlett says to Reed that in his anthology, *10 Necromancers from Now*, 'You included no women poets.' Reed replies, 'I know. It was a mistake.' Bartlett pursues the point: 'Did you get criticized for that?' Reed replies,
>
> 'Sure, but I've changed. Our Before Columbus Foundation used to be called the Boys' Club by various women. Now even our president is female. But in the sixties we had a different attitude. Our workshop in New York always subjected women writers to ridicule. We told them to go make coffee. But look, I grew up with John Wayne. It was dumb, but that was the way it was. We were oppressing other people while we were talking about our own oppression. It's like a circus act where you've got people standing on each other's shoulders. But now my publishing company, I. Reed Books, and our magazine, *Quilt*, publishes mostly women writers.'

(Lee Bartlett, *Talking Poetry*, sub-titled *Conversations in the Workshop with Contemporary Poets*, Albuquerque: University of New Mexico Press, 1987, pp. 173/4.) But people *will* tend to read characters rather than texts. Sandra M. Gilbert and Susan Gubar say of *Reckless Eyeballing*,

> *And Mr. Reed's black masculinist rebel does not find a baroque way to terrorize a series of feminist cultural commissars but is forced to promulgate their position that black men ought to be lynched if they 'recklessly eyeball'* – that is, look at – white women.
> ('Sex Wars: Not the Fun Kind,' *The New York Times Book Review*, December 27, 1987, p. 20.)

They make no further comment on the text, leaving us with the idea that the novel justifies the lynching of black men for recklessly eyeballing white women. Even though they seem to like the novel, they have misread it to fit into their thesis.

Conclusion

1   Ngũgĩ wa Thiong'o, *Decolonising the Mind: The Politics of Language in African Literature*, London/Nairobi/New Hampshire/Harare: James Currey/Heinemann/Zimbabwe Publishing House, 1986.

2   See Ngũgĩ wa Thiong'o, *Detained: A Writer's Prison Diary*, London/Nairobi/Ibadan: Heinemann, 1981.

3   *Decolonising the Mind*, p. 22.

4   Ayi Kwei Armah's novels are referred to earlier in this book. Unlike Ngũgĩ, Armah grew up under an African régime that professed itself to be socialist.

5   Ngũgĩ wa Thiong'o, *Petals of Blood*, London/Nairobi: Heinemann, 1977.

6   'Ishmael Reed Replies to Amiri Baraka,' *Hambone*, ed. Nathaniel Mackey, Santa Cruz, No. 2, Fall, 1982, p. 123.

7   Michael G. Cooke, op. cit., p. 27.

8   Roger D. Abrahams, *Deep Down in the Jungle . . . .: Negro Narrative Folklore from the Streets of Philadelphia*, Chicago: Aldine, 1970, pp. 51/2.

9   *Critical Inquiry*, Vol. 9, No. 4, June, 1983, p. 689.

10 Ahmad Harb, op. cit.

11 Paul Xuereb, 'The Open Doors,' *The Sunday Times*, Valletta, December 8, 1985.

12 Emma Jung and Marie Von Franz, *The Grail Legend*, London: Hodder and Stoughton, 1972, p. 358. Quoted by Michael Gilkes, op. cit., p.41.

13 Mario Vargas Llosa, 'Is Fiction the Art of Lying?', trans. Tony Talbot, *The New York Times Book Review*, October 7, 1984, p.1.

14 However, Bradley Peters says, 'In a curious manner, she might well be "the horror, the horror"; it certainly seems when Marlow tells her that her name was on the dying lips of Kurtz, that he utters the unwitting truth.' ('The Significance of Dream Consciousness in *Heart of Darkness* and *Palace of the Peacock*,' *Conradiana*, ed. David L. Higdon, Lubbock, Texas, vol. 22, No. 2, summer 1990, p. 133.)

15 *JOSEPH CONRAD, Heart of Darkness*, sub-titled *A Case Study in Contemporary Criticism*, ed., Ross C. Murfin, New York: St Martin's Press, 1989, pp. 19, 20, 51.

16 There are scenes in *Reckless Eyeballing* that could have come from Salkey or Ebejer. Brashford tells Ball, 'You guys and your generation, you've fallen victim to the moral laxity of the times,' sounding like Randy talking to Jerry Stover. Ball stumbles onto a feminist newsletter called *Lilith's Gang*, which is like the scene from Salkey's novel when Catullus stumbles onto the racist book in the house of the woman who calls herself Lilith. On page 80 of Reed's novel, Ian

>   gritted his teeth and in his mind's eye saw Paul Shoboater falling from the chair and cracking his skull against one of those stone pillars of the restaurant, or the heavy pot that held ferns. He saw the waiter rise from where Paul lay – blood pouring from his head,

spattering his three-piece French-cut suit – shaking his head before the shocked fellow diners, and announcing, 'He's dead.'

This could come from Ebejer's *Requiem for a Malta Fascist*.

17 Wilson Harris, *Tradition the Writer and Society*, London: New Beacon Books, 1967, p. 57.
18 *Black Skin, White Masks*, pp. 188/9. In 'Carl of the Jungle', Rick Nelson sings of the Man, that is Carl Jung, going to Africa to find the primitive, only to find he is looking into a mirror at himself. When he asks a wise man of the Africans what their dreams tell them, they reply in a falsetto like Prince's that since the White Man came they haven't been able to dream because the White Man knows it all. The chorus keeps singing, echoing the Beatles, 'Go back, go back,' that is, back to Vienna. They repeat this at the end while Nelson says, like a character from Salih's novel, 'Up North.' (Rick Nelson, *Stay Young: The Epic Recordings*, New York: Epic/Legacy, A Division of Sony Music, 1993. He recorded the song in 1978 for an album to be called *Back to Vienna* but it was only released posthumously.)
19 Gregory Rabassa, 'Lying to Athena: Cortázar and the Art of Fiction,' *Books Abroad*, ed. Ivar Ivask, Norman: University of Oklahoma Press, Vol. 50, No. 3, Summer, 1976, p. 543. My italics.
20 Julio Cortázar, *Hopscotch*, trans. Gregory Rabassa, New York: Pantheon, 1966, pp. 191/2.
21 Chinua Achebe, *Arrow of God*, New York: John Day, 1967, p. 55.
22 *Decolonising the Mind*, p. 76.
23 *Black Literature and Literacy Theory*, p. 5.

Index of Names and Works